Hear My Story

What Jews Really Think & Feel

Hear My Story

What Jews Really Think & Feel

Michael Jaffe Garbutt

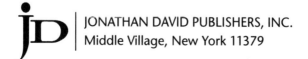

JONATHAN DAVID PUBLISHERS, INC.
Middle Village, New York 11379

HEAR MY STORY

Copyright © 2000
by
Michael Jaffe Garbutt

Jonathan David Publishers, Inc.
68-22 Eliot Avenue
Middle Village, New York 11379

www.jdbooks.com

2 4 6 8 10 9 7 5 3 1

Library of Congress Cataloging-in-Publication Data

Hear My Story: What Jews really think and feel / [interviews conducted]
by Michael Jaffe Garbutt.
     p.   cm.
  Includes Index
  0-8246-0417-2
1. Judaism—United States. 2. Jews—United States—Interviews.
I. Garbutt, Michael.

BM205.H38 1999
296' .0973—dc21
                                           99-24277
                                             CIP

Book design by John Reinhardt Book Design

Printed in the United States of America

*In memory of my father, Cyril Ivan Garbutt,
and his storied world*

Acknowledgments

My thanks to all those people who shared their stories with me and to the many others who provided valuable leads. In particular, I'd like to thank my mother, Betty June Garbutt, for her unfailing love and support; David Kolatch, my editor, who was a tower of strength at all the right moments, making molehills of many seemingly insuperable mountains; Lidia Nemitschenko, who was always there for me through the good times and the bad; and Esther Iwanaga, who first encouraged me to write, and to keep on writing when I was more than ready to quit. Esther was a tireless advocate of the manuscript, closely involved in every stage of its development. She put in countless hours of work, sharing the hopes and many of the adventures. No two ways about it: I couldn't have done it without her.

Contents

CONTENTS

Introduction

---❦---

Memory, Voice, and Identity

"What does being Jewish mean to you?" In a series of informal interviews I put this question to over four hundred Jews from a wide variety of cultural, religious, and geographical backgrounds, inviting them to respond with stories of personal experience. This book contains a selection of their answers.

My interest in the project was triggered by an unsettling encounter while on vacation in the Blue Mountains of Australia. It led me to reflect on my own experience of Jewishness and became the source of an anecdote that I was later to tell during some of the interviews. What follows is a transcript of one such telling. I was talking to Elaine D., a twenty-six-year-old social worker who lives in a small New England town a two-and-a-half hour drive from New York City. After describing the aims of the project to Elaine, I told her my own story to explain how it began:

I have a vacation house in Australia. It's in a small town in the Blue Mountains. And, at the back of the house there's a sunroom and three sides are all window, a bit like here–

ELAINE: *Oh, wow! Sounds really great.*

It really is: eucalyptus trees, clouds, cockatoos, kangaroos . . . But y'know . . . it can get very hot in summer and very cold in winter. And so last year, when I was down there, I decided to have some curtains put up.

1

So I rang this shop in town, which was actually called Mr. Curtains, and . . . this guy came round—Mr. Curtains himself—and took the measurements. And at the time I didn't really think much about him: late thirties, medium build, fair hair, balding. A little . . . um . . . well, nondescript.

Elaine looks mildly quizzical.

Anyway, he showed me a sample book, and I chose the material, a kind of yellow, yellowy gold. And I paid him half in advance—it was . . . Oh, like, about six hundred dollars—quite a lot of curtain! And he was supposed to come back that week to hang them. And . . . a week goes by, two weeks. Nothing. No sign of him. So I ring the shop, and he says he's been busy but he'll come. Tomorrow . . . Next day at the latest. And of course he doesn't show up.

So I called again, and he was like, "Sorrysorrysorry," but he said he could come round one evening. Maybe. Y'know, he was *really* very uncooperative.

So I said, "Well, this evening is an evening."

I was a little insistent at this point. And he, somewhat unenthusiastically, somewhat offhandedly, he said, "OK. Around seven."

And it was a Friday evening, and I had some friends staying with me, a couple of German friends I've known for a long time. They're both tall and blonde and have blue eyes. Sort of typical– Well, this is a cliché, isn't it? Stereotypically German. Not Jewish anyway. And I had made Kiddush* like I always do on Friday evenings, y'know, candles, glass of wine, piece of challah—well, sourdough actually—brocha.*

And we'd just finished this when the doorbell rings. And it's Mr. Curtains. Unbelievable! And because he needed to bring

---

*An asterisk indicates that the term is defined in the glossary, page 349.

the rods and material from the front of the house to the back, to the sunroom, I had to open all the doors for him, and when I arrived in the sunroom, I saw I'd left a book out on the coffee table.

It was called *Modern Jewish Poets* by Howard Schwartz. I don't know if you know it.

ELAINE: *No, I don't think so . . .*

Thing is, it has the word "Jewish" on the cover. Now here—I don't know if this will make sense to you, but [*clicking my fingers*] immediately—instinctively—without thinking, I took the book and I put it under a pile of magazines and papers on the floor—I didn't want him to see it.

And my reasoning was that I thought, "He'll see the book, he'll maybe think I'm Jewish, he's already . . . unhappy about working in the evening . . ." And I didn't want to advertise the fact that . . . I don't know if—Maybe here in the U.S. that reaction is hard to understand, but I grew up in England and . . .

ELAINE: *Well, I lived in France for a time as an exchange student . . . And so, I think I know what you mean. So go on . . .*

So, anyway, he started working, and I went back into the kitchen to have dinner with my friends. And about half an hour later, I went into the sunroom to see how Mr. Curtains was getting on. And the first thing he said to me was, he said, [*casually*] "Oh, I had to move the papers to put the ladder up . . ." And there was the book, on top of the pile. He said, "Interesting book. Are you Jewish?" And I'm like . . . "Me? Jewish? No way! It's not my book! It's *theirs!*" [*indicating my German friends in the kitchen*]

I mean, I didn't, of course. I'm just kidding. But at some level the urge was there, to react that way. In fact, I said, I said, "Yes, I am." And then, of course, I'm waiting for something. I mean, nothing bad bad bad, but something uh, awkward, maybe some morbid curiosity, I don't know, something I don't want to hear. But instead he says, he says, "Me, too. I'm Jewish, too."

ELAINE: *Really? Oh, that is so funny!*

Yeah, it was like . . . relief! Bonding . . . brotherhood. Pogromlessness! [*Elaine laughs.*] And I said to him for a joke, [*wagging an admonishing finger*] "You shouldn't be working tonight. It's Shabbos."* And he said, [*with a smiling tone*] "Well, you shouldn't be employing me either!"

ELAINE: *Touché.*

Exactly. And we laughed. And I looked at him, and I thought to myself, "You *do* have a Jewish face; I wonder why I didn't see it before."

My anxiety at being "discovered" as a Jew might seem excessive, not to say absurd. In every sense contemporary Australia is a long way from Europe and the anti-Semitism that blighted the lives of earlier generations of Jews. But the fact remains: I did hide the book. However much I subsequently tried to turn it into a source of humor, something of the past was undeniably present in that act. And yet, as the story also indicates, I was able to share my version of the Kiddush ceremony with non-Jewish friends, who in an ironic twist just happened to be German. For better or worse, it all reflected much of my own experience of Jewishness: a strong attachment to some of the traditions, feelings of ethnic solidarity, and a corresponding unease in some relationships with non-Jews.

Like every story, it's a part of a chain, reflecting others that I had heard and told. As a child growing up in a Jewish neighborhood of Manchester, England, in the 1960s, my own sense of identity was strongly affected by repeatedly hearing stories about how the world was not a safe place for Jews. The message was conveyed in various languages. In synagogue services, ancient chronicles of enslavement, persecution, and death were chanted in Biblical Hebrew and Aramaic. At home, more recent accounts of pogroms and mass killings—told to me at least on one occasion as a bedtime story about cattletrucks and gas chambers—were related in an English (*Oy, gevalt!*) liberally laced with Yiddish. Outside the home—amongst non Jews—the topic languished in silence. Some things you just didn't talk about with the *goyim.*

Unsurprisingly, it was a background that sensitized me to issues of language and identity, and in part influenced my later decision to study linguistics; I wanted to understand how people use language to talk about their communities, lives, and feelings. In my work as a sociolinguist, this continuing interest has led me to record and analyze many types of oral narrative, ranging from courtroom testimonies to problem presentations in psychotherapy, as well as dinner-table anecdotes of the Mr. Curtains variety. It's a fascinating occupation with only one drawback: it tends to make you a very self-conscious storyteller.

When I shared the curtains story with friends shortly after returning from vacation, it occurred to me that despite the many fictional and nonfictional accounts of Jewish life, informal stories of the kind told around the dinner table rarely make it into print. And when they do, heavy editing almost invariably eliminates the rough-edged vitality of authentic speech.

Certainly, most conversational narratives ("Guess who I ran into this morning . . ."; "Did you see last night's *Seinfeld* . . ."; "We went to this amazing new restaurant . . .") are about events of no apparent historical significance, are generally assumed to be of little aesthetic value, and tend to be quickly forgotten, sometimes even by their tellers. And yet such stories can be a rich resource for understanding something of a speaker's attitudes, feelings, and beliefs. Just by reading the transcript of my curtains story, for example, you already know a lot about me and one kind of Jewish experience. Hear my story, and you'll know who I am—or at least one version of who I am.

Tell me *your* story, and I'll know who you are—or at least who

you'd like me to think you are. Let me hear the difference between the stories you tell close friends and the stories you tell strangers and I'll know you even better. Let me hear the stories told by
other members of your community and perhaps I can understand
how your own stories came to be told.

The experience of recounting my curtains anecdote made me
ask other questions of myself. What other kinds of Jewish story
could I tell? What other Jewish stories could I *hear*? At a time
when the Jewish world has become more culturally, religiously,
and ideologically diverse than ever before, what stories do others
relate about this complex and elusive identity?

Drawing on my experience as an interviewer and analyst of narratives, I decided to record a wide and respresentative sample of
Jews talking about Judaism and Jewishness, though I knew it could
not be a neutral exercise in opinion gathering. Every story exists in
the space created by teller and listener, and so my personal responses to the stories I was to hear would in no small measure
shape the stories themselves.

And I hoped the project would also be an adventure: I had a
hand-held cassette recorder, a bagful of tapes, and a desire to collect stories. This book is a record of that adventure.

Making Connections

I began by taping interviews with family and friends and went on
to make new contacts through religious, cultural, and social institutions. Interviewees often introduced me to others, who in turn
provided new leads. A journey had begun that was to last two years
and take me on numerous zigzags across North America, Australia, and England. By journey's end, some four hundred and twenty
interviews had been recorded, most around two hours in length.
Some were planned weeks in advance, others came out of chance
meetings on a plane or in a restaurant.

It was not only my personal responses that would affect the shape of the stories. My Jewish identity was also crucial to the outcome of the project. I was familiar with a wide range of Jewish attitudes, beliefs, and practices, and at one time or another had shared many of those I was to encounter. But it was not just a case of cultural preparation. During phone calls to potential interviewees, the social distance between us generally lessened after I explained that I was Jewish. Often, on meeting an interviewee, my physical appearance guaranteed insider status, at least amongst Jews of eastern European origin ("You remind me so much of this guy I know in Israel . . ."). But not always: "You Jewish? Really? I never would have guessed. You sounded British to me on the phone."

More or less consciously, every storyteller has an ideal listener in mind, the person to whom they need or would like to tell their tale. For many Jews, Jewishness is an important characteristic of *their* ideal listener. A Baltimore woman who had just returned from a trip to the Ukraine described to me the almost spiritual nature of her connection with other Jews:

> We're a tribe. We're outside of time and space. And that's why I can meet people from the Ukraine who grew up under communism and just bond instantly. It's one thing to meet someone who grew up in San Francisco. OK. We can explain that away. You know, we all watch *Howdy Doody*. But someone from the Ukraine? I really think there is some community of understanding, of knowing, a genetic memory or whatever. I've had enough experiences to realize that I can't explain it away.

Being able to "bond instantly" with (some) other Jews, certainly made it easier for me to persuade strangers to share intimate and sometimes painful stories, although simply being Jewish was not enough to reassure everyone. Some ultra-Orthodox Jews, for example, were suspicious of my motives and reluctant to talk on record. For them, I was not an insider. Fortunately, many were not so circumspect and willingly shared their stories.

Making Emotional Connections

To begin an interview, I would introduce myself, talk a little about my background, explain the aims of the project, and stress that speakers' names and other identifying data would be changed to protect their privacy. And then, since one self-disclosure invites another, I would often segue into the curtains story and end it by saying, "So what does being Jewish mean to *you?*"

For some, the threads of ethnicity, religion, culture, and historical memory remained tightly woven. For others, they had come apart or entwined themselves with other identities. In a pluralist age, Judaism itself has become a pluralist phenomenon, and sometimes a bitterly contested one. Responses to my question were therefore as varied as the speakers themselves, though the themes of connection—and disconnection—were pervasive. For some, the essential connection was between God and the Jews; for others, it was a sense of belonging to a people, of being a link in a historical chain, of sharing certain values, memories, and responsibilities. In other words, of sharing certain stories.

Some personal anecdotes had obviously been told many times before ("Hey, Dad, tell him the one about . . ."). Several Holocaust survivors had even been previously interviewed by others and spoke almost too fluently about the horrors of their past, as if they had a well-rehearsed script that they felt obliged to repeat. In every meeting, however, I tried to focus the talk on very recent events, partly to encourage a greater degree of narrative detail and partly to hear stories that had not been rubbed too smooth by repeated tellings. "Can you tell me a story that includes the words 'I,' 'Jewish,' and 'recently'?" I would ask as a follow-up question. After that, I generally spoke as little as possible, trying to be an empathic, nonjudgmental listener.

This intentional lack of structure meant that the flow of talk could be excitingly unpredictable. Often, however, a subtle change would occur in the emotional atmosphere. A phrase, a gesture, a shift in the speaker's tone of voice seemed to indicate that a connection had been made with something deeply felt. "I think about these things a lot but I never really had a chance to talk about them before," said one woman, referring to her feelings of ambivalence about having "married out." "I'm getting a little tense and emotional," said another, talking about her conversion to Judaism. "Does anyone else feel like this?" she wanted to know. Again and again, I was asked the same question: "Do other people feel like me? Have you heard other stories like mine?" And when I replied that I had, the sense of pleasure, surprise, or relief (often all three together) was almost palpable.

Of course, not everyone was equally self-disclosive. Some preferred to champion a particular religious or political hobbyhorse; others wanted me to act as a sounding board for their dilemmas about Jewish identity; a few were simply eager to promote their institutions or personal ambitions. But my interest was always as much in the circumstances and the manner of the telling as the tale itself.

Intonation, rhythm, speed, voice quality, and body language can reveal character as much as the description of events and attitudes. Similarly, the physical context of talk inevitably affects our understanding of it. During recordings, phones rang and were either answered or ignored; visitors sometimes arrived unexpectedly and even joined in the conversation; children demanded attention from parents; televisions blared; and on one occasion an excited cocker spaniel brought storytelling to a temporary but spectacular close. I always welcomed such disruptions. I saw them as the unscripted, ordinary stuff of life, the tang of which I was trying to preserve on tape.

Sometimes an interruption might even provide an unexpected insight into identity, as in the case of the Australian yeshivah student who was discussing the previous week's Torah portion. He was speaking in the Yiddish-influenced cadence common amongst some Orthodox Jews. Then the phone rang. "Sorry, mate, wrong number. Yeah. No worries," he said in a broad Aussie accent. Hanging up the receiver, he continued to recount the story of Joseph's meeting with his brothers in Egypt, effortlessly, and I suspect unconsciously, slipping back into a singsong Yiddish cadence. Two voices for two different worlds, and both equally authentic. That, for me, was the most revealing moment of the interview.

For two years I briefly entered hundreds of different storyworlds. I was variously moved, amused, saddened, and often elated by the sheer delight of sharing stories. I was also surprised that so many people had such an intense need to talk about their Jewish identity, to share intimate stories with a stranger, and to hear what others had to say. I was eager to create a written record of these meetings, one that would preserve the spirit of the voices and allow them to communicate with others.

Editing

My purpose in transcribing and editing each recording was to create a unique voiceprint that could be read either as a conventional interview or as a dramatic dialogue or monologue lending itself to the more complex readings associated with fiction or verse. Since most transcripts ran to many thousands of words, it was necessary to edit their length to create more focused pieces. Initial decisions were based partly on technical requirements. Removed from its original context, even the most expressive talk does not always read on the page as well as it once sounded to the ear. From the pool of interviews that retained a cohesive argument or storyline on the page, I made a final cut designed to highlight particular issues and points of view.

In establishing the style of presentation, I had to bear in mind that when we listen to a story, it's not just the content that impresses itself on our imagination; it's also the manner of its telling. A speaker's tone of voice, rhythms and cadences, facial expressions, and body language all affect our interpretations of what we hear. However, most of these details are difficult, some impossible to reproduce on the printed page. Inevitably, therefore, the process of transcription results in the loss of narrative vitality. Nevertheless, I have attempted to capture something of the original character by including some of the features of natural speech that distinguish it from prose. To this end, many of the texts include idiosyncratic punctuation and spelling of some of the natural dysfluencies that populate ordinary conversation. These features, I believe, significantly enhance the reading experience, giving an insight into the storyteller's emotional responses to their story and the experience of sharing it with another.

A final note on editing. Since many texts are of a highly personal or controversial nature, most interviewees opted for anonymity. In consequence, names, locations, and other identifying features have been changed. Interviewees who chose to appear under their own names do so.

Representativeness

Some seventy-seven voices appear in this book, just under one fifth of the total number recorded. It would be presumptuous to claim that such a relatively small collection—entirely based on interviews recorded in English in English-speaking countries— could adequately represent the many social, religious, cultural, and political currents that make up diaspora Judaism.

Many voices are missing. The large Jewish communities of Argentina, France, South Africa, and the former Soviet Union are represented only by emigrants now living elsewhere. Other distinctive voices, such as those of Iranian and Italian Jews (to name but two), do not appear at all. Certain characteristic figures are also absent. The rabbi, the mohel (ritual circumcisor) and the fundraiser are included, but the shochet (kosher slaughterer), the shaliach (promoter of immigration to Israel), and the Federation president are not.

How representative therefore is this collection? Although the speakers do reflect something of the social diversity of contemporary Judaism, the collection is primarily designed to present an *emotionally* representative sample. The voices variously express pride, love, hope, and joy. They also speak of sadness, guilt, anxiety, fear, and hate.

If I had met other speakers or perhaps even the same speakers under different circumstances, perhaps at a different time in their lives, I would almost certainly have heard different stories or different takes on the same story. Nevertheless, I believe that the collective emotional response would remain much the same: it rings true to my own experience of what people think and feel about Judaism and Jewishness.

Sequencing

Just as Judaism and Jewishness are a complex and often hard-to-define combination of ethnicity, religion, culture, and memory, so the voices in this book also defy easy categorization. Certain connections—of mood, theme, or topic—do exist. During the interviews, I was often struck by the way one story seemed to respond directly to another heard on another continent. Sometimes the voices were in accord, at other times in strident opposition. The sequencing of the texts is designed to recreate something of this dialogic character.

The opening section sketches in some of the main features of the terrain. *The Memory of Our Journeys* (page 17) relates the psychological value of storytelling as a personal, family, and communal experience, while the second piece, *Words and Worlds* (page 19), explores the ways that stories and storytellers affect each other. *My Kind of Judaism* (page 24) introduces a recurrent theme—synagogue and spiritual life—seen through the eyes of an enthusiastic young woman. *Just Do It* (page 27) counterpoints the story with another person's very different emotional response to the same experience. The section also contains one man's definition of a mensch (A *Twenty-Four Seven Thing*, page 30). It concludes with

Tell Me, Please (page 33), in which I find myself put on the spot by an interviewee who asks the age-old question, "What is a Jew?"

There follows a series of movements that flow almost imperceptibly into each other. *What Was the Point Here?* (page 39) describes a New Yorker's enthusiastic encounters with Jewish law and ritual. It is followed by voices relating their experiences of Orthodox, Reform, and Conservative Judaism as well as those of Jews who feel alienated from religion.

With *Just Like Everyone Else* (page 97) the focus shifts towards an examination of Jewish difference, presenting common stereotypes and beliefs about the nature of Jewish and non-Jewish physical, behavioral, and psychological traits. *My Cousin in Chicago* (page 117) introduces voices of ethnic solidarity, the sense that many Jews have that they belong to a large and tightly knit family. But a family that is often deeply divided.

That discordancy becomes increasingly strident in *Call It Something Else* (page 135), and the section ends with *A Horrible Thing to Say* (page 138), which presents an alternative view of the family as riven by bitter factionalism and dissent.

Developing the theme of ideological and cultural differences within Judaism, *Jewish and Israeli* (page 145) and *The Feel of the Sun in January* (page 148) examine some aspects of the distinctive Israeli identity, counterpointed by accounts of modern Israel seen through the eyes of immigrants and visitors, diaspora observers, and fundraisers.

Returning the focus to the diaspora, *So Natural* (page 177) relates an Orthodox woman's experience of wearing a wig. The headwear theme continues through *A Hat Like This* (page 180) and opens a section on religious law and custom that includes stories about kashrut (*The P Word*, page 188) and life-cycle events such as circumcision (*Why Can't It Be the Toe?*, page 191), and bar mitzvahs,* bat mitzvahs,* and funerals.

However obliquely, the specter of the Holocaust intruded on almost every encounter. For many, it remained the defining Jewish experience of the twentieth century and, inevitably, the reference point for stories about anti-Semitism. From *Suffering* (page 217), an Auschwitz survivor's account of liberation, to *Hidden Violence* (page 238), the Holocaust is recalled by survivors, their children, and others whose lives have been affected by it.

The following section includes the voices of those who converted for religious reasons or as the result of family pressure from a future partner or in-laws.

A *Thousand-Miles-an-Hour Man* (page 266), in which a social events organizer talks about his work to bring Jewish singles together, picks up the theme of relationships. The texts that follow include pictures of one very traditional Jewish wedding (*So Many Different Customs*, page 279) and one innovative one (*Every Step Along the Way*, page 285). Other voices in this section discuss their experience of intimate relationships with Jews and non-Jews, and the experience of growing up in a family where only one parent is Jewish.

From assimilation and the loss of cultural distinctiveness, the theme shifts to the renewal of interest in Jewish popular culture, as younger Jews remember or rediscover their cultural heritage. From *What Remains Here?* (page 317) to *The Dead and the Living* (page 327), speakers discuss their search for meaning and identity through reconnections with traditional Yiddish and Sephardi cultural practices.

From the past to the future: *Running on a Beach* (page 334), a photographer's account of how a single photograph can change a life, introduces a coda focusing on generational change and continuity, ending with *What's Not to Like About That?* (page 341), an exuberant look at a Jewish family that is at once both very traditional and new.

Since each text is designed to be read independently, readers can also construct their own pathways through the book by consulting the index on page 357.

Stories and Lives

Some stories of twentieth-century Jewish life will undoubtedly be told for generations to come. The Holocaust and the virtual annihilation of Jewish life in Eastern Europe, the establishment of the State of Israel and the emergence of a new Israeli culture, as well as the Jewish migrations associated with both events have already become embedded in a collective memory that will outlive the personal memories of those who experienced them.

Other contemporary Jewish stories are far less dramatic and as yet have no clear place in the collective consciousness, though they may ultimately be equally influential in determining the future of Jewish life in the diaspora. Since the end of World War II, Jews in Western countries have achieved more freedom, power, and influence than ever before while other groups have become more obvious targets of prejudice and exclusion.

The social and psychological effects of these changes are far-reaching. While the term "Jew by choice" is commonly used to refer to converts, to some extent all Jews in countries such as the United States, England, Canada, and Australia are now "Jews by choice." The increasing rates of intermarriage and the continued decline in traditional religious observance and cultural practices suggest that at the very least many people are choosing to be Jewish in new ways.

At a time of rapid changes within Jewish society—in part reflecting more general trends—it is not surprising that many different Jewish stories are now being told. The search for meaning has led many to rediscover or reinterpret older Jewish narratives, while others such as Sephardi Jews and Jewish women, whose voices were once marginalized, and yet others who had no voice—gays and lesbians—are finally being heard. In a pluralist age, Judaism itself has also become a pluralist phenomenon.

Is diaspora Jewry experiencing an unprecedented age of opportunity and creativity, or is it in severe and perhaps terminal crisis?

Will factionalism and internal conflict result in an irreparable split between Jewish denominations? Will Israeli identity become increasingly distinct from that of Jewish identity or will the unity of Klal Yisrael—the Jewish collective—be preserved?

This book presents a collection of personal narratives that respond to these questions. Telling a story—or hearing one—can reinforce our beliefs, challenge them, or present us with new ways of seeing ourselves and others. This is as true for communities as it is for individuals, and for storytellers as for their listeners. As Oliver Sacks observes, identity *is* a kind of story, created and recreated through the process of talk itself. In a real sense we are, all of us, the sum of our stories.

The Memory
of Our Journeys

———— ✦ ————

Marjorie Agosin grew up in Chile but came to live in the United States in 1973. A poet, essayist, and human rights activist, she holds the chair in Spanish Literature and Language at Wellesley College, Boston, Massachusetts. Her books include Dear Anne Frank, *a bilingual collection of poems in Spanish and English;* A Cross and a Star: Memoirs of a Jewish Girl in Chile; *and* Always from Somewhere Else: Memoirs of My Jewish Father.

MEMORY IS THE CENTRAL ISSUE. That's why we have survived. The memory of our journeys, that is what has made us a people. And we have been tenacious in keeping our memories alive, and that has been the greatest heritage, maybe more than God. We all have this desperate need for origins, we want to know where we belong, because we want to know who loved us.

MG: *"Who loved us . . ." What do you mean?*

You want to know who were your grandparents, your great-great grandparents. Families have a way to make you feel connected to the world, to feel loved. That's why families are essential, that's why so many people go to therapists here, because they don't have anyone to listen to them. And to trace the history of my own families, to collect their stories, it's a way to connect with their world; it's a tribute to their world, it's an affirmation of my love for them,

17

and their love for me, because they have made me the person I am. So memories have to do with loving.

MG: *All memories?*

Well, there are so many memories that we want to suppress: of atrocities, killings . . . but deep down it has to do with loving because even horrid memories of survivors of concentration camps, of torture . . . the fact that you are able to articulate the memory, to name the memory, to witness, that makes you more human, more vulnerable, but that connects us and that's what we don't want to lose. That's what we all strive for in this world, to have attachments, and that's why I think Judaism is much more than a religion, it's a way of living for me, a way of living. It's to have an active relationship with your community, your family, to be engaged in the world, to live responsibly. And so I write. I write about things that maybe people don't want to hear. I write about torture, about domestic violence, about what needs to be said, but no one wants to say.

And also I am a mother, and my life as a mother is very much linked to telling stories to my children, about where they come from. And I do this and eventually my own children will do this with theirs.

I think people should make peace with their identities. Once you are familiar with the world of your home, you can look at the rest of the world. So being Jewish to me is the shtetl,* and it's not limiting, it's expansive. I know who I am, I know where I come from, I know the story of my family's incredible journeys from Russia to Turkey, to France, to Chile . . . And I am proud to belong to this people that under so much adversity have survived. And that to me is the source of my strength, that's the gift that has been given to me. Stories are going to travel the most primitive way—through people—kind of what you're doing here, what we're doing together now.

---

*An asterisk indicates that the term is defined in the glossary, page 349.

Words and Worlds

———— ❦ ————

Alex L. recently graduated from medical school and now works in the emergency room of a public hospital in Chicago, where I met him yesterday while interviewing a hospital chaplain. It's a Saturday evening. We're in the living room of the Hyde Park apartment he shares with another young doctor. The three of us eat a home-delivered pizza in silence broken only by occasional bursts of laughter. "We always do this Saturday nights," Jonathan explains. "It's kinda our religion hour." When Garrison Keillor's Prairie Home Companion *finally ends, Alex, still smiling, switches off the radio. Jonathan leaves for a date with his girlfriend, and I flick the record button on my Sony. The interview may come to an abrupt end, Alex reminds me, patting the pager on his belt. He's on call tonight.*

FOR ME, JUDAISM *IS* STORIES. Like, when I was a child and we did the seder.* I was always attracted by the story element—the struggle between Moses and Pharaoh, and those really strange, scary images: blood, darkness, locusts, boils, pursuit, death by drowning, and all that. But I guess what really enthralled me was that this never seemed like a long ago event in antiquity, it had a lot of connections with the present.

MG: *You mean in terms of being a symbol of liberation?*

No, no. I mean, later on, I saw that as well. What I mean is that you're not just *telling* the story, you're kind of in it: there's the food you eat, like the matza. Y'know, *we're* escaping from Egypt too; *we* didn't have time for the bread to rise: you're in the loop of history.

So I had this really strong sense that there was a kind of continuity, or better still an identity, between us sitting around the table in America, and the Hebrews in ancient Mitzra'im.* It was almost like you couldn't see where Judaism ended and we began. Or vice versa. And what was most amazing to me was that these stories were brought alive by *me*, because I was the oldest child, and so it was me that asked the Four Questions [*the questions that elicit the story of Exodus*]. And also—because my grandfather—who always used to lead—would talk about how *his* grandfather in Russia used to do it, and he'd talk about the arguments he'd had with his brothers over the meanings of some stories or words or whatever. And I *loved* that idea of this link to other seders, to other conversations, in other places.

And there were others things, too. You know when you go out to see if Elijah's at the door? I'd go into the hallway, open the front door. And this was in Minnesota, in early spring, and I always remember going from the warmth of the dining room, with the whole family there, and the candles and everything, and opening the front door, standing there by myself, and looking into the dark street, and feeling the cold air come in.

And they'd shout to me from the dining room, "Nu? Is he there?" [*laughs*] But, y'know, it was always kind of a little scary. Y'know, "What the hell do I do if Elijah *does* show up?" [*laughs*] And again, for me that was like entering the story. You know the scene in that Woody Allen film? What's it called? *The Purple Rose of Cairo*. You know when the characters step out of the film screen and into the movie theater? And then later on, the real people end up on the other side of the screen? That's how it felt.

And then of course, when I was older, it began to get a little tedious. I just wasn't into it at all. I mean, for several years I just wasn't into Judaism, period. But what happened was that I got involved again through Hillel after I started medical school in New York.

I saw a flier advertising a Torah discussion group, and I thought, "A whole bunch of guys with beards and tzitzis,* and women in wigs serving the coffee. No, thank you." But there was also something a little intriguing about it, so for whatever reason, I went along and . . . Well, there was a real mix of people, not frum* by any means—Well, not that I could tell. And it was led by a literature professor, a guy called Harry Leiberman, who had an interest in Torah. And once a week he would meet with this group and they would read the upcoming parsha,* and discuss it. Totally informally.

And it so happened that that evening they were reading from Shmot, which in fact I didn't know then, but it means Names, and that's the Hebrew title of Exodus. And they were reading the part where Moshe* sees the burning bush, and he's very diffident about becoming the leader of, of the Children of Israel, and convincing Pharaoh to let my people go, and all that stuff . . . And so he says to God, "If—like, when I return to the Children of Israel, they're gonna say, "Who is this God? What is His name? What am I gonna say to them?" And God replies with this phrase *Eh-heh-yeh asher Eh-heh-yeh*, which apparently nobody really knows the meaning of, but some people translate it as "I will be what I will be," "Being there," or "I will be there with you," whatever . . . And so we read this—And then Lieberman sort of asked people to comment about the question. And there was one guy who had obviously done some reading, said that to know a name in those Middle Eastern cultures was to have power over someone. OK.

And then somebody else said that it was like maybe Moshe wanting to discover the nature of God, "Who are ya?" kinda thing. And every time someone spoke, Lieberman was like, "That is *so* interesting, and that's exactly what so-and-so said in the twelfth century." You know, some commentator like Rashi.* Or he'd say,

"That's really fascinating, I never came across that intrepretation before." And to me, this was just great! It was a real trip! And we talked about *yud hei vav hei* [*the four letters of the unpronounced name of God*], and did that kind of reflect the—what do you call it?—the ineffability of God?

And of course, I was reminded of the seders of my childhood. Partly, it was the topic, but also it was like the stories were linking in with all these older conversations and interpretations. And again, it was like . . . I don't know how to put it . . . as if the boundary between words and worlds had dissolved. Does that sound flaky? I don't know how else to put it. It was really amazing. Maybe you just had to be there.

But I was *hooked*! And what was interesting was, after that first class, some of us went out for a coffee, and we were talking about the class, and the meaning of names, and this and that, and eventually the conversation turned to the topic of our own names. And there was one guy there, who talked about how his family name had been . . . I forget now . . . [*glancing sideways*] Shloimovitz! That's right. And his father or grandfather or someone had changed it to, to, to Sheppard or Sheridan. No no no Sherman, yeah, Sherman—and his son, this guy in the group, he decided to change it back. But instead of reverting to Shloimovitz—which is Polish, I think, for "son of Shlomo"—he'd changed it to Ben-Tzion.* And he was telling us how this was a really big thing for him. He said he really felt a hundred times more, more connected with that name. And so he'd been Dave Sherman or whatever, and now he was Dah*veed* [*Hebrew pronunciation of David*] Ben-Tzion. And the funny thing was he was actually specializing in reconstructive surgery, which seemed kind of appropriate. [*laughs*]

And of course, everybody had their own name story. Everybody's got a name story, I'm sure you have too, right? Like, there was the woman who'd changed her name after marriage and then changed it back after getting a divorce, and how she felt about that . . . And

you know, nicknames . . . family names, I can't remember now . . .
a whole discussion about names. So here we are on a Ninety-first
Street café, we started with Moses and God, and now we're talking about Sherman and Ben-Tzion, and personal identity, and
Jewish history and spirituality and all these things . . .

So that's why I say for me, Judaism *is* stories. You know, there's the
Written Torah, and all the stories there, and the Oral Torah, the
Talmud, and the aggadot,* then all the other stories *about* those
stories, including the ones that never get written down. And then
just ordinary Jewish stories. Like even us meeting in the hospital
yesterday, and you coming here, and us having this conversation.
[*His left hand, thumb up like a rudder, loops in front of him.*] And
you writing it down. [*loop*] And then someone else maybe reading
it, [*loop*] and them telling it to [*loop*] another person. Or not, as
the case may be. [*laughs*]

My Kind of Judaism

———— ❧ ————

Manhattan in the evening rush hour: a dull rumble punctuated by an-gered horns, an irregular wailing, and a sudden scream of tortured rub-ber. Twenty stories above the Gehenna of Sixth Avenue, Yael I. is standing on her head. A storyboard for a shampoo commercial provides a resting place for her feet. Yael is a twenty-nine-year-old art director in the cre-ative department of an advertising agency. And a yoga fanatic. Having demonstrated the progress she's made after only six months of classes, she returns right side up and sits on the edge of her desk. Behind her, the twin towers of the World Trade Center are silhouetted against a mackerel orange sky. From talk of yoga to Buddhism, to spirituality and synagogue attendance. Yael, who grew up in Columbus, Ohio, says her family attended synagogue very regularly: "Once a year every year on Yom Kippur!"

MY EXPERIENCE OF TEMPLE was my parents' Reform synagogue in Columbus, Ohio, basically on High Holidays. And that was about it. And then, about a year ago, after I came here to New York, I heard of this Bnai Jeshurun synagogue on Eighty-eighth Street, just off Broadway. A girlfriend of mine, she'd been there, and she was very enthusiastic about it. She was like, "You have gotta go one Friday night, it is *amazing!*" And my reaction was, I'm not really into the religious aspect, and also . . . [*she arches her eye-brows*] to be honest, I didn't think it would be for me, I thought it would be a religious group. And I feel kinda bad saying this now, but people who don't know what else to do with themselves on a

Friday night [*laughs with embarrassment*]. But, I had heard these very positive reports from a number of people, and this friend of mine, one Friday afternoon, she came into my office and said, "Come on, Yael, we're going . . ." So we went.

And when we got there, there was a nonstop line of people all heading in. The line was just solid. And inside it was *packed*. I mean, it holds maybe a thousand, twelve hundred people, and it was literally filled to the brim. And from the first minute, it was totally different than any other temple or synagogue experience I had ever had. There was this incredibly soothing, therapeutic Israeli-type music. And the cantors are both from Argentina, and they are singing this great music. And at the front, there was a woman signing—using sign language for the deaf. And this really added another dimension, because, not only did you get a differ- ent take on the Hebrew—I don't follow Hebrew, but you could sort of get some of the meaning through the gestures—you got a sense of the drama . . . But also, to me it showed how inclusive they were, how much they wanted to include everyone. And there was such a diverse bunch of people there: a lot of people who'd obviously come straight from work, people of all ages, some in T- shirts, sleeveless shirts, very casual style, and also people from dif- ferent countries, and even different ethnicities, some African- Americans, some Asians . . just a very, very diverse group. And I felt completely relaxed, like, "These are my kind of people."

And at one point—oh, this was so neat!—they started getting up to dance, and pulling others up, and they were all holding hands, a hundred, hundred and fifty people, snaking right around the aisles . . . and my friend pulled me up, and we kind of entered the chain, and I didn't know the steps or anything, but I just went with the flow, literally. [*laughs*] This was not your usual winding down from the week with a drink or going out to dinner. It really felt like a celebration.

And after that experience, I started going regularly—and I've even gone by myself, and felt very comfortable doing that, which a lot of people do. And they have a big social side. Like, in the current newsletter, which I have somewhere—I'll show you later—there's page after page of activities, announcements, job listings, trips, retreats, singles' events . . .

And last week was Martin Luther King Day, and so there was something about Martin Luther King and Abraham Joshua Heschel [*U.S. rabbi, theologian, activist (1907–1972)*], who was at Selma, marching with King. And last Sunday, BJ [*Bnai Jeshurun*] did a joint memorial service with an African-American church, I forget which denomination, I didn't go, but . . . actually there was an article in *The Times*.

You know, politically and culturally people are coming from very much the same kind of place as me. It's my kind of Judaism. And after the services, you go out on the street and you forget you're in New York: everybody stands around, talking like it was a small Jewish town in the Middle East, or Poland, or somewhere. And they'll invite you to go have coffee with them, or dinner. Complete strangers. It's happened to me. So like, tonight I'm going with my boyfriend, and we'll probably go out afterwards, to a restaurant—there's a million and one places on the Upper West Side—and if we see someone there who looks as if they're by themselves, we'll ask them along.

It really has given me a lot. You feel like you're meditating, you're in a community . . . you feel at home . . . Even if you're standing alone, you feel at home. Michael, you *have* to see it. You wanna come tomorrow tonight? It is *the* Jewish experience in New York!

Just Do It

———— ❦ ————

*Saturday, 16 January 1999. William Jefferson Clinton's Senate impeach-
ment trial is almost a week old. Over dinner in a French restaurant on
Manhattan's Forty-sixth Street, I've been discussing the trial with theater
critic Mike D. Mike seems thoughtful. He takes his glasses off and pol-
ishes the lenses. He returns to an earlier topic—his dislike of certain
innovations in synagogue liturgy. Last night he was present at the same
synagogue service that Yael I. attended (see page 24, My Kind of Judaism).*

I'LL TELL YOU ANOTHER THING THAT I DON'T LIKE. In the prayer book,
it used to be "Thou": "Thou shalt this," and "Thou shalt that," and
then they changed "Thou" to "You." Happened in a lot of places.
They changed the words. And I don't get it. I mean, what's wrong
with "Thou"? I like "Thou," I do. I mean, God's not supposed to
be your buddy that you're gonna play stickball with. This is "Thou."
He's supposed to be something above you. I do have a problem
with it. It's something for your imagination, this is something unknown, and I find "You" quite offensive.

And last night I had the same reaction, for different reasons. We
went to the Bnai Jeshurun synagogue. My sister was in town, and
she really wanted to go; she'd heard a lot about it, and so I took
her. And she liked it a lot. And I can see why. You haven't been
there, right? Well, you go in, and you say, "Wow, this is great: there
are people dancing, and they're davening* with kavanah, with

27

intention . . ." I mean, it's one of the few places around that attract this *incredible* number of people. You can be very observant, or you can come in with a shopping bag from Zabar's or wherever. And everybody's welcome . . . there's no discrimination—you can be of any sexual persuasion, any ethnic background—there's no judgment, supposedly.

And it's all very, very musically-driven: the rabbi sings . . . There's a guy—I wouldn't call him a cantor—a person on keyboard, like the backup, like The Supremes, and it's all designed—I think quite cleverly—to create a certain atmosphere, and I think that's why people come in droves, because they're creating an environment in which one can feel comfortable enough for the spiritual side to surface. They allow people enough space to be who they are. And that's why they're coming from all over the state of New York. I know people from Poughkeepsie, they go there when they can. They want to experience this. And if you're not used to it, it's very refreshing.

And I'll tell you the truth. I very rarely go there, but I thought last night—maybe for the first time—"Gee, I can understand why people are drawn to this." There's a certain comfort in seeing all these people. You see the guy alone with his son, you see the family, the single person . . . You see the person standing saying Kaddish,* you say, "Gee, where would I go, how would I feel if I'm in that situation?" It felt really good to know it was there, to see these people.

And then the service is over, [*with irritation*] and what happens? The rabbi invites—I don't know who the guy was—some official of the congregation, some guy with a Yemenite-looking yarmulke,* and a goatee, and a ring in one ear, and the guy goes up to the bimah,* and proceeds to announce that there's gonna be an impeachment rally, a State of the Union rally, basically saying, "We think that Clinton's wonderful, and what the Republicans are doing is some grave injustice to humanity and . . ." [*exasperatedly*] I mean, what has this got to do with what I came here for? You basically killed an hour and fifteen minutes of my experience, by imposing your political bullshit agenda on my time. And I found it *highly* offensive, and it's the kind of thing that makes me never want to go into these places. Because I don't find it honest. [*halting abruptly*] Maybe "honest" is not the word. But it's like, "We're all-inclusive *if* you agree with us." So why don't they create a spiritual environment that's nonjudgmental? I think that's why a lot of Jews are attracted to Buddhism. Because the Buddhists don't do all that.

A Twenty-Four Seven Thing

❧

Two days ago I interviewed the father, a retired cardiologist living in Santa Barbara, California. Today I'm with the thirty-three-year-old son, a taxation specialist in a large accounting firm in San Francisco. The view from his office is normally very impressive, he assures me, apologizing for the fog. He seems a bit nervous, says he's worried about saying the wrong thing. I try to reassure him. There are no right answers. And anyway, I say, nobody will recognize you. We'll change all the identifying details. You can even choose your own pseudonym. He pauses to think.

CALL ME NATHAN, IN HONOR OF MY SON. That way, I'll know it re-lates to me. Yeah. You know, I didn't know how to prepare for this. I told my father, I was going to go on the Internet and read. He said, "What are you going to read? It's supposed to come from yourself!" [*laughs*] I said, "I gotta see what other people say, just so I can be in the neighborhood . . ." [*loud, nervous laughter*] But I guess that's boring, to say the same things.

MG: *So did you surf the net?*

No, I didn't! I didn't have time! [*laughs self-consciously*] But I wanted to. You know, I would love to hear from you, what type of comments you get from people. [*pause*] So what would you like to know? How can I help you? Maybe you can direct me a little?

MG: *Well, it's Friday afternoon. Can I ask you, what are you going to be doing this evening?*

Ah! Well, it depends what time I get home. We live about an hour out of the city. My wife will *probably* light the Sabbath candles. Maybe. I mean, sometimes she misses, because she forgets the time, but . . . we will not follow the traditional Sabbath. I mean, we'll try going to temple tomorrow, if we can, but . . . from my own point of view, I don't necessarily view being a good Jew as someone who goes to temple, or who keeps kosher. I've always felt that being Jewish should be a twenty-four seven thing—you know, something you do twenty-four hours a day, seven days a week, and what that means is being a mensch.* You have to be a good person. And that to me, quite frankly, is the most important thing, much more than going to temple. It's the way you live your life . . . that's what it means to live life as a Jew.

MG: *Can you think of anything that's happened recently that could illustrate that?*

. . . sure. We had someone just the other day here in the office who did something to our technology . . . with our system, and absolutely destroyed the whole accounting system! [*loud laughter*] Absolutely destroyed the entire system. Every client in the firm—all ten thousand—had the exact same name.

MG: *What was the name?*

Herman Sterdu. But you'll have to change that, to something else if you're gonna use it, OK?

MG: *Something with the same flavor, OK?*

Great. So we had to undo the whole thing. And this was a huge, huge job. But my way is not to get upset. My way is to think of an action plan. So I did that: developed a strategy, figured out what we needed to do, and started getting it done. But the very *first* thing I did, I went to the person, and I pulled her aside, and I told her not to worry. I said, "This is OK. This is not the end of the world. We'll handle it. I just want you to know that we, we value you and what you do for the firm . . ."

MG: *Usually*.

Yeah. [*big smile*] If I were to respond to her—negatively to her, she'd never try anything again, because she'll always do what she's supposed to do, and that way you'll never get more than the basic out of them. And I said, "Don't worry, we'll fix it. It's gonna be OK."

And over a two-day period, we fixed it. And I think that's part of it. I think there's a responsibility there. I mean, I could have said, [*in an "irate boss" tone*] "You just blew the whole system away! We just spent a million dollars on this thing!! The firm is gonna kill me . . . *YOU'RE FIRED!*"

Somebody else, they might've done that, and felt justified in doing it. But that's not my way. I mean, you have to treat human beings in a certain way. And a lot of that has to do with my upbringing, my Jewish background. And if I didn't do that, and I didn't act in that way, I'd feel I was a failure.

Tell Me, Please

———— ✤ ————

Brighton Beach, New York. A hot, humid evening in mid-August. In the living room of a second-story apartment a block away from the boardwalk, a standing fan arcs across a poodle asleep on a sofa beside her owners, Lilya and Yura K. During my quick microphone test, Yura starts to declaim Yevtushenko's elegy for Kiev's Jewish victims of Nazism: Nad Babyem Yarem pametnikov niet . . . (*"At Babi Yar there is no monument . . ."*).

The K.s are Russian Jews who have lived in the United States for two years. Lilya is an accounts clerk for a Manhattan law firm. She's forty-seven. Yura, a year older, is an engineer who now works as a pizza delivery driver. He's wearing a New York Mets T-shirt, shorts, and sneakers. Lilya's in a light cotton dress with a floral pattern. Throughout the conversation, Yura cracks and eats nuts, occasionally emphasizing a point with a flourish of his nutcracker.

MG: *So what does being Jewish mean to you?*

LILYA: All our friends here are Russian Jews, from different parts of Russia. And we, we have very symbolic Shabbat. We gather together, have something to eat or drink, play cards. That's what we call Shabbat. And always the subject raised: What is a Jew? Is it religion? Or is it nation? All sorts of conversation, but still we couldn't make up our minds. And of course if you talk to three Jews, they will have five opinions!

I strongly believe that it is religion. Now. When I arrived here and started looking for job and had to fill the application form, in field of nationality I used to put "Jewish" or "Jew." And some people in employment agency said, "No. Jewish is not a nation, it's a religion. Which country you from?"

I said, "Why? I always thought of myself as Jewish. That was nation in Russia." In our passport—in our Russian passports, there was last name, first name, place of birth, date of birth, and then you have fifth line: nationality. And it was written: JEWISH.

I *never* associated myself with Russians. It was completely opposite race. I was Jewish, hundred percent, hundred and fifty percent. And then I arrived here and started filling the forms, they said, "No. Jewish is not a nation, it's religion. Which country you from? What's your nationality?" And that's when I started thinking Jewish is a religion. Jewish are all so different, blacks, whites, yellows, and they all Jewish and all under one Torah, something like that. If I meet a Yemen Jew or Jew from Morocco, we have different culture, different kitchen, but we all have Torah.

YURA: If I was applying for job, I wouldn't advertise that I am Jew because you can come across in the gerarchy [*sic*] where they make the decisions, somebody will definitely identify that this applicant is Jewish. And they would rather take someone else, even perhaps Asians. [*cracking a walnut*] Then look at the Dreyfus case, look at Germany—

LILYA: [*taking the nutmeat from the shell*] I was reading now that Germans hate Vietnamese, number one; blacks, number two; Turkish, number three; Serbs, number four; Jews only number five.

YURA: Ach! They feel guilt. In America, the blacks know who are the Jews. *They* know who is the enemy.

MG: *I was talking to someone yesterday, and he was black and Jewish.*

YURA: They take the religious. But they're not Jews. Do *you* consider them that they are Jews? It is like goyim* in Russia, they take Jewish religion just to escape from Russia. [*angrily*] They are not Jews. They're prostitutes!

LILYA: [*admonishingly*] Yura! Yura! Jew now is black, yellow, white, everything . . . There are some Ethiopia blacks in Israel, they are Jewish.

YURA: But that's different. Converted Jews, I wouldn't trust converted Jews. I wouldn't change my religion; why should they change? It is maybe good for them now but tomorrow they become Buddhist. I don't trust them. Can you imagine that I become a Jehovah Witness? Can you imagine?

LILYA: [*turning to me*] I have friend in Hoboken, and their son is dating with non-Jewish girl. But what she's done this girl, she converted to Judaism. But the boy's father is not satisfied.

YURA: He is right.

LILYA: He says, "No, I don't believe her, even though she knows more about Jewish tradition and can teach *us*." Still he's not satisfied. Me, I wouldn't trust her hundred percent, either. But it's a hard situation. Maybe this girl truly converted. How do you know? How do you know?

YURA: When they are alone, without Jews, what you think they say about us? Until the bell will ring, how will you know? Here we have Russian woman converted to Judaism. She become Lubavitch.* But one day someone will say, "Kill the Jews, save America!" I asked her, "What will happen to you then?" And she said, "Oh, then I will go back to Russian."

LILYA: I know her. On the Yom Kippur* she spend all day—the only one—stands from morning to night, the only one in Russian synagogue. We were all sitting, chatting, and this woman— What's her name, Yura? Very funny name . . .

YURA: Hanushka. She became Hanushka! [*laughs derisively*]

LILYA: She was standing all day, her face to the wall, not looking at anyone and praying, praying. I don't know what she was praying.

YURA: [*mockingly*] Baruch atah Adonai Eloheinu.*

LILYA: The others were laughing at her: praying all day! [*chuckles*] I don't know any prayers, I don't know Hebrew, so I was just chatting with my friends. I wasn't eating or drinking. I was among my people; that was enough for me.

The sleeping poodle paws the air and growls. With a smile, Lilya strokes the dog's head.

But who knows? I have very patriotic feeling, always whenever Jewish achieve something: in medicine, in Six-Day War—

YURA: OK! Six-Day War. [*waving the nutcracker*] This is right. You hitting the apple . . . Michael, what you say in English?

MG: *I'm not sure . . . uh . . .*

YURA: I mean, you say exact. You hit target.

MG: *Oh, right. Maybe, "You hit the nail on the head."*

YURA: Hitting nail on head? I don't know . . . Anyway, I want to say, change to Jews only took place due to Israel's existence. That's what I would like to underline. Israel exists, Israel is strong, and we Jews can enjoy life, live a whole life. But if Israel perishes, it would be same it was hundred years ago.

Do you think that you will be safe because you escape to United States? Do you think Jews will always be in this luxury? Goddam bloody Jews! In some time, Americans will blame you that "You are rich, that you got all the positions, you are all doctors, you are all lawyers, all wheelers and dealers, you suck the blood from other nations, from everyone . . ."

And one day, the history will be repeated again and again. I am sure of this. I may not be alive, but your children will experience this.

Jews shouldn't forget who they are. They shouldn't forget their destination. They should not forget why they exist, what they treasure, what they should do: live in Israel. That is what I think. But you see, psychology of Jews in United States is very strange. They think that everything is possible to buy with money. They give money and they think, "Oh, I helped United Israel Appeal." Their conscience is OK. And the Israelis take the rifles and they sacrifice their lives in the war.

As to me, I would send them to serve in the army *their* children. Also, I would like to tell them that it's important to bring Jews from Russia to Judaism. But not to the stupid Judaism what make Lubavitch. Shtetl* is dead. It was five hundred years ago, and it's dead! They should be circular.

MG: *Circular?*

YURA: Circular! Not religious.

MG: *Secular.*

YURA: Yes. What I am saying? Circular Judaism. Not like Lubavitch. But the Lubavitch don't irritate me like Michael Jackson. In comparison to the harm American culture brings to the world, Lubavitch is perhaps like toy. What is good for America is not good for other countries.

MG: *But Yura, you live in America. You chose to come here instead of Israel when you left Russia.*

YURA: [*chuckles*] My life did not end yet. Everything is ahead! L'shana haba'a b'Yerushalayim.* But that's another interview. May I interview you instead?

MG: *Go ahead.*

YURA: Then I will ask you some questions. Can you tell me, Michael, what does it mean to be a Jew?

MG: *Well, that's what this project is about.*

YURA: Yes. It's very important. Tell me. What does it mean to be a Jew?

MG: *It's a difficult question because—*

YURA: Answer me now. What is it? What is it?

MG: *Well, it's all sorts of things.*

YURA: In particular?

MG: *It's not easy—*

YURA: You asking *me.* Why don't you answer yourself? Tell me what *you* think.

MG: *I'll tell you a story—*

YURA: No. Tell me, please, what you think. You, Michael, what do you think? Frankly speaking. Tell me your opinion. I would like to know. Is it a nationality?

MG: *uh . . . no. Well, not in—*

YURA: Aha! Then you are like Stalin. Then what is it? Is it a phenomenon? Is it your blood? Is it your mentality? Is it your religious? What is it? Tell me, please.

What Was
the Point Here?

Seagulls are wheeling overhead. I'm outside on the deck of the Staten Island ferry this blustery March afternoon, sharing a thermos of tea with Alana A., who grew up in Far Rockaway, New York. Alana's parents were members of a Reform congregation, but along with her husband and fifteen-year-old son she now belongs to (and irregularly attends) a more traditionally-oriented Conservative synagogue in Staten Island. For Alana, who is something of a small talk tornado, Judaism is simply an inspiration.

I LOVE THE RELIGION! Whenever I sit down and take time to study Talmud, I think to myself, "This makes sense." Sure, it can be *hideously* sexist! [*laughs*] But not the sexual laws themselves. They have got to be the most liberated sexual laws that any religion has ever created, in terms of a woman's sexual needs. You gotta balance everything! In how many religions do you have to get the woman moist before you enter her? God! I mean, please. Do you ever hear about this in Catholicism? You ever hear that you must satisfy a woman? You ever hear that the woman has a right to say no, but the man must always say yes? Do you ever hear that a woman has a right to divorce a man who doesn't put out at least weekly for her? This is a *great* religion! Jesus!!

And I go to morning minyan* every, every few weeks. And I love it. And they're desperate for people during the winter. The old folks go to Florida, which has more Jews than Israel—God's waiting room—so they kill for people to go to morning minyan. You go through the service like a choo-choo train: twenty-five minutes, outside. If you're staying in New York and you want to go some morning . . . Can you read from the Torah?

MG: *Well, I suppose, uh . . . Yes.*

You know, we were in Israel this summer . . . Why am I telling you this? I forget the point, but it'll come to me. Anyway, I hadn't been in fifteen years. I still have no idea what Israel has to do with Judaism. And if you can tell me, I'd be really grateful.

We spent time in Jordan, too. Jordanians are much friendlier than Israelis. But as I was saying to somebody, "I know Israelis get a bad rap, but they've been bred for survival." And it really is like no other culture in the world. You grow up there and you're having a conversation about, you know, the price of cranberry chip cookies, a plane goes overhead, and suddenly you wonder if you're gonna be gassed to death. So I mean, there's a level of toughening, of paranoia and fear and survival that we can't even imagine. It really has created a very tough culture.

MG: *I'd be paranoid, too, but my response would be to hide under the bed.*

They'll still get ya, honey! I mean, yesterday, I met this woman at a bat mitzvah*—Right! That was the connection! Torah . . . Israel . . . bat mitzvah. OK. And she almost brutalized me to death in the kitchen over the rights of Israelis to kill anybody in order to survive. Now, I brought up Leviticus, where there are any number of laws about how to treat the stranger in your land, all of which request much nicer behavior than you'd ever see from an Israeli! [*grins*]

And she said, "Bullshit, bullshit, *bullshit*! We've been nice to people all our lives, and what has it gotten us?"

40

But I mean, historically, any time Jews become landlords, they've not been very nice. Which is why I think we lost the Second Temple. And when the Hasmoneans won that cute little Maccabee war,* they became more oppressive than Antiochus Epiphanes [*the Syrian-Greek king whose suppression of the Jews led to the Maccabean revolt*]. When you force grown men to convert and have circumcision, this is not a sign of a respectful government. So when Jews are bosses, they are as bad as anyone, maybe worse. Go ask any Arab in Israel.

And in a way, living in exile, living in the diaspora, did wonderful things for us. I mean, a lot of the more beautiful laws and heimishe* behavior—I mean, the sweeter culture came when we were oppressed. We were never the ones that were the source and center of power. We are that self-preserving, witty, intelligent, humorous eye. [*faking a Yiddish accent*] Und venn ve've not binn, you see vot heppens? A nation-state gets destroyed!

And uh, what was the point here? Israel, bat mitzvah . . . bar mitzvah . . . Right! I really wanted my son to know about Judaism and identify himself as a Jew. And the reason we went through the whole bar mitzvah process was that he should know. And not know ritual, but know that there's a bedrock of moral thinking that can help shape your mind, that can affect you wherever you go. His Torah portion was Kedoshim, holiness. Y'know, it says that you should not stand by the blood of your neighbor. What does that mean? He had to think about the fact that there's no such thing as an innocent bystander. If anybody is hurting, you're obliged to do something. And he learned that from one little line.

And the other reason was, "Well, you want something to rebel out of? So here's your board to bounce off of." And it's not a bad board to bounce off of.

But so many of the Jews I know identify their Judaism as "the building fund" or [*in a louder voice*] "We are Jews and couldn't be prouder, if you can't hear, we'll yell a little louder!"—neither of which have a thing to do with it. So, of *course* they hate the religion and have grown away from it.

I think, if, like me, you didn't grow up in a very religious community, you sometimes fantasize about having all your questions answered, knowing what the right choices are, because someone has told you. There's something a little bit attractive about that. [*pauses, leans closer, pats my arm*] Probably when you're not in it!

Do you know Chabad?* They're great. The rabbis are so cute! They're these passionate people. You just have to love 'em! And unlike other Chassidim, they don't pass judgment on you if you're not halachically* right. In fact, they *expect* you to be ignorant. It's their job to bring you over. We're not sinners, we're a challenge! I like the attitude. Now there's a reason why I'm telling you this. And it'll come to me.

Heritage

—————— ᘐᖇ ——————

Washington, D.C. In a meeting room at a Jewish day center for the eld-erly, a moderator reads aloud from an article in this morning's Washing-ton Post. *It concerns the U.S. Secretary of State Madeline Albright's surprise announcement that her grandparents were Jewish victims of Na-zism. The reader looks over his half-frames and invites comments from the twenty-three seniors at this afternoon's discussion group. Did she really not know until recently? Now the truth is out, will it be good or bad for Israel? Half an hour later, the debate is still raging when Artie W., a dapper seventy-five-year-old sporting a blue bow tie, proposes a change of topic. "Let's talk about atheism," he suggests. "We covered that last week," someone retorts. "And anyways," adds the moderator, "it ain't in today's* Post! *As the meeting breaks up, I ask Artie if he'd like to share his views with me.*

WELL, IT'S KIND OF UNCOMMON TO BE A JEWISH ATHEIST. Did you run across many? When I first thought about it, I felt like the ho-mosexual that has to be closeted. For years I didn't tell anybody, I was ashamed to say it. "Hey," they said, "you're Jewish, that means you're of this faith." Fine. I let it go. I didn't stop to argue with anybody about it. But I know there are many people like me, and they are either ashamed or reluctant to say it for that reason. They're afraid they won't be accepted. But I've said it here in front of a large group of people. I've reached an age in my life where it doesn't really matter what they think. I really don't care any more.

I was brought up in an Orthodox household, but when I was very young, when I was seventeen or eighteen, I started to think about various things, and I just couldn't believe in God. To me, if I go to hear a rabbi talk, and he talks about the Almighty doing this and the Almighty doing that, where was the Almighty when they were slaughtering all those Jews in Europe? Some things just don't make sense . . . I mean, if there was such a thing as God around . . . I was an atheist before that, but that sort of codified my thinking and said, "You've got to be right."

Why is it all the people who claim God, they say, "God helped me"? All the winners. All the winners, from football players on, they all say, "We won the game, God was with us." Does God take sides in a football game? If you win a war: "God was with us." God wasn't with us when they had the Holocaust. I doubt whether God was hanging around saying, "Well, it's a good idea, Hitler, keep goin'!" I don't believe in any kind of religion, but I'm not denying myself as being Jewish. I think it's an aspect of Jewish culture and background.

We are the first people that developed into a democracy from our law, the way we interpreted and built it. The old rabbis used to interpret the Ten Commandments like the Supreme Court interprets the Constitution. The Constitution's relatively a small document. But if you've ever read all the cases that were reported, you'd find shelves and shelves of books from ceiling to the floor, wall to wall, covering just Supreme Court decisions on the Constitution, which is a very simple, small document. And this is what the Jewish people developed when they had the Ten Commandments. They took and interpreted various things as they went along. And these interpretations were known as the rabbis' commentaries.

Now there are some things that should be changed by now because they were done many, many years ago. And the reason we didn't change it, we didn't have a country. If you don't have a country, you can't say, "Well, this we're gonna do, and this we're not gonna do." But once we have our own country for several years, that we can develop our thinking, maybe some of the old rules might change, so that we're not restricted to some of the rules of kashrut* like milchiks and fleishiks.*

I remember when I was a kid my mother said, "You can take a glass and drink milk out of it, wash it out, and then you can put soup in it—chicken soup—and it's OK. But you can't do that with a cup, and you can't do that with a saucer." I said, "Why not?" Says, "Because you *can't*! It's not kosher." And as I got older, I started thinking, "It's glazed. If it's glazed, it's the same as a glass. Why not?" The rules didn't change. Those were rules, when we had clay pottery, sure, the particles of what you ate could be embedded. So I can see that. But now things have changed. Scientifically, things have changed, so that some of the things we believed in, we no longer have to follow.

But the heritage of the Jewish background to me is very important. I worked for a company that had about a thousand people, and there were about four Jews. And I stayed out on all the holidays. Just to show them that I am Jewish. I didn't go to a temple, I didn't fast. If you don't believe in it . . . [*smiles*] But I sent my daughter to Hebrew school; she was still interested, and she's very proficient in Hebrew studies. And she's still interested in it. And she keeps a religious household. She sends *her* children to a religious school. It's the heritage. [*looking at his watch*] I gotta run. Been nice talking to you.

This Whole God Thing

Spring in Pennsylvania. On the lawn near the library at Bryn Mawr, the prestigious liberal arts college for women. For a microphone test, I ask Jodie F. to describe herself.

OK . . . I'M NINETEEN YEARS OLD . . . I grew up in California, I'm a sophomore, majoring in English literature . . . I'm almost five nine . . . I'm white—whatever white is . . . I have blond hair—sometimes it's a little enhanced!—but it's blond in the summer. [*smiles*]

And my clothes tell you that I'm the all-American girl, because these are Gap jeans, and Gap is the all-American store! But I'm also the *Western* girl, because my jacket and my sweater are Eddie Bauer—which people make fun of me for wearing because it's kind of like "Mom clothes." And I have on my sneakers—well, actually in California we call 'em tennies, like tennis shoes, but here they call them sneakers. [*fingering her earrings*] And . . . I'm wearing moonstones, which tells us that I like simplicity.

And of course, I'm Jewish, except I feel my Jewish identity is weak.

MG: *What do you mean?*

Like, I have an older sister who's twenty-two, who I refer to as . . . SuperJew! [*laughs and blushes*] She was president of the Hillel organization at her university—which was a place with maybe eight to ten thousand Jewish students. And she was president of that

46

Hillel, really SuperJew. [*smiles*] And she wants to go live on a kibbutz and everything.

And then there's me. This whole God thing is a little out there for me. I mean, if someone asked me, "Do you believe in God?" my honest answer would be—This is very hard for me to say—being raised Jewish; adoring my rabbi, thinking she's the most amazing woman I ever met; having SuperJew for a sister—and I say, "No, I don't believe in God." I feel like there's something wrong with me. And . . . sometimes, I feel hypocritical and confused. Because I *love* Passover, I love Tu B'Shvat* — it's a really cool holiday, even if you aren't Jewish—we just had a Tu B'Shvat seder* on campus—and I go to Friday night services. But this God thing . . . I mean, I don't even want to say I *don't* believe in God, because I'm not sure what that actually means. But I do feel it's hard for me to say I'm a Jew, if I can't say, "I believe."

She picks up a twig and examines it intently. She looks up.

This is very difficult. This is the first time I've actually—Well, the *first* time I talked about it was just this last month, with my dad. I was at home. It was just before I came back to college, and we were having dinner, just the two of us, and I finally told him. Because my dad is someone who feels very religious—although ironically *I* go to Shabbat more than he does, it's weird.

But I told him, I said, "Dad, at this point in my life, God is not in my moral code." And I think that sort of freaked him out. And he tried to convince me—he's a salesman by trade—he's in marketing—so his words are persuasive, but . . . I found what he said . . . very traditional, like, he believes in a Higher Deity, or a connected universe . . . But my dad's a real liberal guy, to say the least [*smiles*]—he doesn't *sound* like one, but he is—and he just said, "It's OK. You can believe in whatever you want . . ."

But that's my problem. I don't believe in anything. Or at least, I fear the future, that I won't take it for all it's worth, that instead of pushing myself, to take the harder job, to take the harder route, I'll just be living an empty life with a lack of faith in myself, in what I'm doing, in everything: God, Judaism, faith, college, work, relationships . . . I think it's all a big web.

I'm very confused. Like, for my sister, being Jewish is a major part of her identity . . . And yet for me, it's so unclear and fuzzy. I don't understand these people who feel Jewish by going to a Jewish film festival, or doing Israeli dancing—To me, that's just going to a film festival or doing Israeli dancing. I would dispute that it's Jewish. Eating Jewish food isn't being Jewish, it's *eating* Jewish. What *is* being Jewish is a belief in God, and an inclination to the texts, and what they say.

Sometimes I'm sitting there in temple, and I'm reading this stuff, and I'm thinking to myself, "Is anyone like, *thinking* about this stuff . . . Or are you just saying it? Do they really believe it?" For me, Judaism is not a race, or an ethnicity, or a culture—it's a religion. And if you don't believe in it, how can you call yourself Jewish? Like, I've heard of Buddhist Jews, and atheist Jews, but it strikes me as odd, as a contradiction in terms. It's like Christian Jewish. To me, it's meaningless. And here in America religion is really important, and if you don't believe, or say you believe, you're outside the loop.

It was interesting actually, about a week after that conversation with my dad, I was working at a local bakery, and two of the women icing the cakes were talking about childbirth—both of them had recently had children—and one of them said, "Man, if you don't believe in God beforehand, childbirth really brings you close to God."

MG: *Do you think she meant the beauty of childbirth, or the pain, or what?*

Well, I think it was more like . . . the beauty of having a child that is now yours, but not completely from you, that's your creation, but also isn't yours . . . And I remember, as I heard that, I really felt a pang, because, I mean, you think, "Is there something I'm not getting here? Am I just so weird that I can't be a part of this Judeo-Christian society?"

But I think my God view, some days it's still evolving, and some days I'm an atheist. Sometimes, when I'm just walking to class, or looking at the trees or something, and I'm feeling just connected, I think, "Oh, maybe *that's* what God is: a feeling of being connected, connected to where I am, to what I'm doing." Sometimes I feel what I'm doing is meaningful, I feel inspired by my courses, I look around me and I feel happy. Is that God? I don't know . . .

I used to be very involved in dance, in ballet, when I was younger. And when I was studying for bat mitzvah, I would tell my rabbi, "Being religious for me is dancing." God was never part of the picture, but when I was training hard, and feeling just like [*makes air quotes*] "in the zone," I don't know if you know that expression . . . there's a whole book on that now . . . Anyway, I think that's the closest feeling I've ever had to being religious.

[*pause*]

I think a lot, I write poems, I read . . . And like, my roommate is extremely religious. She's Methodist, and . . . so the question is constantly in my face. When she says to me, "I'm going to praise practice"—which is her choir—my reaction is, "How is it that it's so meaningful to her?"

MG: *Have you ever asked her?*

We've tried to talk about it, but I tend to get very uncomfortable, very quickly. She's invited me to church and I've sort of—The first time, I really sort of flipped, I left the room and didn't come back for a long time.

MG: *Why do you think you reacted like that?*

I don't know. [*sighs*] That's another thing about me—the most classes I have in one department is in the religion department. I mean, I still have a great bias towards Judaism, but . . . [*self-mockingly*] I'm a twisted soul. [*laughs*] Wow . . . You got more than you bargained for in this interview, right?

I think I did, too. [*sniffs and smiles*]

Fruit on the Tree

Apart from the fellow in the red plaid shirt getting a coffee from the hot drinks machine, the cafeteria of this midwestern U.S. science research institute is deserted. It's six-thirty in the morning. In twenty minutes I have an interview with the institute's director; he's leaving for Europe this morning and this was the only time he could see me. But first I'm going to finish my coffee, glance at The Guardian Weekly, *and go for a brisk walk to try and wake up. As I'm reading the* The Guardian's *Notes and Queries section, a deadpan male voice inquires whether the empty seat in front of me is free. Looking up, I see a styrofoam cup of coffee, a red plaid shirt, a two-day growth of beard, and a pair of dark blue eyes. "Go ahead," I say, folding away my newspaper. I've been in the lab all night," he says. "What's your excuse for being here so early?" And when I explain, it turns out he has a story of his own.*

I LIKE RIGOR. Mathematics, physics: intellectual rigor. And same with religion. It was rigor that I liked. That's why I was attracted to the Lubavitch. And once I was convinced that all the more shallow forms of Judaism—Reform, Conservative—were really not very rigorous, it was easy to ditch them. And when I discovered the Lubavitch wanted to persuade me to give up physics because they prefer to gain knowledge by revelation not reason, I ditched them too. And that was the end of Judaism for me. I purged myself.

MG: *Do you ever have any doubts?*

Well, the interesting thing is there are all these other religions in

51

the world, and they think *they're* right. So whatever answer I come up with has to explain why all these people believe in different things. I think it takes strength to reject, weakness to accept. It's easy to accept, it's the appeal to authority, "Well, they say this, so it must be right . . ."

As human beings we're designed to generalize, to accept things without a lot of critical thinking. If you see fruit on the tree, and someone eats it, and that person doesn't die, you can't assume that you'll be safe. But we're designed to do that. It takes a lot of strength to reject things and test things out.

> *Tony B. is a physicist who studies neutrinos—uncharged elementary particles that are thought to be massless and that rarely interact with other particles. In addition to his love of intellectual rigor, Tony also seems to like desert-dry humor. For the microphone test, I asked him to tell me something about himself.*

I'm thirty-seven and a half. It was my half-birthday yesterday matter of fact . . .

MG: *Well, congra or should I say ulations?*

Either will do. Mazel or tov. OK with the sound system? OK. So what does being Jewish mean to me? Well, I learned to be Jewish by watching Woody Allen films. And I learned that being Jewish comes with a lot of guilt, and a lot of responsibility. Anybody who's Jewish knows that they're born with the responsibility to, to carry on the tradition, to marry a Jewish woman, and have Jewish kids, to go to shul,* to support the community, to send money to Israel . . .

MG: *And have you?*

No. But it took a lot of years to overcome the, the sense of responsibility. I felt guilty for a while, about not doing it: my wife's not Jewish; my kids aren't Jewish; I don't support the community . . .

MG: *So how did you overcome it all?*

The first time was after leaving high school. I felt like the values I'd been instilled with were not the ones I wanted. So instead of going to college, I took off, hitchhiking around, seeing other cultures, losing myself into them. So when I came back I didn't feel the same level of attachment.

The next time was when I decided to get married to a woman who wasn't Jewish. I was living in London, studying for my doctorate, and I'd joined the Lubavitch. So for a year I'd stay with families on Shabbat, have Wednesday afternoon sessions where we'd study. I even wore tzitzit* for a while. I started getting into all that. It was actually taking over my mind, for a while, but fortunately the wedding forced all that to a close—I'd hate to think where I'd be now.

And then for a couple of years I'd have dreams of rabbis where they'd be telling me I should be doing this and that.

And then when I left London, I didn't get involved in any Jewish communities, so the whole thing goes into the past. But I do still feel an attachment.

MG: *In what way?*

Well, I was in Israel for two months this year, working at the Technion, and when I go over there, I feel a sense of attachment, of history. So it feels good. On the other hand, I'm very careful of what I say—the avoidance of being judged by others there. People automatically assume that you're doing everything that is expected. So it's better to, to play the game, which involves not saying too much, and let people assume you're doing everything. I mean, a friendship overcomes that—It's not the friends I worry about— No, that's wrong. I don't *worry* about it, it's just a concern.

MG: *Are you concerned about being judged here?*

I'm not involved here. I'm not connected with the Jewish community. So there's a sense of release.

MG: *So where's the attachment then?*

You know what I do? I go to China every year for research, and when I'm over there, I'm there for about a month around the High Holidays, and I go to a pseudo-temple. There's a grouping there, mostly American, but various others, one Chinese family—an interesting grouping—and I participate in that. Yom Kippur, they get hundred and twenty, hundred and thirty people. So when I go away from family, and I'm on my own, then it's nice to have a connection, that's what I find when I go to China! [*laughs, scratches his stubble*]

MG: *And how about when you're at home? Nothing at all?*

Well, interestingly, we lit one Chanukah candle this year. You see, my daughter's eleven, and my son's ten, and this year—God forbid—we even had a Christmas tree, which is crazy, because my wife's a Hindu, and I'm Jewish . . . But the kids wanted it, and I stopped saying no as vigorously as I've said in the past. So there was a tree. I just avoided that part of the room.

And then I figured, the reason this is all happening is because my daughter is fixated on culture and ceremony, so I decided that it was my fault for not teaching her my ceremonies, and so I managed to get out the chanukiya*—couldn't find a book, but I remembered some of the stuff by heart, and then we lit a candle on the first night.

Turned out the night was actually the night *before* the first night—got the day wrong, and then I had to go to Canada for a week, and when I got back, we didn't bother to light it again. So that was Chanukah. Pesach* we're probably gonna do something too. My kids take Hebrew lessons, at school.

MG: *Really?*

Yeah. Partly because they want to—they know their parents are from two different cultures, they want to know more about them, and part of it is . . . because they think they're Jewish. I haven't broken the news to them yet, that Jewish people reject them because their lineage comes on the wrong side. You know how prejudiced we are against the Y-chromosome. But I'll probably start doing more Jewish things, I don't really want them to get into Christian things. If they need a ceremony, then I'll give them the Jewish thing. I don't mind if they're not Jewish, but I don't know if I can live with them being Christian.

Angels

Mid-afternoon in a café on Beacon Street, Boston. Marthajoy Aft, a former consultant with the local Board of Jewish Education, now teaches Jewish mysticism and healing practices. She tells me she's been suffering from chronic fatigue syndrome, but the voice and manner are decidedly allegro vivace as she describes her discovery of the Jewish esoteric tradition.

FOURTEEN YEARS AGO WHEN I TURNED FORTY—now you're supposed to say, "Oh, Marthajoy, you don't look that old!" [laughs] Anyway, fourteen years ago when I turned forty there was a door that opened in my head, and I became interested in Jewish mysticism, which until then I had not been interested in at all. And that was a very big turning point for me, and I began to meditate in a serious way, and to study mysticism.

I used to wake up crabby. When my kids were growing up, I wasn't so pleasant in the morning until I had two cups of coffee. It's abusive I think, but I've made my amends on that. Anyway, now I wake up and the first thought I do is *Modeh Ani,** the morning prayer. And when I first began to do that it felt unnatural. Like I *wanted* to wake up crabby. But now instead, that comes to me first. And that's helpful. And there are songs. I sing *Adon Olam** in the shower. I don't know why. I began to do that when I first had chronic fatigue and I couldn't think straight, and my mind wasn't right. So I started working with doctors, I found herbs and various medications, and I'm much better, Baruch haShem.*

56

But anyway . . . So I sing *Adon Olam* in the shower, and if I'm driving or I'm riding on the bus—which I did today—I make it my business to look at the sky and be aware of the order of the universe. Y'know Nachman of Bratzlav [*founder of the Bratzlaver Chassidic sect (1770–1811)*]? Nachman says, "Watch the sky every day. In fifty years it's the only thing that will be the same." And that's why I watch the sky. Because Nachman said. Nachman said. [*laughs*]

MG: *What do you do when you watch the sky?*

I'm aware of beauty. And the light. I watch the light, I watch the birds. I'm particularly interested in birds. I'll tell you my eagle story.

When I first got chronic fatigue I was really sick. I was sick for six months. And we were scheduled to go for our twenty-fifth anniversary to Nova Scotia. And I said to my husband, "I'm too sick to go." And he said, "Look, you can sleep in the car, you can sleep in the hotel, we're going!" So we went. And I said, "OK. I have one goal. I want an eagle in the sky." And that would be a sign for me. Because of the whole idea of where it says in Exodus, "I brought you to me on eagle's wings." I said, "OK. I wanna see an eagle."

So one day we were up on Cape Breton, parked over an overlook. I'm leaning on the car because I'm too weak to stand up. And I see an eagle soaring. And I said, "Oh, my God! This is wonderful. This is just what I wanted. Thank you so much. You know, you made a beautiful bird."

Then there were two. Then there were three. Then this big eagle—I don't know if it was mother or father, though I *suspect* mother—goes into the woods and starts flapping around and all these little eaglets come up popping like popcorn. There were thirty eagles circling above us. And I said, "This is a sign I'm going to get better. These are angels."

So when I watch the sky, I'm looking for birds, I'm looking for light, I'm looking for angels. So I work at it. It isn't always easy. I work at it. That's what I'm doing when I watch the sky.

MG: *I didn't realize there were angels in Judaism.*

Most people don't. In the Siddur,* in the Orthodox Siddur, in a prayer called *Sh'ma al HaMitah*, the *Sh'ma** you say on your bed, talks about four angels that are around you when you go to sleep at night.

So Michael is the angel on your right side. It's mi-cha-El: he who is like God, the angel that delivers — 'cause the angel's a messenger — delivers awe before God.

And on the left side is Gabriel, gibor-El: he who brings strength and support from God. So people who are sick particularly, this is a really wonderful prayer to use. Shlomo Carlebach [*U.S. rabbi, folksinger (1926–1994)*] set it to music. So, those two angels are like — go through your body, you know, with strength and support on your left, and awe on the right.

And then in front of you is Uriel, or-El: the light of God, giving you direction, showing you where to go, if you listen and watch. And in back of you is Raphael, rofeh-El: the angel of healing, who brings healing.

And all of these angels work on all four worlds, so they work on the physical realm, and they work in the emotional realm, and they work in the intellectual realm, and they work in the spiritual realm. And over your head is the Shechinah* who just showers down love and blessings all the time. Luria [*Rabbi Isaac Luria (1534–1572), a theologian and mystic*] teaches that after a person has cried so much they cannot cry any more, they're going, [*sobbed in breath*] "Huuuh," then the Shechinah Herself comes, and strokes your head, and says, "There, there, my child."

So that's mainstream Judaism. You can understand it literally, that there are these winged beasts, or you could understand it energetically, that there are these messages being delivered in energy form. Or metaphorically . . .

MG: *How do you understand it?*

Oh, it happens. It's real. Absolutely real. My parents are eighty-five. They live in Chicago. My dad has been sick a lot, off and on. Three months ago I was there and we didn't think he was going to make it really. He was lying in a fetal position in a hospital bed. He was wrecked. So my mother—I taught my mother, and we did the angel prayers for him every day, and on the third day, he turned a corner—Baruch haShem—and we'd leave the blinds propped open so he could see some light, and he recovered. He's home now. I'm going to see him this weekend.

They're real. It's not that they can necessarily cure. They can cure on the emotional realm, or on the intellectual realm, the spiritual realm, but not necessarily on the physical realm, that they're going to undo whatever. You know, just as much as is possible can be delivered, as much energy, as much light, as much healing, that's all. So that's angels.

A Long Way to Go

⌒⌯⌒

Lunchtime in Central Park, New York City. In the spring sunshine, tourists and office workers picnic on the grass. Children play on nearby swings. Thirty-one-year-old Shoshana W. works as an administrative assistant in an Orthodox girls' high school. She's wearing a black jacket, a matching ankle-length skirt, and an auburn sheitl.* Discovering the joys of Orthodox Judaism has transformed her life, says Shoshana. Her voice is soft, measured, and also intense: she has experienced the beauty of Orthodoxy and is eager to communicate the feeling. "It's like a big jewel," she tells me.

IF MY HUSBAND GETS UP LATE AND MISSES DAVENING,* he gets very upset. So I'll be in the kitchen getting stuff ready for our lunches, and I see him put on tefilin* in our living room. And the first time I saw it—I cry a lot, I'm gonna give myself away here—I couldn't stop crying: looking at our progress, at how we started out and here we are today, living as Orthodox Jews. It's mind-boggling. Sometimes you can't look, it's painful to see. You remember all the arguments, the struggles, the decisions.

And it's a really beautiful journey, you really see how much you've grown together. But sometimes you'd really love to have just grown up with it, not had those conflicts. But we don't get mad about it. God gives you a path for a reason.

My family was very, very unaffiliated. And quite assimilated, a lot of intermarriage on both sides. And it was very hard finding a way

60

back. But I always had an affinity for Jewish culture, and as I got older, also for Jewish religion. For a while in college I experimented with Eastern religions—not experimented like living them, but read about them, studied them, talked to Buddhists, Taoists, whatever it happened to be. But I had no connection at all to that, no interest in becoming that way.

My husband and I kind of worked our way up through the ladders. I don't mean this to be offensive to anyone but we started reading Reform books, because that seemed the closest to where we were. But we kept finding holes in the theories, and said, "Well, why would you choose to do *this* and not do *this*? OK. So maybe we'll be Conservative." So we bought books from the Conservative press. And that was even more difficult because they were trying to walk an even finer line: they were teaching their children about kashrus,* about Shabbos,* and yet the parents are dropping them off at synagogue and then driving to the mall. So, of *course*, the kids are getting mixed messages.

And we started thinking about how will we teach our children what it means to be Jewish. I think when you grow up assimilated, with the outside culture's version of religion, you perceive that there's a separation between your life and religion. And we really found the beauty in Orthodox Judaism is that it was not separated at all. You are just as responsible as a religious Jew in your business affairs, in your relations with people, as you are in the synagogue. That was very powerful for us. And then we started studying more about the religious precepts.

And of course we didn't become observant overnight. We had no idea we would end up here. It was a process, a long, painful process, because as you move through these questions of trying to understand if there's a God, and if there is, what are our responsibilities. You have to question your families' decisions, you have to question your own lifestyle choices, you have to make priorities.

We've been on the road for about eight years, but really trying to observe very carefully I'd say for the past three and a half. Those first years were really a lot of philosophical dialogues. It does incredible things for your relationship. And for a while it was touch-and-go, because one of us was moving faster than the other.

MG: *Was that you or your husband?*

I'd rather not say which one, out of respect for our relationship, but one of us was saying, "I'm not going to work on Saturdays or Friday nights, and holidays that come in the middle of the week," and the other saying, "I'm not sure it's so black-and-white."

But it deepened our relationship to such a degree, it raised it to such a level, we started talking to each other differently. We started really trying to understand who this person that we were with was, and what they wanted out of life, what their value system was based on. And that was an incredible thing. Here we were trying to really figure out what was our understanding of the universe.

And still we have to be careful. One of us gets very excited about a new thing we want to do. We want to make a point to give exactly ten percent tzedakah, righteous giving, the other person says, "I don't know if our budget can take it." The other says, "But we can do it if we have faith. Everything is always provided. Have we ever gone without?" "No, we haven't." "So we can do it!" And so we learn to make do with less.

It's been a real shock, I have to say, growing up in this culture, learning to say you don't need to have it now. I mean, we still have a long way to go; it's never finished. Like, my mother has this idea that once you're Chassidic, that's the ultimate, then you're done. [*smiles*] "No," I said. "These people, they study full-time. You *always* have things you can improve on. You always have things you can learn." There's so much in the liturgy, you could study your whole lifetime. *Six* lifetimes, there's too much.

And people sometimes think you're a freak that you're making this change that the rest of society thinks as going backwards. They think you're shutting yourself off. As a woman especially, it has such connotations. People really think you've pulled out your brain through your ear, and put it in a jar and pickled it; that you're a sheep, and you're this, and you're that . . . instead of understanding that women find great beauty in living a lifestyle that puts its priorities in order.

For a while I thought I would have real problems that women don't participate so much in the synagogue service. I thought I'd have real problems with the idea of women covering their hair. I said, "I don't know if I can do this, because everyone's gonna think I'm stupid, and I'm an intelligent woman."

Then you mature, you say, "It really doesn't matter if people don't like what you do. People don't like it? What do I care?" I feel callous to say that, but I can't help it. I had a conversation with a friend of mine. She thought she was a feminist. She said, "All this wasted potential."

I said, "What do you mean, 'wasted potential'?" I said, "Someone has to raise children, and if a woman wants to do that, that's *her* choice. Isn't it a feminist belief that a woman can choose?"

She said—[*trying to recollect the exact words*] "Those are choices that have been made for you. You have to make your own choices."

And then I realized: I was totally at odds with this belief system. I don't see men and women in competition. I see them as different types of people that have to find a way to work together in the world. Even in the most Orthodox communities women do work. Sometimes it's a reality; you cannot get by on one salary. But it's not a career. It pays the bills. It's not a priority. The family's the priority.

I don't *want* to be a CEO! I want to learn how to be a wonderful Jewish mother, for when, please God, we have children. I want to learn how to be an educator for the next generation. I want to learn how to be a hostess, that when people need a place to come for Shabbos, they can come to us.

Constant Love

Susan H. is thirty-eight. She lives with her five-year-old daughter in Palo Alto, California. Three mornings a week she attends a Torah study group for women. Afternoons, she teaches yoga in the downtown studio where I am now. An advanced class has just finished. As students file past, Susan comes over, recognizing me by my tape recorder. She's wearing a purple leotard and black leggings. Palms pressed together in the traditional Buddhist greeting, she explains that unfortunately she won't be able to talk for long. In forty-five minutes she has to pick up her daughter from kindergarten. In an office decorated with a framed color photograph of Tibetan monks creating a sand mandala, Susan relates how in recent years she has become increasingly attracted to Orthodox Judaism.

WHEN I WAS SEVENTEEN, I wanted to go and study in Israel. I wanted to go to a yeshivah. And I wasn't allowed. So instead I went to Japan and studied Buddhism and stuff. And for twenty years I struggled. I really struggled in the desert. I did wonderful things, but I got very hurt in doing them, because they were very away-from-Torah things. I really, truly wanted to have a family when I was twenty something. But I didn't know it. I was so into going with the flow, going with your feelings, fuck who you want to . . . And that's what I did. I went with the gestalt, and I followed the garbage pail. I had an amazing time, grew as a human being . . . But I also actually got very hurt, had serial relationships, and then finally, got totally lost.

And then I rediscovered everything through the birth of my daughter. And the more I learn, the more I know that all the answers are there: in Torah, and you just have to find them. But first, you have to find a person who's been there. There has to be some mentor, someone who can put you on track. And I've been fortunate: I've found Rabbi Mermelstein.

Like the first time I met him, my issue was—I had been going through enormous guilt feelings about marrying a Catholic-born person, and I was relearning the Torah, felt more and more guilty, that I'd sinned . . .

And I had a session with him, and he clarified all of the issues: If you do something consciously, then it is a negative, but if you've done something without being aware of it, it's not a sin! He gave me an enormous amount of encouragement that I had not sinned. He felt that I was really unique in the way I'd handled the situation, and it was understandable why I'd married the person I married. He *really* empathized and accepted me and my soul. There was no judgment, just total acceptance. He saw right through the garments I was wearing and right into the neshuma* and what that had to do.

And from there I could deal with the real issues. It's all about moving on, it's about forgiveness, life, normality, challenge, no guilt. This is Buddhism! [*laughs*] I was telling the rabbi this just yesterday! And he loved it. I told him it's Buddha's birthday on Saturday, and of course it's Shavuot* on Saturday night, so we decided Buddha was a Jew. [*smiles*] It all comes together beautifully.

And for me there's a total crossover between yoga and Judaism. For the rabbi, it's like, "Ugh!" but I keep bringing it in, and he's becoming quite comfortable. I imagine one day I'll even get him into the lotus! At the moment I'm very busy on his diet, and trying to get him into ayurvedic cooking, and stuff like that, really trying to incorporate these things into the teachings. He's doing OK, too.

He's given up caffeine and sugar, and I've given him books, and now he's not threatened by the words any more.

MG: *What kind of words exactly?*

Like "India." [*laughs*] There's just an incredible two-way flow of information. And Rabbi Mermelstein's there for me, at all hours of the day or night, on e-mail or phone. And my friends in the group, they are just *so* spiritually connected, offering a constant love, understanding, lack of judgment . . . Which is so different to my secular friends who are more about me-me-me, I - I - I.

And I forgot about my other teacher: my daughter. She's a little walking neshuma. She's just so close to all these messianic beliefs, and she keeps my light going. Kids are so open, such open daisies. She swings on a swing, and she sings, "Moshiach,* Moshiach, Moshiach is coming!" She really believes in the cycle of life, and we'll be reborn, and saved, and it'll all be fine, and the world will be happy.

I only learned about Moshiach myself last July. It was a bad time for me, and I was really in the depths of depression. I got hold of a videotape of this Rabbi Friedman's, and decided that the man is a mind-blowing mind. The Rebbe* said to him, "You are to teach women," so he's in Northfield, Minnesota, doing women's retreats. So I called and decided that I'm going. Never left my daughter before, but I left her with my mom, and flew there the next day.

It was quite mind-blowing. He is *amazing*. We did *Tanya** and a few other sections from the Torah, and then there were two women: one was very Venus-oriented, doing a lot of the feminine stuff from the Torah, and the other was in and out of kabbalistic stuff. We laughed, we played, we studied. I felt so full. I felt I was on the right path. I wasn't flying, I just felt real.

And according to the rabbi, Moshiach is a sense of time and space and being. So it's, it's a period where people are doing good things, where the world is more good than bad, where bad is overcome by good, people start caring, rather than I - I - I, me-me-me and it's all about giving and sharing, and warm, fuzzy good deeds.

She glances at a digital wallclock.

But I come from a secular world, and I'm conscious of an enormous chasm between the two worlds. And I'm on the fence myself. I haven't got there yet. Well, I'm slightly off the fence. I wouldn't call myself strongly secular, but I jump back on the fence every now and then. [*laughs*] Let's say my tush is still on the ledge; I'm not there yet.

To be a single mother living far away from a shul, surrounded by very secular families, exceptionally secular, antireligious, I find that an incredible struggle. I mean, I have friends who *really* want to get involved but their partners are atheists. It's impossible. You cannot keep a kosher home when someone's bringing seafood into it every day, and takes the kids to Burger King. You can't do it.

I have a fantasy about . . . if I was with a man who was committed to learning with me, then it would be a cinch. Maybe that's my ledge. I want a hand to hold. I've met a handful of men, because I'm supposed to be meeting men. [*laughs self-consciously*] I'm single and this is the way it should be done. But so far, Rabbi Mermelstein hasn't come up with the right person, because I'm not looking for someone who's already there.

A True Chassid
of a Rebbe

The late leader of the Chabad-Lubavitcher Movement, Rabbi Menachem Mendel Schneerson (1902–1994)—the Rebbe—was believed by many of his followers to be Moshiach: the Messiah.

Rabbi Moishe S. is twenty-seven. He directs a Chabad House in New Jersey. Chabad is an acronym based on the Hebrew words chachma (wisdom), bina (understanding), and da'at (knowledge). Chabad Houses are centers for prayer, Jewish outreach, and education. Rabbi Moishe sits at the head of the table, some cookies on a plate in front of him. He invites me to help myself. The rabbi's two-year-old son, Naftali, plays by his side underneath the table.

MG: *Did you ever think . . . Y'know, a lot of people . . . Well, some people say the Rebbe was, uh—I mean, what did, did you make of . . . ?*

Rabbi Moishe smiles at my awkwardness.

Messianism is very much part of the foundation of Judaism. And in every generation, every Chassid who is a true Chassid of a rebbe* should think no less of his rebbe than that he is the Moshiach. And if he doesn't think that, what kind of Chassid is he?

MG: *Right. But, I mean, did you* personally *believe that the Rebbe—*

69

He guided us in all life's most pressing questions. He inspired us, he lifted us up, he was the center of our lives. He was regarded with *unbelievable* reverence. The Rebbe was a beacon of light to the entire world. No major event in my life happened without consulting the Rebbe. The Rebbe was perceived by the eyes of Chassidim, by many in the Jewish community, as the leader of the Jewish people, a person who singlehandedly, *singlehandedly*, breathed life back into world Judaism after the Holocaust. He built a whole new generation, reached out to the Jewish people, had a message for everyone of acceptance and love.

Everybody acknowledged that the Rebbe was truly *the Rebbe*. There's certainly a void that hasn't been filled.

Naftali tugs at his father's trouser leg.

Hey, hey, hey! Stop that please! Be a good boy. Go on, go play with your toys. [*to me*] But the organization is as before. The network has experienced a tremendous growth spurt in the last three, four years, almost as large as in the previous ten years. Hundreds of new Chabad Houses. And now the world is waiting to step up to the next level of consciousness, of Godly consciousness.

That is part of our mission, to bring about a sense of God into the world. A time will come when God will be obvious, not the other way round, as now, when the world is obvious, and God is not. A time will come when we will find ourselves spiritually, and intellectually, and emotionally able to experience the most subtle truths, and see them in a very vivid, clear manner, and understand that God is in everything.

Naftali pulls vigorously at his father's trouser leg. The rabbi gently but firmly pushes him away.

You wanna cookie? OK. There ya go! Good boy.

Naftali unceremoniously throws the cookie away, yelling with rage and frustration. Rabbi Moishe bundles up his son and car-

ries him into an adjoining room, where a housekeeper is vacuuming the carpet.

Yeah, so, as I was saying, the side effects are all very nice, in terms of world peace, a Jewish brotherhood, the Jewish people establishing themselves once again in Israel. All nice things. All part of our tradition, part of our faith system. I can give you some literature if you'd like.

MG: *Thanks.*

So why don't you come to shul tonight, come back here, eat with us? How would that be?

MG: *That's very kind of you. But I have to catch a train back to New York and the last one leaves fairly early.*

Stay overnight. We have room. Sleep here, come to shul tomorrow. Get a train when Shabbos is out. Five-fifteen, five-thirty, you're at the station. Think about it. It's up to you.

Place to Go

Steven H. is thirty-five. He teaches in a university department of romance languages in Chicago. A few months ago he and his wife came to live in this pretty lakeside town a ninety-minute commute from the city. Steven's sitting on an adirondack in the backyard gazebo he recently built. The lawn is a lush green, surrounded by a dense stand of oak and birch. Gentians grow in profusion. A dragonfly darts between us. Steven's wearing shorts and an open neck shirt. At first, he seems a little tense, his hands clasped tightly behind his head, but gradually relaxes. It's a Saturday morning. I ask him if he ever attends services at the local synagogue.

I HAVEN'T BELONGED TO A SYNAGOGUE since I was fifteen years old, and that was my parents' membership. And yet when I sought a place to live up here I really didn't want to move to a town that didn't have a synagogue. And the synagogue's just three blocks away in an old Victorian building. I think it's a bit of a hybrid denominationally because it has to serve the whole district. I think it's Reform-Conservative, probably drifting towards Conservative, which appeals to me.

Yet we haven't joined. But we like the fact that it's there. In fact, it's more than "like" it; we needed it; it was a requirement. I remember feeling in the other towns that we looked at that were nice: "I'm not sure I'd feel comfortable here." It's not that I was worried about not being welcomed, but I wasn't sure that I wouldn't feel alien.

It was the first time I'd lived out of the city too, so I needed something familiar.

See, the synagogue says to me, "Jews are allowed here" and that they have been here. I draw all kinds of assumptions—some of them may be false—that Jews are tolerated here, that there isn't a problem. But I still haven't joined.

We did call, I must say that. We called because we'd thought about it and were put off by the cost of joining. It would cost us something like twenty-five hundred dollars to begin. You pay a foundation or building fee to contribute to the structure. I think the annual wouldn't be as much, but it could be sixteen hundred a year. And then they wanted five hundred dollars for the tickets for us to attend High Holy Day services. And I was really put off by that and didn't feel that I could afford it. And I know that they would allow me to come for a reduced fee, but I didn't pursue it because I know that I'm still ambivalent about joining.

And I know my wife is too, because it's alien to her. Well, it's both familiar and alien at the same time. She has a much more ambivalent feeling about Jewishness. She knows she's a Jew, she knows that she can be treated as a Jew, yet she feels completely outside that building. She doesn't know the language, she feels—I know she feels embarrassed in front of other Jews for what she doesn't know. Yet interestingly, she wanted to marry a Jew . . . So *there's* Jewish identity for sure.

So I haven't been inside that synagogue. I've thought about it, though. There are a number of influences to draw me to the synagogue, even though I haven't taken the plunge. One is intellectual. I saw a way in for me back to the religion in terms of study. If I knew that the synagogue had a reading group where people were discussing Talmud or Torah, and, and, and Jewish philosophy, I'd be there next week! And I suspect that if I joined, and they don't have something like that, I might want to start a group.

I would also like — I mean, really, really, *really* would like to polish my Hebrew. Studying the Bible as literature has made me crave the language. However, I'm not sure how I feel about the religious side. The spiritual side is still filled with uncertainty, so . . . It's like something I crave — but don't necessarily believe exists — as a source of comfort or relief. But I have definitely circled that synagogue, both mentally and physically. And sometimes I wonder why it's so hard to enter.

My experience of my parents' synagogue in Chicago, in probably one of the richest suburbs of Chicago, was that the important thing was making sure you had the finest clothes for the High Holy Days. Always felt like a fashion show to me. Not that that's so bad but it's what *wasn't* there in terms of intellectual and emotional content. And all they did was squabble. They had a huge fiasco over a rabbi, and it was all political, and there was nothing there for me. Misplaced priorities. I don't want to repeat that.

Yet I don't want to be a snob in the other direction and make assumptions about what I might find here before I learn. But I am . . . concerned. I don't think it's unusual for a Jew to worry about alienation from without *and* from within.

And another impulse drawing me to the synagogue is suffering. I've had a lot of problems in my life over the last five years — my wife's been sick — and she's — I'd rather not go into details, if that's OK. But it's been very, very difficult for us . . . And that can make you think that there may be some relief in this kind of community, in this kind of place. Is the synagogue a place you can go for the kind of comfort that I seek? My fear is that I will encounter a rabbi who falls short of my idea — which I think is very idealized. I'm afraid of a rabbi who won't understand me. Or who will be more political than caring. Or more showy, more superficial. That's the big thing I'm afraid of, that it'll be superficial. And I cannot bear that it would be that way. There are times when I've thought of just parking the car in front, going in and seeing if the rabbi is there. Not joining, just going and talking to the rabbi. And I haven't.

Judy called the rabbi to talk about it and she said he sounded very nice. But to me, he sounded like I remembered rabbis to be: like cheerleaders for the community, and the children's group, and this and that. Useful . . . but I need something else.

I'm not sure there's an adequate model to care for real suffering within a congregation. I watched my father argue with a rabbi who wouldn't come to visit his mother when his father died. He was very angry. His feeling was very much like a businessman's: "I pay my dues to this synagogue, I've been a part of it for twenty, thirty years, and I've never asked for anything. I ask once, and you're too busy." And I didn't know who I was more troubled by. Because my father just wanted the rubber stamp, and I didn't see that that was going to help anyway. And then my father said he was going to leave, he was that angry. I think he stayed away for a while, but he didn't, he didn't leave, you know?

My fear of disappointment in the synagogue is intensified by my wife's illness. That's what started all this. It's almost as if I'm not approaching the synagogue because that is safer than if I go and don't get what I need. Because what's beyond the synagogue? Then I would feel I really don't have a place to go. And before I can go, I have to adjust my expectations, and maybe even my needs so that they're not so great. I don't know . . . I think there will be a point at which not investigating will be more annoying and more troublesome than finally just seeing for myself.

A Marketing Exercise

———— ✺ ————

Richard L. owns a fried chicken takeout chain in Los Angeles. He's thirty-two. We're in a café near his Santa Monica office. The cell phone in the breast pocket of his linen jacket rings.

Excuse me.

[*Five minutes later.*] OK. I'll call you back. I have someone with me right now. Bye. [*to me*] So uh . . . what was I saying?

MG: *You were telling me about your business.*

OK. I've been in the chicken business about a year and a half. Saw there was a big demand for it. Saw that it was a good thing to invest in. And it's going well, thank God. Varies with the seasons of course. Summer's best. But once a franchise is established, the turnover — the fluctuation is not huge.

> *After receiving another three business calls in as many minutes, he switches off his cell phone. "I can give you fifteen minutes, OK?" In a nutshell, then, Richard feels the problem with Judaism is bad marketing.*

Unfortunately, being Jewish doesn't mean a helluva lot. Religiouswise it doesn't mean a lot. But I still have a strong Jewish feeling. I get very offended by anything anti-Semitic that I see. So that means to me — that confirms that I'm Jewish. That I'm still Jewish.

And I'd have to say I feel more comfortable with other Jews. But synagogue? Nope. I find it to be very boring. All it means to me is sitting next to a guy, probably my brother, and talking about what business he's been doing. And ninety percent of people who go there I'm sure are like that.

There's no real incentive or motivation to be Jewish. I don't believe that the kids today look up to the rabbis and say, "I'd like to be like that."

It's a marketing thing. Judaism is a marketing exercise. And so's anything. And I think it's been marketed very badly. I mean, for the amount of brains that Jews generally have in business—and in marketing!—this is the one crucial area that has been neglected. I really believe that. Things like tefilin* and going to synagogue and Rosh haShanah* and Pesach* . . . it means nothin' to me.

But I think it's fairly—well, relatively easily solved by havin' this whole change of leaders. It might be as simple as when you go and buy a house. The things that you look at most, the thing that impresses you most are the cosmetics. You walk in there and there's nice tiles and there's nice wallpaper, but the actual house could be crumbling. And yet people will still want to buy that house. Sure, they might reassess things after doing further research, but then again, they might not.

Same thing applies to Judaism. If you have role models that look the part. And that act the part . . . They may not genuinely *be* the part, but at least they're gonna bring people in. It'd be a start. At the moment there's no—there's not even a starting point.

MG: *Can you think of anybody who'd be an appropriate role model?*

It's a good question. I think . . .

He distractedly massages his left temple.

I mean, I've got people in mind that, that could do it. But they—they may or may not be the right people. I think of my brother, for example. He's a well-respected guy. He's an honest guy.

And uh, well, I suppose *I* could be a fairly good role model. Y'know what I mean? I could be. But . . . There's two—there's two things. There's firstly a time factor. As you can see [*points to his cell phone on the table*], this is what my life is like seven days a week. And the other thing is, I don't know whether I've got a genuine interest. Because it is a big responsibility. And it's a time-consuming thing.

Now, you might regard that as being a copout, and it probably is. But I gotta look at the practical side of things. If I'm gonna commit to something, I like to do it one hundred and ten percent. Y'know what I mean?

Or maybe even someone like my business partner. Larry's a good example of the—the cosmetic side of things. He's a good-looking guy. And he's an intelligent guy. [*laughing at the joke he's about to make*] But you'd have to be careful of the risk of attracting only women. You might find that you've got a huge female following. [*laughs*] It's gotta be appealing to guys as well. [*sighs*]

And I don't know what the formula is.

He glances at his watch.

Maybe the right thing to do is go to a marketing company. Treat it like a project. Say, "This is our problem. We wanna market Judaism to Jews. The problem is—[*He jabs an index finger around his coffee cup.*] This this this and this. The opportunity is this. These are the risks." Have you ever been to a marketing presentation? What they do is, is you go there and say—Well, let's take my chicken business. What they'll do is say, "Well, what market are you after?" OK? "The market that we're after is . . . kids or people between sixteen and thirty-five." And the answer on the Jewish side of things would be . . . fundamentally, pretty much the same market.

And then they would say, "What are the problems that you have with your product?" And we would say, "The perception that the food is not healthy, that it's greasy, and this and this and that." And that's something that has to be fixed. And the perception on the Jewish side of things would be that you are basically a jerk if you are a religious Jew. And that is a perception thing— 'cause I know a lot of religious Jews who are not jerks.

The marketing people would do their research. And they wouldn't do it in the synagogue. Because those people are the traditional people. They would do it in the sports bars. In the street. Down on the beach. The people who don't know us. And don't come to us. If someone took this initiative, I figure you'd come up with some very, very novel and interesting ideas. And I guarantee you it has never ever been done in the whole history of Judaism.

Surviving the Jews

A beachside café in southern California. In the middle distance a scatter-ing of surfers catches the last waves of daylight. In manner and appear-ance Rabbi Aharon P. gives a sense of tight, coiled energy released in short, intense bursts. His large navy-blue felt cap barely restrains an ir-regular mass of brown curls. The grizzled beard, however, is unencum-bered. During the interview, Rabbi P. runs his fingers through it, twisting a strand into an irregular corkscrew. The rabbi's volubility and marked southern accent—he grew up in Memphis, Tennessee—attract the stares of a number of quieter patrons, though he seems unaware or unconcerned. His is also a voice of concern and exasperation—over the years he's worked in many Jewish institutions and become disillusioned with them.

FOR TWENTY YEARS I'VE PLAYED THE ROLES OF RABBI, chaplain, mash-giach,* teacher, counselor, New Age meditation workshop leader. Well, that's not really mainstream, is it? But working for institu-tions that are basically mainstream.

I've done almost everything that a Jewish professional can do. Ex-cept stay in a job. And it's important to tell you this objectively. I'm not going to freak out here and tell you all my complaints . . . I've been there, too. I've lost jobs complaining; that's the Jewish institutional mentality: "You come here, you shouldn't be think-ing of changing *anything*!" The most absurd thing.

The institutional culture is backbiting, politicized, ego-tripping, loshen horeh* ad infinitum, putdowns, scorn . . . It's a style. And to survive professionally, you have to be very Machiavellian. What's going on is really bad news. There's a lot of spiritual and psychic abuse, so at this point in my life, I think, "How do I survive the Jews?" Matter of fact, I was thinking of writing my autobiography: *Surviving the Jews: The Autobiography of a Jewish Mystic.* [*loud laughter*] But I think people would call me an anti-Semite, that's how crazy Jews are.

There's no sense of self-critique. You won't find that in the Jewish world. I have not seen it. I'm forty-five years old and I have not seen it. Have you?

MG: *Well, I—*

See, what the Jewish world wants is Jewish humor, simplistic responses to Jewish tradition, information gobbledygook. It's just hype. Big-time hype. American Jews don't want to be woken up. They want to be pacified. They're satisfied with the basic: Rosh haShanah, Yom Kippur, Passover and Chanukah. [*sarcastically*] Sweet, nice, feel-good.

They want to enjoy their affluence, and they want a Judaism that reflects that concern. That's very limiting. There's no real practice in the community. I mean, to hear over and over again that to be a good Jew means "to have a good heart." Such a crock of shit I've never heard in my life! "All a Jew has to do is to have a good heart." It's the biggest copout in our generation.

And then the Orthodox say, "Wait a minute! We're in direct lineage to Sinai. There's nothing else to talk about. You don't like it? You don't exist! We love you but you don't exist."

And kids, kids, kids, kids, kids. "We don't need big Torah scholars, we don't need philosophers, just kids, kids, kids. We're going to take over everything. And all the nonreligious Jews, they're cute and sweet, but they're going to disappear. They don't count."

These guys may be geniuses in actual learning of the Torah, but in compassion—Well, the frum* world makes a big thing of everybody has to have food. They have massive organizations giving food to poor people, visiting the sick all over New York City. But in personal relationships, in the appeal to compassion there, they're shmucks all over the place!

At the same time, at the opposite end you have the most inventive, most interesting Reconstructionist Movement, who have *completely* warped the most fundamental principles of Judaism without even blinking a wink. I have an ultra-Orthodox cousin who's studying in a very prominent rabbinical seminary, and he was telling me that at every period in history, obviously people have thought differently, had different interpretations of the Torah. That's why you have a Rambam [*acronym of Rabbi Moshe ben Maimon (1135–1204), also known as Maimonides*], in the thirteenth century, a Vilna Gaon [*Rabbi Elijah Ben Shlomo Zalman Kremer (1720–1797), scholar, religious leader, and opponent of Chassidism*] in the eighteenth century, and blah blah blah.

So I said to him, "Are you aware that this position is the basic rationale for the Reform Movement, the Haskalah* in the eighteenth century?" And he was blown away, he didn't even know how to respond. He barely knows what the Reform Movement is, except they're goyim* and you have to kill 'em wherever you find 'em! [*chuckles*] But you see how really close they are? You've got to find a balance.

And that's what I'm trying to do. My main energy now is to translate Kabbalah and Chassidism, and to transmit it to people as a living reality. It's desperately, *desperately* needed. But you think I can get a job in a mainstream Jewish institution?

A Very Private Person

The secretary of Grand Rabbi Y. A. Korff, the Zhvil-Mezbuz Rebbe, hereditary leader of the Zhvil-Mezbuz Chassidic sect, calls to say that the Rebbe will be available following tomorrow's lunchtime prayer meeting. He invites me, she adds, to attend prayers.

At the end of the short service in the sect's headquarters in downtown Boston, the black-clad figure of the Rebbe leaves the first-floor chapel and takes to the stairs. I run after him and breathlessly introduce myself on the second-floor landing. With a spring in his step, the Rebbe leads the way up, past the Austrian Consulate to New England (the Rebbe is the consul), past the offices of The Jewish Advocate, *Boston's Jewish newspaper (the Rebbe is the publisher), until we finally reach his private suite on the top floor. According to* The Jewish Guide to Boston and New England *(published by* The Jewish Advocate*), the Rebbe is also Boston's Jewish chaplain, representing the Jewish community at public and civic events and acting as rabbinic liaison to the Boston mayor's office and to the city's police and fire departments. The position, the guide adds, was previously held by Grand Rabbi Korff's uncle and grandfather.*

IN OUR NECK OF THE WOODS, when we use the term intermarried we mean between two Chassidic dynasties. [*chuckles*] And I sit with the burdens of being related to many of the Chassidic dynasties, because Zhvil was at the crossroads. My great-great-grandfather was R' Baruch of Mezbuz, the grandson of the Baal Shem

Tov ["*Master of the Holy Name*," *Israel ben Eliezer (c. 1700–1760), founder of the Chassidic Movement*], my grandfather was the Chief Rabbi of the Ukraine, appointed by the Czar with the power to pardon.

As a child there were constant reminders that we were the descendants of the Baal Shem Tov and other great rebbes. We heard about it at home, we heard about it at school. The teachers would teach about the Chassidic Movement, saying, "This is your great-great-grandfather, this is a great-uncle of yours, this is your cousin . . ." It was inescapable. And we found it very edifying.

We always had an interest in history and how we have come from where we come. Nobody ever said, "You're going to be a rabbi," nor did I ever really make the decision. Earning smicha* was something that was simply a natural result of my desire, which was cultivated at a very early age to study and to learn my heritage, to study the history of our people, to study the laws of our people, Talmud, Gemara,* Kabbalah, et cetera.

And then I was very strongly encouraged by my father and his two brothers, all three of them rabbis (though none of them felt worthy of accepting the title of rebbe once their father passed away), to get a secular education. Getting a law degree, which might at first blush seem inconsistent with the rabbinate, upon slightly deeper analysis is productive, supportive and complementary. And so I merrily pursued two—What today would be called a dual career, and accepted invitations to lead various congregations.

It was only some twenty years later that there was a little bit of pressure to accept the title of rebbe. It came from various quarters. It came from Chassidic rebbes who remembered the heritage and felt that it was time for someone to pick up that mantle of leadership, to be what we call mamshich, to continue what had been.

It came from my uncle, who was diagnosed with cancer and saw this as a mission of his that someone in the next generation should pick up the mantle. It came from various of my own congregants who over the years had learned the history of my family. It came from certain rabbis and people in the community who knew— either still remembered or had learned about it.

And with great trepidation and fear and unworthiness we agreed to accept the title, knowing that we could never live up to what had gone before.

There's a story, I forget which Chassidic heritage it comes from, which dynasty. The young son of the rebbe, with a bit of arrogance, was with one of his friends and was bragging: "Who are *you*? Your father's a butcher, a laborer," whatever. "Look where I come from," et cetera.

And his friend replied, "That's right. I have had to work a little harder, a little longer, study a little deeper to get where I am. But you, you had it all handed to you, you grew up with it, you have this heritage, and we're at the same level."

And the rebbe, later upon hearing this, seeing how it impacted on his son, said to this other boy, "Thank you for making my son a Chassid, inspiring him not only to be humble, but to realize that he has to go further . . ."

So you know, I never really wanted to accept, because it brings with it, uh, an awesome sense—and that's the proper use of the word—I never like to use the word except in the sense of awe from Heaven. It is an awesome responsibility. One should try to live up to it, even if one is absolutely certain that one can never get there. I tend to be a very private person. I don't like a lot of hoopla, I don't like a lot of publicity. I would prefer to hide.

On the other hand, as I've been told over and over again, there are times when one can contribute something by making a statement and being more visible. This tends to be a more regal choice. That is fate. Not by choice. God puts opportunities in front of us, and God determines where things will go.

We were in a small community out of town, and at the respectful urging of people here who said, "Rebbe, when are you going to get out of that loch"—loch is a hole—"and let people enjoy what you have to offer?" a little seed was planted. So we looked for somewhere downtown, and there was absolutely nothing. Not "there's something but it isn't quite right." Nothing! And then one day something came along—this building—that was absolutely perfect. There were no other choices. It was there. So what do you do? You do it! [laughs]

MG: I imagine Zhvil is rather different from downtown Boston. Have you ever been there?

I have heard of many people who went to visit the graves of my ancestors, and came back with pictures of the various locations. One couldn't help over the years develop a sense of being there. I have pictures, I have travelogues, the whole thing, but I have never been to Zhvil in terms of physically being in Zhvil.

But when my son was born—most recent son—he was screaming and yelling, he was a handful. [smiles] And the nurse brought him—I was behind the curtain because I can't be with my wife, but I could hear what was going on, and nurse brought him around seconds after the birth, and he's screaming.

She looks at me, says, "Do something!" And I started to sing, traditional Zlochover niggun.* He immediately stopped crying, opened his eyes, and there was peace. And so the story got around the community, and one of the people said, "Simple! He's heard it before. It's very comforting."

So, yes, [chuckles] I've been to Zhvil, but not in the ordinary sense, but in other ways. You go places in your dreams that you've never been to before, or think you've never been to before. We have souls that, to use the current terminology, may have been recycled. We go places and see things unlimited by our physical being.

Have you ever been in a situation where you recall something and you're not sure whether you were actually there, whether you saw it in a movie or read it in a book? And in fact, that's what you're doing with this book. You are sharing with others what you've experienced; and they will, maybe, in years to come not remember whether they actually met that person or only read about them in your book.

When Every Door
Is Open

---꒷꒦---

The rabbi's husband, Steven, greets me when I arrive at their home. It's a little after ten in the morning. "Judy won't be long," he says, as he brews some coffee. On the refrigerator, a Hebrew flier advertising McDonald's. Steven notices my gaze. "We've just come back from Israel." Ten minutes later, Rabbi Judy L. arrives. Steven places her coffee on the table in front of her and leaves to work in another room. Rabbi L., who leads a Progressive congregation in New York, seems tired at first, but soon becomes much livelier.

JUDY: My congregation is kind of a—less now, I would say, but certainly at one time—the last-stop-on-the-way-out kind of place. You know, "We've tried this our whole lives, it really didn't work but let's give it one last try . . ." Nobody wants to be the last one to turn off the light.

There is something very incredible about the way people hang on to their Judaism. I mean, if they've come to me, they're hanging on. Many people don't come to me: they're gone.

And I love Jews. And I'd like to meet all of them. It's like meeting a member of the family. It's like they're people in your family that you don't know. It's not that I'm not interested in other people, I am. But it's like every time I meet someone new, it's like I've met a new member of the family.

Of course, the family is changing in some respects. Well, certainly, my congregation is always one or two steps ahead in the direction of change. We have kids of every racial grouping . . . In our community, there's intermarriage among Japanese Americans, blacks and American Jews. We have black kids, we have Korean kids, we have Native American kids—adopted—You just have a racial hodgepodge. Which never threw Judaism at all. In Israel, certainly, you have every shade of color.

But in terms of just being able to visually identify, or by names identify who's in the family, I think it'll get harder in the next generation.

She sips her coffee. A thought makes her smile.

The other night, at Friday night service, two women were talking. One is an O'Sullivan, and the other is an O'Brien. The O'Brien converted to Judaism, and the O'Sullivan's mother was Jewish. And the O'Sullivan's new to the congregation. And she said, "Oh, I heard you had an O'Brien here," and did I know that the O'Briens and the O'Sullivans come from the same part of Ireland? And off they went together and had a wonderful time. And they're both Jewish women!

A phone rings in another room.

And Mary O'Brien is the president of our youth group. For a while she was talking about becoming a rabbi. And it wouldn't surprise me if she did. She'd be the first Rabbi Mary O'Brien. [*smiles*] You know, in a community where there's a great deal of intermarriage the O'Sullivan kids *may* be Jewish. But the Goldbergs, these days, you have to wonder. . . . You can't be sure anymore.

Steven returns to the kitchen.

STEVEN: Office called. Computer's working.

JUDY: Oh, that's good news. Who was it that called? Freddy? Good. [*to me*] Yeah, we're losing a lot of the old markers, which means that we're culturally deprived, though I don't think people in my congregation would see it that way. We eat anything, we go anywhere, we do anything, our friends are not Jewish . . .

STEVEN: [*who is on his way out*] How about hunting? That's one of the last things to fall.

JUDY: But we don't live in a society where—The non-Jews that we hang out with don't hunt, either. You know, maybe if we lived in a Southern community . . . I would go so far as to say that if our friends hunted, we would hunt.

Steven nods in agreement and leaves.

[*almost plaintively*] Or Jewish jokes. We have kids studying Jewish humor, you have to *explain* to them what's funny because they don't understand. Which means they don't understand the culture of Judaism. So you have to start explaining the culture to the people who are in the culture. They're deprived.

And you're sitting there, explaining the most basic things to adults. Like, when things aren't good, like—if someone dies, in American society I guess you just want to be by yourself. In Jewish society the whole world comes. And I've had to teach people to open their doors. And I'm not always successful. And of course people who do open their doors and who allow this to happen are just so happy that they did. But not everyone is Jewish enough to do it. And of course at that moment you're not going to force them.

I mean, just a couple of weeks ago, there was a family sitting Shiva.* And they did a number of things that were not the norm to do. The father died on Sunday morning. The funeral wasn't until Wednesday. That's very unusual. And they said, "Well, is that wrong? Do you mind? It isn't convenient for our son to come before Wednesday. He's got a test." [*with intense exasperation and bewilderment*] Like, "convenient"? Somebody dies, you drop everything! You go! But they don't seem to *know* that. They attempt to continue on with a test tomorrow, as if they could go and do that.

And they don't learn, until it happens, that they didn't really want to be there, they wanted to be here. They didn't know that, until they did it the other way. Or they wanted Shiva to be longer. They only sat Shiva three days.

One of the members of my congregation is on TV. A television personality. And his mother died. And he buried her. And the next day—within two or three days, he was back on television, doing one of those cheery morning shows. And to make it worse, it was Mother's Day week. I watched him on television every day. I just didn't know what to do. I mean, this man was *suffering*. He was like mourning on television. "Get off! Go back. Do what you have to do."

People just don't get it. As they become farther removed from who they are, they really lose something important. When every door is open, when every family welcomes a Jew—Well, not everyone, I suppose, but not so's you'd notice . . . all you have to do is eat what's on the table, and be willing to give up who you are to sit at that table.

The denial of who you are, and the value of being who you are, that saddens me. I think if you haven't resolved your Jewish identity, you haven't really resolved your identity as a person. Just like if you weren't comfortable being what sex you were, what nationality you were, you'd be wandering, psychologically lost. I think a lot of Jews really need to resolve the Jewish part of them.

Cheesecake

Saturday, ten-thirty A.M. Hendon, England. A secular Sabbath in Raye N.'s kitchen. Raye's preparing a cheesecake, assisted by her daughter Talya, who's seven. Thirteen-year-old Sharon is watching TV in the living room. Helen, fifteen, is still in bed. Raye's husband left earlier to play a round of golf.

RAYE: Sorry about this. I'm normally not—I'll just prepare this cake mix and stick it in the oven . . . [*switching on a blender*] My friend Anne's having a fortieth birthday tomorrow, and I'm the official cheesecake maker! And this [*pointing to Talya*] is my helper. She cracked the eggs, and she put all the ingredients in, didn't you, precious! And here's the recipe . . .

Raye scans a handwritten note in front of the microwave.

I've got such a bad memory. I only made one yesterday too! OK. Here goes the lemon juice. [*to Talya*] Do you want to pour it in?

A picture of concentration, Talya pours the mix into a baking tray.

That's it. Very good. [*to me*] So you wanna talk about being Jewish. Is cheesecake Jewishy? What do you think, Talya?

Talya is having difficulty with the last drops.

OK. I'll do this. [*laughs*] It was funny, we actually didn't have anything for dessert last night, because I was saving the cake for the

92

party. So we had to sweet-talk my husband into going out to buy some at the deli. [*She opens a carton of cream.*] OK. This is the sour cream. [*pours it in*] Whoa! That was good. Better than yesterday. What did I do yesterday?

TALYA: [*laughing*] Put the carton in, too!

MG: *The secret ingredient.*

RAYE: So anyway . . . Oh! I forgot Golda's still outside.

Raye opens the patio door. A large golden Labrador bounds into the kitchen and makes straight for my bag on the floor.

Talya, go and ask Sharon—[*to me*] Did she just take something from your bag?

Golda has a C-120 cassette between her teeth. It contains an interview with a social worker discussing drug and alcohol abuse amongst Jewish adolescents.

Come on, Golda, give it back. Good girl! Come on, let go, give it here! That's it!

A saliva-coated cassette returns to my bag. Tongue lolling, Golda pads out of the kitchen.

You should really interview Golda. She's a Jewish dog, after all. It was funny actually, when we got her, my mother-in-law, who's one of the old school, she said, "Raye, What on earth got into you? Jews don't have dogs." I said, [*incredulously*] "What?!" I said, "Alex and Sam—" That's her brother and his wife—"Alex and Sam have had poodles for years." "Ah!" she said. "That's different. Poodles are *poodles*." [*laughs*]

So anyway, getting back to the cheesecake . . . Like I said, it's Anne's fortieth, and of course it's Israel's fiftieth anniversary [*the interview was recorded in May 1998*], so she decided to have a Jewish theme, and we all have to come dressed up as our favorite Jewish character.

To be honest, we all thought it was a little nerdy, but anyway . . I'm going as Groucho Marx, and I want my husband to go as Harpo. But I'm having a very difficult time finding the right kind of wig for him. We thought of all sorts of people: Abraham and Sarah; Golda Meir and Moshe Dayan; David and Bathsheba . . . Moshe Dayan would be easy, but the others were a bit harder to dress. Actually, first of all I thought of Krusty the Klown, but I wanted us to be coordinated.

MG: *Krusty the Klown? Who's that?*

RAYE: [*with mock horror*] He doesn't know anything, does he, Talya? Tell him who Krusty the Klown is.

TALYA: He's in the Simpsons!

RAYE: There's a famous episode: Krusty's father, the rabbi, won't speak to him, because Krusty doesn't wanna follow in the religion and become a rabbi. So–

On the countertop, a phone rings.

Hello. Oh hi, Adam. No, she's still asleep. Do you want me to wake her? OK. I'll tell her when she gets up. Bye.

That's the other thing: I'm an answering service for my children. So anyway, I was looking for a Harpo wig yesterday and I didn't think it'd be so difficult. Like, when the kids were younger, everybody had Harpo wigs at birthday parties. So we went everywhere. It was *very* frustrating, I had a million other things to do. And we had to do food shopping and take my daughter to a friend's, and pick up my other daughter, and bake. And pick up Talya from her sleepover. [*to Talya, with a smile*] Didn't I? That was my day shlepping.

MG: *And what did you do in the evening?*

RAYE: Y'know, usual: dinner, TV, fight, and then it was bedtime. Sometimes I do the candles and stuff, but y'know, the kids just aren't into it, except Talya, likes it, don't you? [*brightly*] You wouldn't believe we sent them to Jewish day schools, would you? And we took them to synagogue on all the chagim.* But my two oldest have absolutely no feeling for it.

She checks her watch.

Is that the time? Ooh! Look, I'm sorry about this, we're going to have to go out in a few minutes. I have to get some cash and uh, I've still got to find that Harpo wig. And—Talya, do you have your shoes on? OK, let's go and find them. [*to me*] Come on, I'll show you some photos.

In the hallway, Raye points to a framed black-and-white photograph of a mustachioed young man and his dark-eyed wife, to whom Raye bears a passing resemblance.

This is my grandparents, in Istanbul. And this [*pointing to a gold-framed color print*] is my parents. I'd tell you about Istanbul if I had the time. We lived there till I was eight, and . . .

We enter the dimly lit living room, curtains drawn to keep out the morning sun.

And . . . Ah! Here are Talya's shoes. And this is my TV addict.

A teenage girl is lying on the sofa, one hand in a bag of potato crisps on the floor, her face illuminated by the screen in front of her. "Dry, lifeless hair and an itchy, flaking scalp?" inquires a concerned voice. Golda the Labrador, tongue lolling, nods in agreement.

We're just going out, Sharon.

SHARON: [*distractedly*] Mm hm.

RAYE: And *please* pick the crisps up off the floor, and don't let Golda have any more. You know what happened last time.

SHARON: Mm hm.

On our way back to the kitchen, we bump into Raye's eldest daughter coming down the stairs in her dressing gown.

RAYE: And this is Helen: sleeping beauty. Helen, this is Michael; he's writing a book on Jewish people. Would you like to be in it?

HELEN: [*sleepily*] Did anyone call?

RAYE: [*to me*] You see, not "Good morning, Mum," not "Hello, Michael," but "Did anyone call?" [*to Helen*] Adam called.

HELEN: Which Adam? Adam Seligman or Adam Beenstock?

RAYE: I can never remember. The one without the eyebrow ring. The one that lives with his father. Which one's that? Anyway, he said can you ring him back . . .

Five minutes later. Cake's ready. Helen's talking to Adam, the phone cradled between her ear and shoulder.

RAYE: Here's Helen having breakfast, licking the cheesecake bowl. And yeah, note the permanent fixture. Helen, hold the telephone properly, please. [*to me*] Y'know, I would sit and talk all day, but I really have to get some cash at the dispenser, and if I don't get that Harpo wig . . . OK, Talya, are you ready?

Two minutes later, on the doorstep.

MG: *Well, thanks very much for your time. It's been great. I appreciate it. Hope you find your Harpo wig!*

RAYE: I'll show you the photos if you come back. Say bye bye, Talya. Say "Shabbat Shalom,* Michael!"

Just Like Everyone Else

Jeff S., twenty-six years old, has the face of a young Kirk Douglas and the physique of a light heavyweight fighter. Born in South Africa, he now lives in Vancouver, Canada, where he runs a family-owned electronics store. An amateur power-boat enthusiast, he's invited me to join him for a lunchtime ride in his pride and joy. As we bounce and thump across the harbor, Jeff explains that he has no doubts about the nature of the Jewish character. He has to shout to make himself heard above the roar of the boat's engines. It's going to be a nightmare to transcribe.

I THINK JEWISH PEOPLE HAVE A SENSE of arrogance about them. Which is good and bad. I suppose it comes from knowing you're probably superior to the other religions and races. Which I definitely feel. I shouldn't really say that but that's definitely the way I feel. As I would imagine most of my Jewish friends feel, 'cause we've discussed that.

We're a minority race and we have a different outlook to the goyim.* We really do. It's something that only a Jewish person can understand. You just have to sit with a Jewish person, talk to them, then sit with a—somebody who's not Jewish and just see the difference.

MG: [*shouting*] *Do you have non-Jewish friends?*

Yeah, of course! It's important to mix. I have my non-Jewish friends.

I would have no qualms about being a good friend of somebody who wasn't Jewish. I don't know if I'd trust them as much . .

MG: *What was that?* [*louder still*]

I DON'T KNOW IF I'D TRUST 'EM AS MUCH. But I think it's important not to be narrow-minded and insular. And that's what can happen.

MG: *What about non-Jewish women?*

Mm. [*grinning*] Very nice! Really enjoyable. I'd just never marry them. The shiksas* are to practice on. That's what they say, don't they? [*laughs*]

MG: *How about business? Notice a difference between your Jewish and non-Jewish clientele?*

Yes! Very different. I must be honest with you, I prefer non-Jewish. The Jewish people are too shrewd. They wanna buy wholesale. They've got contacts with this, contacts with that. As much as I love Jewish people, they're very difficult to do business with, I find. And they want everything for nothing, and they want this, and they want that, and not like this, and then like that.

Some of them are unbelievable. Very, very tough to deal with. If you make money off them, you're a very clever businessman. I mean, why did God invent the goyim? For retail. [*laughs*]

We thunder past a small dinghy. Jeff waves to the occupants and leaves them bobbing in our wake.

MG: *Do we have any other defects?*

Well, I find a lot of Jews are physically weak. They're not able to defend themselves. They're too academic. No balance.

Is he looking at me?

And I think that's why they're picked on a lot, because of their appearance. I was brought up to do sport, and a lot of South African Jewish men are much bigger and much more able to defend themselves than, let's say English Jews.

He is looking at me!

Because I lived in England. They're much smaller, they're more timid, they're always picked on. I wouldn't like my children to be like that. If someone says to them, "Ah, you fuckin' Jew," they'll turn round and give 'em a smack, not to have to do it with their brains. And that's what Jewish people have always done.

Jeff spins the wheel to make a wide curve to starboard, heading us back towards the landing. At the end of the maneuver, he picks up his train of thought.

Except in Israel, obviously. That's what I like about Israel. Jewish people are tougher there. They know how to look after themselves. Love Israel. Wouldn't like to live there though! Purely out of fear. [*laughs*] But uh, yes I love Israel. It's our protection. It prevents what happened with Hitler from ever happening again. Which could very easily happen. There's a lot of anti-Semitism.

And what is *crazy* to me is that people criticize us, say the government in Israel is right-wing. Well, why shouldn't we have a few right-wing people in terms of anti-Arab, anti-Nazi, and anti-this, and anti-that? I think it's only fair. You can't expect Jewish people to be any different, really. We're just like everyone else.

Engines roaring, we thump past the dinghy again. Jeff waves.

A Very Bad Jew

Southend, Essex, England. Three o'clock on a summer's afternoon. I walk around the back of the large detached house and, as per telephone instructions, knock on the garage door. No response. I try again. Just as I'm about to give up, Leonard N. appears and ushers me in. "Punctuality is not a common Jewish virtue," he grumbles, pointing to a wall clock that shows five after three. A dozen or more timepieces lie in various states of disassembly on a large wooden tabletop. I discover that Leonard, a retired London restaurateur, has always enjoyed repairing watches and clocks. Scores of miniature cogwheels, springs, and winding mechanisms are embedded like fossils in the linoleum floor. He rubs his creased face, pushes his glasses up onto his forehead, and readjusts a lank lock of hair that was hanging over his ear. "It's just a different mentality," he adds, stifling a yawn. Indeed, according to Leonard, the Jewish mind works differently from all other minds.

I THINK MY MIND IS MORE COMPLICATED than the average English person's. I think in a Jewish way. To a certain extent. I don't think in straight lines. I never take anything at its face value. I look at all the ins and outs, the various options, look at it from every angle. I don't look at things straight on.

I don't think *anybody* thinks in the same way as Jewish people. Probably the British and the Americans never wrote the law for Jews, because the Jews can always find a loophole. And this gives us a bad name, because people like to see justice done. Now, unfortunately, wherever you go, justice is never done. It's the richest, the person that can pay for the smartest lawyer that wins. And the Jewish people use the law to their advantage.

MG: *Doesn't everybody try to do that?*

Yes, but Jews are probably smarter than a lot of people. You see, we can think in circles.

He illustrates with both index fingers.

We can think round a subject, and through a subject, and use the law to our advantage. It isn't only the Jews that are crooked, of course. But I suppose when you get a bad Jew, you get a *very* bad Jew. Because the law can be manipulated. It's so easy. If you're going to be sued, get yourself a Jewish lawyer.

Take my Uncle Arnold. He wasn't very keen on work, I don't think, and wasn't a particularly good businessman. He made his money mainly from gambling. I remember how at sundown on Saturday night, soon as Shabbos was out, he'd shoot off, because he used to go to the dog races. And he also made money from falling down holes and suing people. I remember one court case he had — this'd be in about 1948 or thereabouts. Now, according to Uncle Arnie, he was walking along in Hyde Park, and they were digging a hole, and there wasn't a barrier, and he fell in the hole. Now, how anybody could've fallen in a hole [*chuckles nostalgically*] in the middle of Hyde Park, I just don't know! But this was how he made his money.

And he always lived quite well. The family always ate well; dressed well; they lived in a big house in Hampstead. You see, if you go back to where the Jews came from, we had to be smart, we had to use our brains to survive. That's why we think in circles.

MG: *Right. Forty years in the desert, going round in circles.*

Yes. I'm not sure I'd say all this in print though, if I were you. Racism is so near the surface that it just needs one tiny spark for the fire to catch on and nobody can stop it. And anybody who's seen to be slightly different is a target. And the Jews, because we're clever . . . You know, you're sitting on a time bomb with this book, if you say this kind of thing openly. You'll spend your whole life defending it, and you're going to have to use your brain.

Hype and Nonsense

Eve T. and her Israeli husband, Rafi, run Blow Up, a store specializing in balloons and other festive decorations. It's a quiet Thursday morning. Eve, a large, cheerful woman with a marked New England accent, is standing between the counter and a large tank of helium. She's wearing a plaid flannel shirt under denim overalls. A badge on her shoulder strap says "HAPPY BIRTHDAY!" Around the walls a chorus of heart-shaped silver balloons wishes us "MAZEL TOV!"*

WE DO A LOT OF BAR MITZVAHS.* We did a space theme recently for a bar mitzvah. They turned the whole Sheraton ballroom into an outer-space theme. They covered the walls with black cloth. They had stars and planets and moons made out of foam hanging from the ceiling. We just did the balloons and the robots.

MG: *Robots?*

We put robots as the centerpiece of every table and had three foil balloons with "BAR MITZVAH!" on them, on the robots' heads. Just so people didn't lose sight of the fact that it *was* a bar mitzvah. Then on top of the bar mitzvah balloons we put plain balloons, with a ring balloon around them to make them look like Saturn. And above the center of the dance floor they had this, this great big gold dome, like an upside down crater. So we filled it up with helium balloons that had stars on them.

MG: *Stars of David?*

No. Sort of planet stars. But from afar it could've been either way. You could see the gold through the balloons, and with the lights they'd set up all around, it set off the scene wonderfully. It was quite a sight. There were about three hundred, three hundred and fifty guests. One of the bigger ones. We used over a hundred of the big foils. We also did latex bunches around the room using blues and whites.

Lots of people, even to this day, don't like to go too far from tradition, so they use the blue and white, denoting Israel. Some of the brave ones, I call 'em, choose hipper colors: greens, purples, oranges, multicolors, whatever. But nine times out of ten, they stick to the blues and whites.

The mother came in on the Monday, to pay me. She said that it was amazing, all went very well. And I've had a few people come in since then that had been there, and wanted to make bookings. They were like, "Wow! You walked in there and you thought you were in outer space!"

She shrugs.

I'm here to take the money. It's a business; I gotta survive. But to me it's a waste, I have to tell you. I have my personal beliefs about bar mitzvahs but I don't say anything 'cause I'm in the business. I'm part of the hype. But if I had a kid, I know what I'd like to do: get back to basics. The service in the synagogue, and the family.

Today, everything's gone to extremes. Decorations not so much, because we're last on the list. But the best food, the best bands, and the best presents. It's gone way overboard. For the money some people spend—and I know how much they spend—you could put twenty, thirty percent deposit on a condo, put it in a fund for the future.

With non-Jewish people there's less of the hype and the nonsense that surrounds a lot of the Jewish community. I go shopping and, quite frankly, I wouldn't behave, act and speak like a lot of the

Jewish people that come in here do. I don't know what it is. Maybe with some of the older people, they had servants and they're used to ordering people around. Maybe it's because some of them went through the Holocaust, and so everything to them is like, "I'm not going to let anybody get the better of me anymore." I put it down to that, and I hope that in the next generation we change.

I'm Jewish, and I look at Jewish people and I—I stereotype them so you can imagine what non-Jews think. I've had non-Jews in the store when Jewish people come in. And afterwards they say to me, "What's goin' on?" It doesn't help.

I had a couple in here a few days ago—a non-Jewish couple for a big wedding. They'd booked everything, put down a deposit. I'd spent about an hour with them. Then this older woman came in, fur coat, pearls around the throat, two gallons of Chanel number whatever—you know the type.

She said, [*abruptly*] "I've got a bar mitzvah." So the couple said, "Take care of her," because I'd given them some colors, they were going to look at some colors I'd given them. I showed her this, that, colors, went through the whole rigmarole. She said, [*brusquely*] "I'll think about it." OK. "With pleasure. Thank you. Have a nice day." And out she went.

The couple came to me. They didn't know I was Jewish. I don't have a Star of David sitting on my head. They said, "Are Jewish people always like that? Are they always so rude?" As a Jewish person I have to protect my own. But as a realist, I have to be honest. I said, "Well, yes, in this case she was rude. But in most cases no, they're not."

But it's off-putting, it's not good. There's enough trouble. Jews have been persecuted throughout history, and to add to it with their childish behavior . . . It's a shame.

MG: *Do you ever get Israelis in?*

From time to time, sure. They might want a bag of balloons or something for a friend's party. Nothing serious. But we've done a few parties for those who've been here longer. They're in a category of their own.

See, I speak Hebrew. Having lived in Israel for several years, and married to an Israeli, I understand their mentality and the way they present themselves. A lot of people think they're pushy. They're not. It's the Israeli manner. It's how they live and are brought up. If you live over there, you understand this. You don't take offense, you understand it. They can say something that in *literal* translation in English would put them in the other category. But it's not to demean you or be rude. It's just the Israeli way.

The Jewish Test

In 1994, after filming Schindler's List, *Steven Spielberg set up a world-wide project to record on video the oral testimony of Holocaust survivors. Londoner Naomi S., a forty-nine-year-old high school history teacher, is one of the many people who trained as interviewers for the project. I ring the bell outside her East Finchley apartment. A tall, fair-haired woman answers the door. A visiting friend? For some reason I had the impression that Naomi lived alone. "Hi. I have an appointment with Naomi. Is she in?" "She is indeed, Michael. And she is me."*

YOU'VE GOT HUNDREDS OF YEARS OF ANTI-SEMITISM, and then you've got the Nazis, all saying that Jews are ugly little people with dark, curly hair, dark eyes, and big noses. And somewhere along the line, we started believing it too.

Quite a few times with the survivors I had a real problem with credibility as soon as I arrived. Especially with the women. I didn't notice it so much with the men. One of the first things they would say after I walked into their home was, "Oh, but you look like a shiksa,* darling. Are you sure you're Jewish?" Before I ever got to ask *them* questions, they'd put me through the hundred questions, I call it. "What's your family name?" "What country do your parents come from?" "Do you have children?" "Where did they go to school?"

I'd have an emotional reaction to that. I'm always very offended by that because I've had to justify myself all my life. I have a girlfriend called Pat Levine, and Pat used to teach boys bar mitzvah* Hebrew. And her Hebrew was excellent. Her father taught Hebrew, too. And Pat has blue eyes and—I don't like to use the term, because I'm already using the stereotype I'm disputing—a fairly nontypical Jewish appearance.

And she and I used to go out together a lot. And when we went out, we were never taken as being Jewish women. And people would sometimes make jokes about Jews, or anti-Semitic remarks that were very nasty, and expect us to laugh at them. And we always took a stand and said, "That's offensive. We're Jewish." And they'd say things like, "Oh, that's bullshit. You don't have the nose, the brown eyes . . . you're having delusions. You're not Jewish."

I must say, if I'm really honest it hurts me more when Jewish people—particularly survivors, often mature women—say, "But *you* don't look Jewish. You're too tall. Your eyes are blue. You look like a shiksa."

I developed a joke about it. I used to say, "If I had a pound for every Yid* that said that to me, I'd be a rich woman now." And that used to embarrass them. But it really freaked me out that I had to go on proving I was Jewish for hours on end just because of their judgments of my physical appearance. It's not an easy thing to live with when you're supposed to be part of a community and it continually makes you justify yourself, or rejects you.

Like, recently, I went to a Jewish women's function, and I was there with my daughter who was back from college for the weekend. And Mim is small and olive-skinned, has brown eyes and dark hair, and most people there didn't know that I was her mother. And it seemed easier for her to socialize there, even though she has very little to do with the Jewish community—far, far less than I do in fact. It was a feeling that people were friendlier and approached her. It seemed like she got through the Jewish test and I didn't.

It's very hard for me. I used to get taken as her babysitter or a housekeeper, never as her mother. It is a big issue for me. I can't resolve it.

I went to a Jewish singles party last year and I haven't been back since. It was so alienating. Oh, I knew a few people, that was OK, but the rest . . . "How did *you* get in here?" [*wearily*] Oh, I'm so sick of it. It's so boring to hear.

But sometimes you can't tell. [*laughs*] We've got a little cottage up in Hertfordshire, and one day I was in the back garden chopping out blackberries, and I let slip an "Oy vei!"* I didn't even notice there was a woman in the garden next door. She came rushing over, and she said, "Did you say, 'Oy vei'?" I said, "Yes." She said, "We have to talk."

I've been going up there for ten years and we'd seen each other many times but we'd never said much besides "Hello," "Nice day." And we had never known that we were Jewish. It's an emotional impact. It's hard to describe but it's very emotional. Everything changes when two Jewish women recognize each other. There's an immediate rapport, there's "Who do you know? What are you involved in?"

That's why it hurts so much when they don't see who I am.

Not Good Enough

---⚜---

Max N. was born in Lvov, Ukraine, in 1946, moving to the United States with his family in 1992. He's a large man, his grey hair closely cropped, his face dominated by a Saddam Hussein mustache. He's a cellist in a prestigious West Coast symphony orchestra.

Sunday afternoon in the N.s' apartment. Max and his twenty-year-old daughter, Sophie, are in the living room. Mrs. N. has just gone out to buy cigarettes. On the arm of Max's chair, a precariously-balanced full ashtray and an empty pack of Marlboro. Sophie, who has a ring through her lower lip, sits opposite Max, feet curled up beneath her. She's wearing a Lilith Fair festival T-shirt over a sarong. Her hair is even shorter than Max's. As he begins his story, Sophie smiles at me wryly, as if to say this is not the first time she's heard it.

MAX: A childhood memory, at the age of eight or nine. I remember, there was a game: boys should find the girl in hiding, and if boy find the girl, he should kiss her. And in this game boys were Jews, I and a friend of mine, Viktor Shteynman, and girls were Russian or Ukrainian, I don't remember. And I heard a conversation between the two girls who were hiding, and they were discussing what happen if Viktor—I wasn't identified as a Jew for some reason—"What happens if Viktor finds us?"

"He will kiss us."

"But how you will allow him to kiss you? He is Jew."

They were afraid: [*with disgust*] he was Jew, how can he kiss you? And immediately, I felt that I am inferior, I and he. It was like starting developing this inferiority complex. I was not good enough. Stigma from very, very early childhood, and the only way to escape it is not to look like Jew.

But, I *was* looking like Jew. And increasingly I was looking more and more like Jew. [*smiles sardonically*] I was watching myself in mirror and saying, "Yeah, I am Jew. Look at these eyes, this nose."

MG: *Could be a Roman nose, or a Greek nose.*

MAX: [*dryly*] Very, very Greek, amounting to Jewish.

I was disappointed: everyone who look on me could tell, "He is Jew." I used to live with this assumption, that wherever I appear the first thing will be: "He is Jew" and therefore . . . "You bad person, out of normal person." In Russian the word is *izgoi*. [*to Sophie*] You know what is *izgoi* in English?

Sophie shrugs.

I should find this word . . .

He takes down a Russian-English dictionary from the bookshelf behind him.

[*reading*] *Izgo* . . . Ah! *izgoi*. "Social outcast." [*closes dictionary*] Immediately, social outcast. And if you develop something in crucial years, it stays with you, you can fight it but . . .

Jews are strangers in a Slav population. They are different. Some people are tolerant. They are sympathetic if they have, say, a Jewish daughter-in-law, but basically Jews are condemned to live amongst themselves, to be comfortable. I am comfortable in my family. [*with a sardonic laugh*] The only anti-Semite in my family is my daughter.

Sophie rolls her eyes.

But here in the States, they can't identify if I'm a Jew or not. They don't care. If I'm saying I'm Russian, it's enough. But if I'm meeting Russian, this problem could appear again. I feel uncomfortable. I know what is in their mind. You can imagine what image Jews have in Russian mind.

SOPHIE: I can see how for my father it was a bigger problem, but times were changing. When I was a kid, what was permissible was changing, your response would be different, you could do more about it. Like, I remember I was walking home once from school with this girl—she was new in our class—and she lived pretty close to me and she was saying something about Jews, I don't remember what, and I said, "But I'm Jewish." Well, I said, "I'm half Jewish."

She said, [*surprised*] "Really?"

MG: *Why did you say you were* half *Jewish?*

SOPHIE: I don't know . . . I didn't want a confrontation, for her not to feel too bad. I don't know. I was a kid. I wanted to educate her, I wanted to ease it on to her, not give it her fullblown, so I wouldn't alienate her . . .

Her father turns to me and smiles his own wry smile.

But here it's not a big deal at all. People ask me what my accent is, it's hard for them to figure it out; it's not really Russian—Well, it depends on the day: sometimes it's Irish, sometimes it's more American . . . And I just say I'm from Ukraine. But if people do mention something about Jewish, it depends what their attitude is, what I wanna let them know. Depends if I can be bothered going into it. It's not such a big deal. I wouldn't be cautious about saying it like in the Ukraine.

MAX: So now you don't need to be a half Jew. [*with heavy sarcasm*] Maybe three-quarters Jew? Or not Jew at all?

The Desire to Pass

————— ✧ —————

A weekday lunchtime in a crowded diner in midtown Manhattan. Tamar S. is a senior buyer in a nearby department store, specializing in jewelry and accessories. When I remark on the attractive chai* pendant on her necklace, she tells me she bought it in Israel in 1969. As a teenager living in Baltimore during the late 1950s, she would never have worn it, she adds; back then, she desperately wanted to blend into the main-stream and avoid being identified as a Jew. The lively style of Tamar's observations about her "desire to pass" soon engages the middle-aged couple at the table behind her. They eat in silence, nodding with recognition at many turns in the story.

IN THOSE DAYS, THE MELTING POT NOTION was very prevalent and being different was not a good thing. You didn't see Barbra Streisand on the big screen, you saw Doris Day. And I had, you know, kinky hair and a big nose, and I always felt ugly. I literally sat in school like this:

She pushes the palm of her hand against her nose.

. . . thinking if I did this long enough, my nose would turn up. But it never did . . . [*smiles*] And when I was in high school, my parents wanted me to have my nose done: "So, you're gonna have a nose job? You're gonna have a nose job, aren't you?"

And why I resisted it I cannot tell you. I mean, my sister had her nose done, but I didn't. I mean, I always *hated* my nose. But it's a

Jewish nose, and I instinctively knew that my face wouldn't look right without it. You know . . . that you're meant to be put together in a certain way? And that's the way it is.

But I mean, *everyone* had their nose done. There was this girl Ruth in my high school and she had her nose done so many times she didn't have any nose left! All she had was a little rise and two holes!

It wasn't funny but—[*laughs*] I used to go to the same summer camp, Jewish summer camp every year. And you'd meet kids there from all over, and there was one girl at camp—Marsha—and she was ugly, OK? She had this *big* hooked nose, she had frizzy hair, big thick glasses . . . She was really a homely girl, chubby. I'm sure they said the same thing about me, but whatever . . . [*shrugs dismissively*]

And one year, we must've been fourteen or fifteen, I went to camp, and there's this *gorgeous* young woman I'm looking at her, and I'm thinking, "Who *is* this?" I mean, we all went there for ten years. We all knew each other. Who's this new face? "*Marsha*?!!"

Indeed. Contact lenses. Hair straightened. Nose done. Chin done. Lost the weight. All I could think of was, "My God! One day she's gonna marry some man, she's gonna have a child and [*starts to laugh*] and he's gonna say, "Aaagh! Where did this child come from?"

We both laugh. So does the couple at the next table.

Because she was really homely, and she became really beautiful. I've heard since she's become an alcoholic. And it's not surprising, because how can you do that? And that was in one year. That's how it was. And why I resisted it all I cannot tell you. But the good news is: as I was growing up I learned to talk the talk and walk the walk and I could do it. I could pass. And people—I mean, it's embarrassing—but people would say, "Oh you're Jewish? But you don't seem like a Jew to me . . ." I mean, I took it as a compliment. It was sort of like, "You don't think like a woman."

All these things were seen as compliments in those days. I mean, it's *totally* horrifying to me now to realize that, but it's absolutely true. And even—I literally used to wish I could have an epiphany: that Jesus would come to me and I'd just get it, and be like everybody else . . .

The thing is Jews have never been allowed to pass. I mean, I think we would have passed ourselves happily out of existence, a lot of us, if we could have . . .

I tell you what I think. I think that when I was growing up, there had to be an underlying terror of being Jewish that we weren't fully conscious of. I mean, if you didn't have it before in the shtetl with pogroms, I mean, *hello*!! I can't really imagine that the shadow of the Holocaust didn't incredibly fuel the desire to pass. Must've been somewhere in grade school I realized that not only were you different—'cause I was already for a whole lot of reasons—but also you got this feeling that what you did *mattered*. In the sense that if everyone thought you were a jerk, they'd think Jews in general were jerks.

And you were surrounded by a lot of anti-Semitic stuff. It was subtle, but not that subtle. I couldn't join the dancing school that all my friends joined in the sixth grade. Why? Because I was Jewish. In the seventh grade I couldn't join the skating club. When we'd go up to New England to camp you'd see signs: "NO JEWS!" "Do not try to stay here!" I mean, that was quite blatant, you know? So it was big time to try to think like, look like, act like everyone else. Don't talk loud and all that.

And I never really understood this until the first time I went to Israel when I was twenty-four, twenty-five, and, and I just totally fell in love with it.

My husband and I were taking this little tour bus to go down to Ein Gedi and he was late. And I'm on the bus and he's there and I'm, "David!! Hurry up!!" And I'm *shriekin'* at him. He comes runnin' and he's, "Why are you screaming at me, you sound like a fishmonger's wife!"

[*whispering*] And it's like, "What the fuck do I care! This is a bunch of Jews."

And I realized then, for the very first time, how much I always did care. I mean, I wouldn't have done that in Baltimore if my life depended on it! But there, it was like, "Who cares? What are they gonna do to me? Think I'm a jerk? Well, they're jerks too." And I never knew how self-conscious I was in that way till I wasn't anymore.

My Cousin in Chicago

In the cafeteria on the campus of Stanford University. Howard L. is a Ph.D. candidate in international relations. Last year he was over in England, and we've just been wondering if we have any mutual acquaintances there, but have so far drawn a blank. This is unusual for Howard, who turns out to be a masterful player of that other kind of international relations known as "Jewish geography," the popular game in which strangers try to figure out whether they're related or have common friends. But Howard and I might still find the missing link. If only he could remember the last name of that woman he dated a couple of times in Leeds . . .

WAY BACK WHEN THE PLAY *Six Degrees of Separation* was popular, I used to say that Jewish relations are *two* degrees of separation. The more I live, the more likely it is that I go somewhere—a synagogue, a conference—and I meet someone and it turns out that we're related or we have a common friend. This has happened too frequently for my sanity. Really.

In England last year I ended up meeting a relative. I'm related to Joseph Hertz, the Chief Rabbi of the British Empire in the early twentieth century. The same Hertz that did the commentary on the Pentateuch. Actually, he's only related by marriage [*chuckles*] so I can't say I have anything genetic! But my great-grandmother's sister was his wife—that's essentially it. So it's not a direct relation, but, I still feel very close, and it's yichus* in its own way. How can I complain? [*beams*]

And in fact there's a story that when they were appointing the Chief Rabbi, they had to choose between Hertz and another rabbi—the rabbis themselves were equal—but they chose based on their wives. [*smiles*] I can garner some honor from that.

And so I went to a service at a synagogue in London. And I got talking to this guy at the Kiddush* afterwards, and he offers to drive me back—this is on Shabbat, it's no big deal—to drive me to the local underground station, and, uh, on the way he talks about his grandfather, Joseph Hertz, the Chief Rabbi of the . . . I look at him, I say, [*portentously*] "I think we're related to each other."

He stops the car, we move over to the side of the road, we start explaining how it is we're related, we start figuring it out, and saying, looking at each other, and saying, "I guess there is some resemblance there."

And the next week I went over to dinner at his place, met his wife, met his children, who are my third cousins, I guess . . . saw my family tree dating back to the seventeenth century, was able to clarify some family history: I wasn't born in 1973, I was born in 1972, things like that. It was *very* exciting.

And it happens *all* the time. I walked into a synagogue in Atlanta just a few months back—Well, same thing just last Friday night. I was at a Reform service, and I was walking out, and I literally ran—well, not literally—into someone, and we get talking, we compare notes, see who we know, and I find out she's good friends with my cousin in Chicago! It's kind of an embarrassment of riches to make those connections.

MG: *Pity you can't remember the name of that woman in Leeds . . .*

I only wish I could. Tip of my tongue, too. But tell me, do you have any connections here on the West Coast?

The Mishpocha

WHAT DOES BEING JEWISH MEAN TO ME? To be perfectly honest, I don't ask myself questions like that. I'm just too busy. I just get on with it.

On the four days of the week that Londoner Pearl W. manages a pharmacy, she has a very tight schedule. She's been working today. Fifteen minutes ago she locked up the store and is now at the wheel of her Toyota Camry, en route to see her mother, who lives in a nursing home. Pearl visits her every day, though she can't stay long on the days she works in the pharmacy. It's already ten past six and she has to be home by seven-fifteen to prepare dinner for her husband and son. The heavy rush-hour traffic on the Edgeware Road is making it a slow ride.

A recent Jewish story? [*shifting up to second gear*] Let me see. Friday afternoon, I'm not at the pharmacy so I get everything ready for Friday evening, so last Friday I made kneidlach* but I must confess [*shifting down to first*] that the chicken soup came out of an Osem can. There's a very good kosher deli down the road.

Then we had chicken, baked potatoes—which are very easy to do—and a mixed salad, which is also . . . simple . . . And . . . then I was a bit pushed for time, so I didn't bake—which I normally do—and just picked up a bilberry pie on the way back from seeing Mum.

I spent a couple of hours with her in the afternoon. We played dominoes, and she was having a good day, she could more or less

119

follow at times. Which was very good. You know, she has Alzheimer's, and on a bad day she really hasn't got a clue what's going on . . .

It would have been lovely if you'd met her oh, maybe five or six years ago. She had *so* many stories. My kids used to love hearing them, and it's all gone now . . .

Traffic in our northbound lane is bumper to bumper. We inch forward towards a distant set of lights.

So anyway, I left Mum, picked my son up at the station. He always rushes home from work for Shabbos—he's a medical researcher—and one of us always picks him up. I have the heater switched on for him in the bathroom, so he can have a quick shower and get organized. And I make him a cup of tea. Such a nice mother! Ah! And then—[*sudden intake of breath*] Oy gevalt!*

A northbound ambulance, sirens screaming, dashes past us in the less congested southbound lane.

So . . . uh . . . so . . . [*remembering*] Oh yes! And then, it's Shabbos. It's so nice to sit quietly and read, waiting till we have dinner. You just sit down—my husband, my son, and me. Candles are lit, everything's in the oven and ready, and you just sit quietly. I was reading Gore Vidal's autobiog—No, I think I'd finished that . . . Yes, that's right. I'm reading a Ngaio Marsh, which is very good. And I just sit quietly, enjoy sitting in a tidy room. Flowers in the vase. My husband always brings flowers home, always for Shabbos. And then we make Kiddush.* It really is an oasis for me.

Then, this weekend, Jack went to shul, I spent the morning with Mum, gave her lunch, then went home. Fortunately, it's very close by. We're very lucky in that way. And then, then the three of us had lunch—Sorry, four of us—my son's girlfriend was there too. You think I can remember what we had? Oh yeah! Gefilte fish, beetroot and potato salad. It's all ready, in the fridge. Just have to serve it.

And then in the afternoon, I must confess, I had a shlof* for a couple of hours, on the bed. And then after Shabbos was out, I did some shopping at the deli, and then I went on duty in the shul kitchen because a friend of mine's daughter was having an engagement party and I'd promised to come and help. I was cutting up the vegetables for the dips. It was for a hundred and fifty people, so lots of cakes, lots of salads, dips. Professional staff as well, but all the friends rally round, and all catered for by the ladies' guild. What was funny was that a lot of people who came, they were so impressed, they asked, Could they have a card for the caterer! [*laughs*]

Then on Sunday—I normally work in the pharmacy two Sundays on, two off, and I was off last week, so I went to see Mum in the morning, and in the afternoon I went with Jack to a bar mitzvah* do in Romford. It was a cousin's child. Yes, so some weekends are very socially Jewish, some . . .

Finally at the lights, Pearl makes a difficult right turn into a less congested street.

. . . some, some aren't. Now this coming weekend, is going to be rather hectic. My other son, who lives in Jerusalem, has just got engaged to a girl from New York—lovely girl, she's a doctor, at Mount Sinai. Mount Sinai? I always get mixed up between Sinai and Carmel, which is where he used to teach English. Some big Jewish hospital in New York, anyway.

And, they wanted to meet everybody here before the wedding in Israel. So they're flying in on Wednesday, and then this Sunday afternoon I'm having everyone round for afternoon tea. Our family, my son's friends, our friends, it all mounts up. Probably about eighty people.

MG: *Just a quiet affair . . .*

Well, [*laughs*] my two sister-in-laws . . . sisters-in-law? . . . Anyway, Wendy and Adrienne came round on Monday, and we had this all-day bake-a-thon: apple cakes, carrot cakes, lemon cakes, chocolate chip biscuits, chocolate caramel slice, uh, fruit squares. And all this is now ready. Plus the smoked salmon and savories, of course. Then I get some help in on the day, to serve and that sort of thing. It's just easier that way. You'd think my life revolves around the kitchen, wouldn't you! But it doesn't. Normally, I avoid it! I have the shop to run.

A traffic light changes to green. Pearl makes a left turn, passing a block of council flats, an Indian restaurant, and an off-licence. She slows down, pointing to a carpark next to the off-licence.

That's where the old shul used to be. That's where Mum got married . . . long since demolished . . . [*breezily*] So was that OK? I mean, is that the sort of thing you wanted to hear?

MG: *Exactly! It was terrific.*

Are you interested in family history, the mishpocha?* We're related to the speaker in the Knesset.* Do you wanna hear about that kind of thing?

MG: *If you'd like to tell me . . .*

[*delightedly*] Sure! Well, on my father's side, my grandfather was Meyer Feinblum, and he married a woman called Miriam Jacobs, and her sister married this guy who was a fiery orator exhorting people to go and live in Eretz Yisrael* et cetera et cetera and eventually they did and they had three sons—

Oh! First I should tell you first that my husband's late father, his family went from Russia—or wherever it was—to Manchester, and his parents . . . I *think* it was his parents, had a matza factory or was it his sister? Anyway, the children went to South Africa, South America, disappeared completely. But the one I want to tell you about is one of the sisters who stayed in Manchester and married a man named Levy.

The more animated Pearl's story becomes, the slower she drives. We're doing thirty m.p.h. in a sixty zone. A car behind us toots.

122

Oops! [*laughs and accelerates*] And . . . and . . . and they had a family party, but they didn't invite Mr. Levy's brother, and he got feribel* that his family weren't interested in him, and so he decided to leave. This is true! So he went down to the docks, but the boat for Argentina had just gone, so he went to Canada instead, and he got a job as a picture framer in Montreal. And you know who he was? He was my mother's boyfriend, before she met my father. She would have *so* many stories to tell you. And now it's all gone. [*sighs*]

Now, the speaker in the Knesset—actually he's the ex-speaker now—you're probably wondering what the connection is. I'm coming to him. It all ties in . . .

The Extended Family

———— ❦ ————

At a Jewish young leadership convention in Atlanta, Georgia, I meet Frances G. She grew up in Anchorage, Alaska, but now lives in Dallas, Texas, where she's a marketing director in a computer software company, often going overseas on business. Over coffee in a hotel lounge crowded with other delegates, Frances takes me on a whirlwind trip through the world of Jewish travel. Traveling alone can be difficult, she says, especially for a woman with strawberry blond hair.

I GUESS MAYBE SOME POLACK raped one of my great-grandmothers! Or married in. Somewhere along the line someone married in, something happened. Who knows! It's terrible when you're in Japan. You get hassled a lot. And Turkey. Same in Morocco. Anyways, wherever I go I look up the local Jewish community. It's the extended family. When I travel for pleasure, I try to make it around the Jewish festival time.

But even when I'm working—like last year I went to Florence for work, went to the synagogue, met the local Jews. That was Saturday morning. Then I had a day off on the Sunday, and went up to Venice and actually saw a Jewish wedding in the old ghetto area. So I met some Italian Jews. Really interesting.

And when I was in New York I heard about this synagogue in Sutton Place just for singles. Have you heard of that? No? Anyway, the special service for Yom Kippur was in the Waldorf Astoria.

I thought, "Gotta do this." [*laughs*] Like, "Waldorf Astoria, whoaaaaa!! I gotta be there."

And I met some amazing people. One guy said he had a model agency on Fifth Avenue. I thought, "Oh yeah, great line." But he *did*. He took me there. No job offer, unfortunately.

It's like another family, I guess. If you don't get along with your own family, there's always somewhere else to go. There are always these resources. It's a safety net, culturally. That's an important part of being Jewish. There's a book on it actually: *The Jewish Traveler*. You know it? I used it when I went to Fiji and met some great people.

It's got some unusual places too, like African countries, far-flung places. They say Jews are everywhere, right? It's like a password in a way. You say you're Jewish, and then it's OK, you're in. I went to Russia in 1989 with a friend, a few months before the Berlin Wall came down. In Moscow we went to the synagogue but we knew the KGB was there because they were taking photos on Shabbat. A real giveaway, right? [*to another delegate*] Hi, there. OK. I'll talk to you when I'm through here. [*looking at me*] Fifteen minutes?

MG: *Whatever* . . .

OK. Went to Vilnius—or Vilna—in Lithuania, with another friend in 1994, and tried to find records of my grandmother, but there weren't any. I was only in Vilna for a few days, but there was a family I was introduced to that uh, were going to emigrate to Israel. They took us around to the synagogue. There's just one left. Then they took us to the forest where there were all these mass graves, big round slabs of cement in the forest.

I said to Susan, "Do you hear that? We're in the middle of the forest and there's no sound. No birds, no insects, nothing." I'm sure it had such a bad feeling about it that even the animals wouldn't go near it. Really eerie. And then I thought, "A number of my relatives could be here." There were quite a few of my great-uncles and aunts who didn't make it, so I figured maybe they were there.

And uh, after that we went to Tbilisi in Georgia. They're like the Italians of the USSR: boisterous, singing, dancing, drinking wine. And some of them looked sort of Semitic. And one afternoon we were walking across this street and there was this like, building with domes on it, which looked a little bit like a mosque.

We wandered in there, and there are all these guys sitting in a room, drinking tea or something. And they waved us in. It turned out it was a tea room—you know, they're famous for their tea in Georgia. And they speak a different language to Russian, so we tried words like: "Israel . . . Judea . . . synagoga . . ." All these different words.

I finally hit the right word: "Magen David."* That was it! They understood. "Ah! Mogen Daveeeeed! OK!" This guy started motioning us: "Follow me." So we walked and walked through all these back streets. Didn't know where the hell we were going. It was a really cute town too, Tbilisi.

And finally, we ended up in a synagogue with all these Magen Davids all over the ceiling. He introduced us to the rabbi, who was also the shochet,* who spoke a few words of English, few of Russian, few of Hebrew. We sort of got along with that. He took us around the back and there was an old factory making matza. Bizarre. That was a real buzz.

And later on, we were walking around the streets, and someone invited us up to her apartment for tea. Just like that. "Oh Americans! Good! Good!"

And it was a really *beautiful* place she had. She was like, an artist making carpets. And on the wall was a menorah* with some candles and a crucifix hanging from it. [*her eyes widening*] It was like, complete bewilderment really. So I went through this little drama again: "Israel, Magen David, et cetera" to get her to understand. Finally,

I drew the Star of David and I said, "That's *me*. And that" — pointing to the menorah — "that's *Jewish*." And then she got it! "A-ha!"

I tried to find out how she'd got the menorah, was there anyone in the family? . . . It came out that they'd had it for many, many generations. I'd figured it was pretty old because it had the Lion of Judah, which is an old symbol. She said it was from 1708. I offered to buy it because I thought, "Maybe I can give it to a synagogue here." Because it's not doing what it's supposed to be doing, and it kinda hurt me to see it used that way. But, it was in the family and she wouldn't part with it. So that was two things in Tbilisi. I thought, "Isn't that bizarre? I'm only here for a day and I've run into two Jewish things." And it wasn't hard.

The Whole History
of the Jews

———⟆⟆⟆———

A corner table for two in a quiet café in New York's East Village. Shelley M. is a thirty-two-year-old bookseller who defines herself as a "cultural Jew." She enjoys reading about Jewish history and culture but also has a passion for Jewish film festivals. It's not just what's on screen that attracts her; she likes the audiences, too.

I ACTUALLY—I DON'T OBSERVE JUDAISM. It's just I feel Jewish. [*nods rapidly*] And I feel like Jewish film festivals make me feel more Jewish. It sounds silly but when you're there with all these Jewish people going to, ten, fifteen, twenty films, which sometimes, some years I've done. . . I don't know, you just feel like there's a lot of commonalities and that we're really a big culture . . . So I don't know . . . I guess that's about it.

MG: *Do any particular films stand out in your mind?*

Well, a couple of years ago I went to a festival, and there was a showing at a school auditorium so it was smaller, it was a smaller thing and you could see the people there. And it was a showing of *Because of That War.* Do you know this? It's an incredible film. It's about rock musicians, two rock musicians who put out a record called *Ashes and Dust* in Israel. And they're both children of Holocaust survivors. And the movie is their story and their parents' stories, and why they did this. It's incredible. And it's rock music.

She mimes a headbanging drummer.

So anyway, I went to this festival and . . . [*knitting her eyebrows*] I *think* it was this movie. Coulda been a different movie. But it doesn't matter. And I sat down . . . No, I think it *was* this movie. I saw this movie twice, and something happened to me at each, each time and . . .

So a woman in her eighties—seventies or eighties—sat down next to me. She was kind of a stocky woman with white, snow white hair in a bun. And when she spoke to me, she sounded *exactly* like my Aunt Miriam, who's dead now, who came over in eighteen . . . in nineteen hundred or nineteen-oh-five. From Russia.

And this woman came from Russia too. She had just come a year ago or less. She sounded *exactly* like my Aunt Miriam, which kind of flipped me out. I don't know how to explain this. I mean, she was Jewish. And her name was Anna. She was a Russian Jew who'd gone to—Well, she was a Russian Jew, and she spoke the way that my grandmother did. And anyway, we started talking, and she told me her life story. This is like, before and after the film. I asked her if she liked Russia, and if she was sorry she left.

And she said, "Russia is a terrible place." And she told me how her mother was killed during a pogrom. Was shot in the head. And I think it was either Anna or another child who was—Her mother was pregnant and the child was born. Or something. It's very confusing, but that's what she told me. And then when she got older, she married. And her husband was killed at the Russian front. And then—Oh! Hang on—Her, her husband was killed at Babi Yar [*site of the massacre of Kiev's Jews during World War II*]—Does that . . .? She . . . lost . . . her husband, I think, at Babi Yar. And someone else in her family, I don't remember. Maybe—

She pauses, gently chewing her lower lip.

Someone was killed at Babi Yar. I can't remember who was killed at the Russian front. Someone. But the point is, there were all these tragedies in her life. And I felt, as I was talking to her, that the whole history of the Jews, of the Russian Jews was before me. That she lived through these major events . . . I mean, [*wonderment in her voice*] I've never met anyone who had a relative who died at, at Babi Yar. I mean, that's—To us that's a legend.

So . . . I don't know . . . It was just a very moving experience. And we were in this really safe place. And we were all Jews watching this movie, or we *assumed* we were all Jews. And anyway . . . so things like that often happen to me at this festival.

And I learn a lot from the films too. That's how I learned about the Falashas* and about Dominican Jews, and all the different kinds of people who are Jewish. It's history, it's community, it's memory, it's, it's . . . it's everything. It's like a secular form of synagogue! Yeah, I think, that's it. I'd go to services every Saturday if they were like that. [*laughs*]

Apart from the Missiles

TOYBA: A lot of people think it's just the hora. But as Israel developed, the dances developed too, and they added more steps, more style. Now, they take from everywhere: from Russian dance, from Greek, from Yemenite dance, Arabic debka, partner dancing . . . Then we also have Latin American, we have line dances, rock 'n' roll, It's unbelievable. We get maybe eighty people at the club on a good night. But that'd be a very good night.

But in Israel, it's *huge*: five hundred people in a gymnasium! Dances every night of the week . . . Dance camps, dance competitions, dance marathons . . .

Late evening in the kitchen of Israeli dance teacher Toyba O.'s home in Los Angeles. Toyba, who grew up in Los Gatos, California, is at the kitchen table with her husband, Asher, a native of Nahariya in northern Israel. Sleeping at his feet, Hector, the family dachshund. At the other end of the table, Toyba's mother is making a face at her crossword puzzle. A CD player on the countertop enlivens the atmosphere with the Latin rhythms of the Israeli song "Imbal." The CD is in single-track repeat mode: "Imbal" has been playing for twenty minutes.

TOYBA: I think of it as a physical form of Zionism. When you're doing Israeli dance, you feel that you're there, in Israel. And a lot of people who dance with us have lived there, and it's like they go home one night a week. And it's aerobics, it's fun, it's a great place to meet people.

I was talking to some friends who've just set up a new club in New York, and they said, "We've already had three couples getting engaged in the first month!" And I said, "That's amazing. All we ever get at my club is divorces." [*laughs*] Really. We get a lot. One partner goes dancing, the other stays at home . . . You start dancing with someone, you get to know them. I mean, I don't think it's *just* the dance. It's probably they're not happy with their spouse or whatever . . . and then . . . Well, it happened to me, actually.

MG: *Really?*

TOYBA: Yeah. Asher is my second husband. And I met him dancing. I was his teacher!

ASHER: I danced since I was thirteen. In Israel, you grow up with it. I always danced. When I was in the army, I'd run away from the base, just to go dancing. They never caught me! [*laughs*]

TOYBA: It's a terrific experience. And like—I mean, in Israel— where it's really mega—they have these dance marathons.

MG: *Have you ever been to one?*

TOYBA: Sure. Last time we were there. I was seven months' pregnant with Bailey, and I'd just spent seventeen hours on the plane with two children, and Asher said, "You know there's a marathon on tonight?"

I said, "Excellent!" So we got off the plane, drove to Asher's parents' place near Haifa. I put the kids to bed, I said, "Lemme just rest coupla hours." I said, "Wake me up, promise me you'll wake me up." And he didn't—he was sleeping himself! But fortunately I woke up anyway. And we drove to this big open air place. A couple of hundred people there.

And we danced till, like, four or five in the morning. I danced nonstop, but Asher caught up with some people he knew.

ASHER: I know a lot of people in Israel.

TOYBA: Once you're used to it, you can last for hours, dancing.

MG: *So what d'you do next morning?*

I woke up to my kids! [*laughs*] You don't catch up with sleep when you're a mom.

MG: *And this was in Haifa?*

ASHER: No, near Nahariya. Beautiful place. You have the sea, the valleys, the whole Galil in front of you. Beautiful, peaceful place—apart from the missiles they're getting from Lebanon. You been there?

MG: *Oh, quite a while back . . . late eighties.*

ASHER: Last ten years, it's changed a lot. Before it was bananas, avocados. Now it's all houses.

MG: *And dance venues.*

ASHER: Right. Like you go to a bar. Ten-thirty at night, it's empty, then at eleven, a few more people. At twelve, it's full. And there are *hundreds* of places like that in Israel, and everyone's dancing till three, four in the morning. And they work the next day. Israeli dancing in the States, it's not like that. [*a loud noise from under the table*] You wanna record the dog snoring? [*laughs*]

TOYBA: We try to keep up with what's happening in Israel. I have a guy there, sends me all the new videos and cassettes. And we get Israeli choreographers coming over here, too.

I was talking to a guy that was here last week. God, it was so funny— You know, a lot of people here, they really idolize the Israeli dancers, think they're like God or something. They try to copy every movement. And this guy Uri from Tel Aviv was saying how he was in New York or somewhere, in a Jewish community center, teaching some new Israeli dances. And it was a sunny day, the sun was in his eyes, and so he's shielding his eyes with hands [*demonstrates*] and like, the whole class start doing it too. [*laughs*]

The three of us raise our elbows to do the new Israeli dance.

TOYBA: Seriously, you should come to the studio and see what we do. You've never done it, right? We have a beginners' class at seven-thirty tomorrow. Come along, and get a feel for it.

MG: *Oh, I couldn't. I'm severely dance-challenged. No sense of rhythm; two left feet.*

ASHER: People coming there, some of them are cripples. No problem.

TOYBA: Right. My lawyer'll be there. She's a really intelligent woman, but she gets frustrated with right and left, so it's a whole new challenge for her. So come along, loosen up, and meet some people.

Call It Something Else

In the living room of an apartment overlooking Central Park, New York City. On the wall, a reproduction of Ben Shahn's portrait of a Japanese fisherman dying of radiation sickness, the victim of an American bomb test in the Pacific. Louise A. is an attorney who specializes in cases representing the victims of human rights abuses. She is a member of Amnesty International and the American Council for Civil Liberties. Judaism, Louise explains, provides the ethical basis for her work. She's belongs to a Conservative congregation on the Upper West Side. Louise's religious beliefs and practices have led to friction with some of her Jewish friends.

WHEN MY DAUGHTER HAD A BAT MITZVAH* up here at our Conservative synagogue, an Orthodox friend of ours—and one of my best friends—wouldn't come to the service. His wife came, but he didn't. And at the party afterwards, we didn't have any dance music, we had it completely kosher—totally kosher—we had it here so that they could walk, so they could feel perfectly comfortable. And they both came to that.

And y'know, it was never laid out there why this guy didn't come to the service, but she said—his wife said, "I've never seen a girl read from the Torah before, and I can really see why it's so distracting: because it's so beautiful."

And clearly, her husband was not meant to hear this Torah being read by a girl. And I was very, very offended. I was very, very offended. And I think that was the kind of . . . the beginning of things—this was a couple of years ago—dropping off between us.

It's one thing to say you have the truth, but to say that it's the *whole* truth, and other people's truth isn't, it's just so offensive. I mean, everyone does have a truth for themselves. [*exasperatedly*] And these are thinking people! In other respects they're liberals! But there's this sense that what we have is not a religion. This is a joke. Or it's not Judaism, call it something else.

Their concept of Judaism is about the law, and my concept of Judaism is the Prophets, that we are here to help God—whatever God is—to bring about the Messianic Age—whatever that is . . . that there is something in the Prophets about ethical living: "You were strangers in the land of Egypt, and you owe it to other strangers . . ." That's the basis of my life. That's how I got into law. Everything I do in fact probably is because of Judaism [*outraged*] and to say that that's not really Judaism!

My husband thinks I overreact to this, that I should just say, "Forget it," be friends with them on other levels. And I try. But it's too much. This guy would not come to the synagogue, he would not listen, he would not listen to a girl reading from the Torah.

And the Orthodox Jewish day school is getting more and more right-wing. And they tell those children, "If you happen—God forbid—to have a close friend who belongs to the Conservative synagogue, and worse, you go to that bar mitzvah* on Saturday morning, you still have to go home and pray, because what they do there, that, that's not prayer."

And I have Orthodox friends in Israel, and they say, why don't we go to Israel to visit them? And they would treat us royally, and why didn't we have our son's bar mitzvah in Israel?

And I have to admit this, I don't have the guts to say, "Because you can be as frum* as you wanna be there but I'm considered secular. And I'm *not* secular!!" They just don't get that. And they also feel that American Judaism is clearly dying, and that really, if you identify as a Jew, you've got to go to Israel. And my feeling is, "Wow! If that's the kind of Jew that I'm supposed to become, for . . . geddit!"

I love being a diaspora Jew! I'm very interested in diaspora history and the whole—the problems that go with it. That's me. That's what I want to hear about, and I don't consider it "less than," whatsoever. But the Orthodox too—I feel I have an inside a lot of the time on what's going on. I know some Orthodox feminists. They have their struggles too. But they don't talk to each other. And it's interesting, maybe because I'm a good listener, but sometimes they to talk to me.

They don't like the mechitzah.* They don't—One woman said to me they love Thanksgiving because it's the one holiday they can go in the car, and go shopping. You know, it's such a relief to have an American holiday. And they're all on medication. It's hard for them, too.

137

A Horrible Thing to Say

Early Sunday evening in a Chinese restaurant in Melbourne, Australia. Belinda H. is forty-two. She teaches French and English in a local high school. As a teenager growing up in a small town outside Brisbane, Belinda thought she knew all about anti-Semitism. She was in for a surprise, however, when she and her family moved to Melbourne. Her voice is colored by anger, guilt, and bewilderment—often simultaneously.

MY PARENTS WERE SECULAR, humanist intellectuals. Their circle of friends were like them: educated, cultured professionals. That's what I thought Jews were. Then when we came to Melbourne, I discovered there were these other creatures who called themselves Jews: men with beards and black coats, and their wives with wigs, and ten kids in tow, and that horrible Yiddish whine. You see them going to shul* on Saturdays, long lines of men in front, women and kids behind. It's the Middle Ages. They even seem to look down when they walk, as if, if they take anything in, it might change the furniture of their mind. And they don't want to do that. Everything's got to be as it's writ, as it's passed down.

It makes me so angry that other people, non-Jews—noninitiates—will see them and think: "That's Jewish." And yes, that is Jewish, but it's not coextensive with Jewish. There are people that are Jewish that are not like that. Like me: the secular, ethnic, tribal, humanist kind.

But the others take up so much space in the gentiles' mindset, this kind of Jew with his black coat and his peculiar view of the world, there's no room left for someone who looks just like anyone else, and ninety percent of whose beliefs are the same as anyone else's. I think they make it hard for me in the real world.

She rests her chopsticks on her rice bowl.

Isn't that a horrible thing to say? It's the way I've been brought up. I mean, there are lots of reasons to be against these people: they're sexist, racist reactionaries. But those are rational grounds. I have some very irrational feelings too.

I was driving earlier today — just a few blocks away from here — stuck behind a delivery truck, and he was really crawling along. "OK. Maybe the guy's looking for a number." I'm quite a fast driver. Finally, I passed him, and it's a Chassid. "Fucking religious Jews!" I thought. "You drive the way you walk the way you think!" It's a closed world that can't let in other influences. Jesus, I sound like an anti-Semite, don't I?

And when I lived in Israel, they came down the street and banged on the door, shouting, *"Zman, zman!** Time to get ready for the Sabbath." Fine. It might be time for *you* to get ready for the Sabbath, but what I do on my Fridays and Saturdays is up to me. They make me so angry.

The "Blue Danube" waltz is playing on the restaurant's sound system.

I remember when my son was about seven. We were driving along and we saw a bunch of Chassids going to shul. He said, "Who are they?" I said, "They're Jews." He said, *"They're* not Jews. We're Jews." Uh-oh! I said, "There's all kinds of Jews, sweetie, and that's another kind."

It Frightens Me

———— ❦ ————

Walter R. is eighty-two. He and his wife, Margot, live in a harborside town in Connecticut. On their bookshelves, a jumble of colored spines. Titles that hit the eye include Eva Hoffman's Lost in Translation, Leo *Rosten's* The Joys of Yiddish, *and J. H. Hertz's translation and commentary on the Torah. Above the fireplace, an oil painting of a gaff-rigged schooner. Walter sits in an armchair, his right hand held firmly in his left to suppress the tremor. Mrs. R. is unwell and went upstairs to bed before I arrived. Her hacking cough is audible throughout the recording. Walter talks about the changes he's observed in the Jewish community over fifty years. It used to be anti-Semitism that worried him. Now it's the rift within the Jewish community.*

SINCE I WAS A LITTLE BOY I ALWAYS WANTED TO SAIL. Sailing was what I wanted to do more than anything else. So we moved out here from Brooklyn in nineteen hundred and fifty-one.

Our first experience of driving around town, we drove to a certain area—I tried to find the photograph for you today but I couldn't find it. I took a photograph: NO JEWS AND DOGS. That is a scary, scary thing to see. I had never seen this before. Had a camera in the car and took a photograph of it. It was in a field, right next to the road. On a vacant lot. Houses hadn't sprung up then the way they have in the past ten, fifteen years. I said to Margot today, "Where the hell is that photograph?" We got photographs up to here. [*chuckles*]

But we came here in spite of it all. There were very few Jews in those days. But as of the early eighties the school system shut down on Rosh haShanah* and Yom Kippur.* What a change. There was a huge influx of Jews. Where a Jew could not belong to the yacht clubs—the two major yacht clubs—they created a Jewish club right next door to the others! They brought the property and they made a Jewish yacht club.

We had a daughter and a son. I didn't belong to a temple. And we—fifteen of us here started a Reform temple. We didn't have a building. On High Holidays we went to the Protestant church, and they had a meeting house, not the church but a meeting house. We asked if we could use it. They said, "Definitely." We said, "We'd be glad to pay you." They wouldn't allow us to pay 'em. For the first time, we turn around, "Hey! There's some nice people here."

And from then on we started a building fund and we built our own temple. It now has six hundred members.

[*stonily*] We don't belong now. I quit a time ago for a reason.

MG: *Why was that?*

My son, having been bar mitzvahed* there, was going to confirmation classes. And in order to be confirmed, you had to go to class so many days a week. And my son was playing football; he could not go to class. So he was supposed to go to every Friday night service. Margot and I used to go with him. I loved going to Friday night services. It's an amazing thing. I'm not imbued with Jewishness, but there's something very nice about sitting in a service and listening to . . . whatever little lecture goes on that night, to the prayers, singing a few songs . . . It's kinda very heimishe.* That remained with me. That I couldn't give up. I would go and take Ken with me.

But he never showed up on Thursday to class because he had football practice, and Thursday you were supposed to sign that you'd been to the Friday night service, the previous Friday night service. And when it came time at the end of the year for Ken to be confirmed, Ken went up to the rabbi and said, "These were the days I was here." The rabbi looked at him and said, "Ken, I'm puttin' you down for half that time." My son was *furious*. If he had lied, OK, but this was a guy who went there 'cause I took 'im.

I quit because of that. I couldn't believe it. I confronted the rabbi. I put in my resignation. They said, "You can't quit, you're a charter member. You can't quit." They wouldn't accept it. So I stopped going Friday nights and just showed up on High Holidays. We stayed for two more years, then my yacht club jumped its prices, my company folded, I was out of a job, so I decided—I had a choice: either stay with the temple or give up my boat. So I quit the temple.

[*with feeling*] But I missed it, I missed it. I love being a Jew. I love the history of the Jews. I spend a great deal of time reading about it. We have our finger on what's happening to Jews. We cry for those who are being hurt, and we try to do whatever we can for some of the injustices that Jews are doing to Jews. I'm not talkin' about Christians doin' to Jews. Now Jews are doin' to Jews.

I'm thinking that there's quite possibly going to be a civil war in Israel. You have almost fifty percent of the population one way, fifty the other. People are saying, "Let me be a Jew in my own way in this great State of Israel." And they won't allow 'em to do that. The right-wingers, the fundamentalists have taken over the power. Freud used to say that Abraham and Moses talking to God were hallucinating. They were so obsessed with God, and the word of God, that they heard voices. I buy that. I buy that.

But the fundamentalists do not. And that's perfectly all right. But unfortunately, they say, "We are right and you do it our way or you don't do it at all." They will drive the Jews out of Israel. It frightens me. It frightens me a great deal, because I care what happens to Israel.

We're gonna be called on Sunday to give money for Israel. For the first time, I'm gonna refuse. I'll say, "I will give you money if you can tell me it can be used for something else. But I'm not giving you another goddam cent for Israel while this is going on!" No.

I'm sure there are a lot of friends of mine who'll say, "Oh, you're a bastard for doing this." But no. Israel is a land of milk and honey, where if you're a Jew, you're a Jew, no matter how you pray to God. It's the same God.

Margot and I were reading the Torah the other night and we realized that Jews used to sell their daughters as slaves! The culture said it was OK. So things have changed a lot. And we don't want to go back to those days when you had to put a veil on a Jewish woman. What I'm trying to tell you is, we're a different kind of Jew. I want to drive a car on Saturday, I'm not a bad Jew for that . . .

But you know, we are the Jews that many conservatives are worried about, because we're intermarrying with other faiths. Our rabbi will marry somebody of a different faith. The ultra-conservatives say that the Reform temple is nothing but a spawning ground for intermarriage.

My son and daughter did not gravitate towards Jewish people. It didn't bother me. Because there are many Jews I don't gravitate to either. You pick your own. But the one thing I've always wanted for my children—My wife and I feel the important thing is for our children to be happy. My daughter married a Jew and was very unhappy with him. Married a Jewish man who went on drugs and made her life miserable with two children. So . . . And now she's sharing a home with a non-Jew, who's the most wonderful guy in the world. He treats her like a princess. Am I gonna say, "Because you're a non-Jew I don't want you to have anything to do with my daughter?" I don't believe that. I look at my daughter and see how happy she is.

My son lives in Holland with a girl, been there many years now. He brought her out here, we fell in love with her. He never married her, they never got married; we can't understand why. But that's not our business either. But we fell in love with her. She's a gentle, wonderful girl.

There are other families who if my son did this, would put him out of the house. They'd put a cloth over the mirrors, as if there was a death in the family. What a horrible thing to do to a child. And for what? It takes the living hell out of yourself. You have to wake up every day and curse yourself. You don't want to do that.

Jewish and Israeli

Although diaspora Jews have tended to identify strongly with Israelis and the State of Israel, some secular Israelis feel that they have increasingly less in common with Jews in the diaspora. Ezra Z. is thirty. He grew up in Dimona in Israel's Negev Desert but for five years has lived in San Francisco where he's the assistant manager of a music store. This Sunday morning Ezra's at home, sitting on the floor of his second-story apartment. A Black Sabbath CD is playing. He's wearing a pirate shirt over black jeans that are ripped at both knees. A spiraling column of blue smoke rises from a freshly-lit cigarette between his fingers.

ISRAELIS HERE, THEY'RE EASY TO SEE. If it's at the bus stop, they'll go first and push. When you see someone pushing in: he's Israeli. They're pushy. If they want to get discount on things, they'll hassle. In department stores! This is the Israeli. If they want something, they'll take it. If they have to give a kick to someone and it won't be nice, they'll do that. No problem. If they have to work twenty-four hours, they'll do that too.

And they shout. They don't know how to talk soft. If they're coming here and he wants to call me, he won't go upstairs and knock on the door. He'll just shout: "EZRA!!" Doesn't matter what time it is. Screaming. Two o'clock in the morning.

[*drawing on his cigarette*] I used to do it too. Why bother to go upstairs to go downstairs? This is the Israeli. I can recognize them. I grew up there.

Here, you can understand that life is not only war, fighting, rushing, being rude to everybody. If you live here, you start to calm down and relax. Just listen to that.

He indicates the absence of street sounds. A dog barks in the distance.

In Israel, I never thought about being Jewish. You don't have to. It's only when I came here I realized that there was Jewish and Israeli. In Israel there is no alternative. [*laughs*] Well, there is, but you don't think about it because, hey, the Muslims they are your enemy, and the Christians are such a small community and so far from me. I was an Israeli. It's like you are a man, and that's it, there is no other way.

In Israel you don't have to think about when is Rosh haShanah* or when is Yom Kippur* and all that. The Jews here expect me to be a Jew. "What did you do on Rosh haShanah? Where did you celebrate that?" And I didn't. I never been to a synagogue here. I never did anything in Israel unless I went to see my parents. My brother is with Chabad.* He's a very religious guy. He's doing the work for me. [*grins*] The only one who doesn't expect me to be a Jew is Israelis.

At home in Israel, it doesn't make any difference if you celebrate or not. Yom Kippur in Israel is dead. People won't put loud music, people won't drive cars. From respect. They will do whatever they want to do in their places: they will smoke, open the lights, put music, but it will be soft, not loud. But here, it's just another day.

MG: *What did you do on Yom Kippur this year?*

Don't ask me that!

He laughs, throwing up his hands in mock shame.

The truth is I don't know it's Yom Kippur. I didn't talk to my parents the week before, that's why I didn't know. I realized that something was happening in the morning. I saw people going to the

146

synagogue. I told my boss, "Something is happening here. What is it?" And she said, "It's Yom Kippur." And I said, "Oh . . . fuck!" That was the sign that, "Hey, you've gone a bit too far." I was disappointed that I didn't take the day off. So I asked my mother to send me a calendar for next year.

I don't have lots of contact with Jewish people to tell you the truth. I'm not going with people because "Oh, yes, you're Jewish. OK. Let's be friends." I don't go that way. But I have lots of customers that are Jewish. They're always happy to see me, tell me about their experiences in Israel or whatever. But they're not like Jews in Israel. For me the Jewish here are Jewish, but I don't feel close to them as I do to Israeli.

Like, Israeli talk dugri. You know what is dugri? Straight talk: "Tell me what you *really* think. Don't be afraid to insult me. I want you to talk dugri." Y'know? This is one of the things that the Israeli have that the rest of the Jewish don't have.

People here ask you to be honest. So you are honest, and then they say, "Shit, man! Why did you tell me that?"

I had a customer. He asked me what do I think of his band and how was their gig. He say, "I want you to be *really* honest." And to me, honest is honest. I say, "Well, I didn't think it was so good. I didn't enjoy it. There is lots of things you need to change. You have to change this, this, and that." I don't remember what, maybe the instrumentation, some of the songs, lighting, and stuff like that. Just things I thought.

He said, [*flatly*] "OK." [*with mild bewilderment*] I never saw him again. In Israel, if you say that, you will see him again. They appreciate that. I've been here five years, but I'm sometimes wondering why I'm still here.

The Feel of the Sun
in January

Professor R. sits behind her desk in the North Carolina college where she teaches media studies. Her pale face is framed by the dark back of a video monitor on one side and a desktop computer on the other. She has short blond hair and two extremely large hoop earrings that almost reach to her shoulders. It's early evening, winter. The window behind her reflects a large framed poster of a David Hockney interior and a still from Jean Renoir's film La Grande Illusion. *As Professor R. talks, her Israeli-accented voice becomes gradually softer and less animated.*

I WAS ACTUALLY BORN HERE IN AMERICA, but I grew up in Israel since two months old. I had a very Israeli kind of upbringing in the forties and fifties. Served in the Israeli army, did the whole thing. And, I come from a family that's deeply rooted in the Israeli tradition. My mother's family are there from the nineteenth century and my father's family came there in the nineteen twenties.

And I never expected to come back to America. It was just not in the agenda at all. And then I married an American Jew, came here, the marriage broke up and I stayed here anyway. I had a job offer from the Hebrew University in Jerusalem and another here in the U.S. And after tremendous conflict and crisis I decided to stay here. As I understood it in the nineteen sixties, at a time when

America seemed like such a revolutionary and exciting place, Israel felt really claustrophobic and constricting to me.

In retrospect, with greater wisdom, I also realize that I was trying to put as much distance between me and my family as I could. I found it impossible to live with my parents. But I feel really sad that I had to do it that way. But I'm glad that I did. It was survival really.

But the danger for somebody like me is that my entire identity here goes unknown. And unrecognized. Because I'm not a Jew like American Jews: I grew up in Israel. And my friends here don't know what it's like, haven't gone through that. So there is a way in which things resonate I cannot assume that anybody else will pick up on or understand. Even though we are all Jews.

Like you. I don't know what your background is, but if we can assume that at most you've been a tourist in Israel then you probably wouldn't know that either. Most of the time I don't think about it at all, but sometimes it feels lonely when I really wished somebody connected to my version of it. I'm very often with people and I know I could tell them some *fascinating* stories. And I don't because I feel like I will enter on a long monologue.

So there is a lot that people here don't know about me actually. And that's a little weird. But they haven't shown that much interest. They're perfectly happy to simply know me as who I am here. I've just been to Israel and come back. And they say, "How it was?" And I tell them, "Oh, my parents are now old. We didn't do very much . . . " And I let it go at that.

So maybe it's my fault . . . But I don't feel that for me there is really a context to make it known. So I sit on my history a lot. And I feel like what constitutes my history, beyond those stories that I could tell, are things like the feel of the sun in January in Israel as contrasted with the sun in July in Israel, and the smell of a certain plant, or a place, or my recollections of walking barefoot in a certain field. I mean, all these incredibly tactile, sensory things that define certain expriences for me.

If I go to Florida or to California, I sort of try to get out of it something familiar. Maybe something about the smell of the earth, something that . . . [*wistfully*] I say, "Ooooh, it's like Israel." Oh, but it's *barely* like Israel. And it also—As you know, Zionism really extracts a tremendous commitment from people. Being there and leaving is really a heavy burden. Everybody in Israel when you visit used to—if they don't anymore—says, "So, when are you coming to settle?" or "So why aren't you settling here *yet*?" That question is always in the air, the expectation is always there. And for me to have left Israel, and to have made it as a conscious choice, as an ideological choice, not as an economic choice, not as any accident, but a very conscious choice: I could've gone back, I chose not to go back. That was very hard. Extremely hard.

And I don't think people here would even have an *inkling* of what that means to me. And continues to mean. It's just a tremendous sense of loss.

She cries softly.

It's a kind of bereavement really.

Three-second pause.

And I do love the warmth of the people, and the kind of unqualified acceptance that they give one. You know, I realize that the one I'm talking about is a Western, Ashkenazi Jew. And I'm not sure if it's quite as embracing for . . . But I think people like us *are* embraced. And it's a wonderful feeling.

I have a . . . a great sense of responsibility about my own contributions. And I'm giving them here in the U.S. I feel like I have not contributed enough to Israel. I contribute financially, but that's not—In my last visit, I thought to myself, "Gee, when I retire, maybe I should go and do some work there." I would like to do something, like go and work in a development city. As an educator. That's what I really would like to do.

At the same time, I spend there a bit of time, and that claustrophobia for me comes right back again: everybody knows everybody there and everybody gossips about everybody. I'm sufficiently quirky and sufficiently eccentric that it would be very hard for me to be myself. And people are not just meddlers and busybodies; there is a certain amount of ill-will in the gossip I hear there that I don't hear here. It drives me nuts. But it's family. I mean, I don't mean literally family. Metaphorically family. So . . . I don't know. I can't imagine what my life would've been like had I stayed there. I don't think it would've been good. I really don't.

If Moshiach Would
Come Tomorrow

He concedes that his proposal is impractical, but still feels that the Israeli government could have quelled the Intifada if only it had adopted a tougher policy. Brian F. is in his early thirties and works for an Israeli investment bank. He grew up in South Africa but has lived in Jerusalem for the past fifteen years. He and his American wife, Susan, are vacationing in the U.S., staying with Susan's parents in their home off Pico Boulevard, Los Angeles. In the living room, Susan is nursing their six-month-old son, Ehud, whilst talking on the phone to friends in Israel. Her father is reading a newspaper. Her mother is in the kitchen preparing lunch. In December 1987, just as the Intifida was starting, Brian F. completed his basic training in the Israeli army.

IT TOOK ME A WHILE. No question, it took me a while to get the army out of my system. Took me a long time. You see things you don't want to see, you're involved in experiences you don't want to be in, and yet it's all done as a mitzvah.*

People often have the idea that right-wing Orthodox people aren't sensitive. You're very sensitive to everything that goes on around you. But unfortunately, you take a position in politics which forces you to sacrifice tolerance for what you think is correct.

We don't need the Palestinians in our state. They're not contributing anything. You might say, "Well, they make the workforce. Without them no buildings would go up." That's unfortunately true. But I think it's about time that the Jews learned to build their own buildings.

My ideal is to have no Palestinian in Israel. A Palestinian state, they can have it and gesundter heit,* they can choose anywhere in the world, but not Eretz Yisrael.* I don't care where. They got plenty neighbors, millions of hectares of land which is uninhabited, millions of friends and so-called brothers. That's where their place is.

If they want to live in Eretz Yisrael, they live by the rules. If they start throwing stones and challenging the security of the state, that's treason. They have no political rights whatsoever in my mind. They have *human* rights, but they don't have political rights.

Brian's father-in-law looks over the top of his newspaper, clears his throat, and resumes reading.

We weren't equipped for the Intifada. I think as a South African I had a lot more knowledge than the Israeli officers of how to quell a riot, just because I'd seen the South African police deal with apartheid over the years. [*hastily*] I wouldn't call them role models, but in terms of quelling a riot, they really had it down to a tee. Whereas the Israelis were just learning the basics of what it meant.

I remember challenging my officer. I said, "Where are the dogs? Send in the dogs! Why do I have to run after somebody who's gonna throw a stone at me? The dog will dodge it better than I will. He'll grab the guy a lot faster than I will, too. What are you sending *me* there for?"

He said, "Dogs? What's an army with dogs?" [*laughs*]

Now this was the most stupid thing I ever saw them do, the officers. We were in a place called Jibalya in Aza,* and they wanted to take a street. Apparently, this refugee camp is the most heavily populated place in the world. There's something like fifty thousand people in a two-mile radius. I don't know if you've ever been to Gaza . . . I don't know how they'll ever clean it up. I think if Moshiach* would come tomorrow, he'd just get everybody out, bomb the place to nothing, just level everything there. It's an absolute disaster. I mean, the refugee camps are disgusting. The whole place is squalor, is dirty, is filthy, is terrible.

And the officers decided—They were looking for troublemakers on a certain street. So they pulled out the whole—They pulled out the residents of that whole street. They were brought out of their homes at two o'clock in the morning to be punished. One block, one block that had about five thousand people. What do you do with five thousand people? They brought 'em, put 'em into a stadium—I don't know who gave this order—

He shakes his head in disbelief.

I wasn't part of the people rounding up the normal crew. You know, I was with the troublemakers, the ones caught throwing stones. So they were taken to another part of the stadium and they were either beaten up or arrested and thrown in jail et cetera et cetera. I was part of that. You try to teach 'em a lesson, you try to teach 'em something.

I said to them, "This fight's been going on since time immemorial. What must I tell you? There's no such as 'occupied territory.' It's ours. God gave it to us, gave it to Avraham, Yitzchak, and Yaakov.* And that's it. Make the best of it. I don't want to hear your stories. If you don't like it, you can always leave!"

And with all the others, they collected all the passports—not the passports, the IDs. You've got five thousand at least! I couldn't believe how many people there were. One massive pile. Now, how you going to give 'em back? Call 'em out by name. For five thousand people! We never slept the whole night. The most stupid thing I ever saw in my entire life! What did it achieve? Nothing.

But what can you do? Who you going to blame? An example of a debacle.

As a thinking individual, you walk up to the officer and you say, "This is stupid." "This is not my thing," he says. "It comes from above." So what you going to do? You going to go to above? Where's above?

I never had a problem identifying what should happen. Here was a people that was living in our country as guests. And therefore, any political insurgence should've just . . . should've been quelled. I don't know how, but should've been quelled. The leadership should've been taken away, should've been arrested. There should've been a clamping down. They should've been thrown out.

But the honest truth is, I'm talking as a little boy, you know, without the political ramifications and knowing what the intelligence is and knowing how America's going to react, and sanctions, and the world view. I'm acting as an idealist, as a young man without the experience of life.

A Lot of Fuel

I DO BELIEVE THE LAND HAS SIGNIFICANCE, but I'm not so sure about the state, the political state as it is. I cannot say there isn't any religious significance to the State of Israel's coming into being, everything has a reason, God plans it. At the same time, I have mixed feelings because the beginnings of the state were very secular. It's trying to be a democracy. But can a Jewish state be a democracy? But I'm very thankful it's there, that I can look at the land. And I really believe I should be there. We plan on making aliyah* at some point, because I believe that's where we find the most fulfillment as a Jew: you're connected to the land.

> *Shoshana W. (see also A Long Way to Go, page 60) is thirty-one. In 1997, on her last trip to Israel, she visited the Tomb of the Patriarchs in Hebron (Chevron in Hebrew). According to Jewish tradition, the city is the burial place of the Patriarchs—Abraham, Isaac, and Jacob—and three of the Matriarchs—Sarah, Rebecca, and Leah. It is home to around five hundred Jewish settlers and more than 120,000 Palestinians. At the time of Shoshana's visit, Israeli troops were still occupying the city, in breach of the timetable for their withdrawal set by the 1993 Oslo Accords.*

We stopped on the way in Bethlehem to pray at Rachel's Tomb. It's like, on the side of the road, it's not a big built-up area, and they've built this nice building to enclose it. And I went inside, and it was very dark. They're still constructing it, so the ground was dirt. And there's this beautiful—They've got it covered with, uh, like a velvet cover with plastic over it. And people are davening,*

156

the women on one side, the men on the other. I didn't daven a specific service, because I was just—I was a little overwhelmed and I couldn't really focus.

So I davened, special things in merit of Rochl,* and then we got back on the bus, and we headed to Chevron. And, here I was thinking, "If my mother knew what I was doing, she would *kill* me!" [*laughs*]

There are parts of the area that are just desolate, just crumbled, like blown-out cars, and, I feel bad to say this because it sounds a little bit, um . . .

The Arab area—this is what I don't understand—The Palestinian Authority has millions, billions of dollars. If Chevron is a city that's so important to them, where's it being put? These people are living in squalor. No one's forcing them to live that way. I felt a lot of anger that all this money– I keep hearing about all these palaces that all the senior officials in the PLO have. Why are they not trying to help their people? They're being used as a pawn, because the PLO wants a certain amount of this and that, not because they want to help their people.

Anyway, when we got close into Chevron, we pulled up at the Cave of the Patriarchs. And there were a couple of other groups there. And the guard escorted us up, and there was another security system and it was all very . . . I had this constant state of tingling. I kept thinking, "I'm going to one of the oldest places in Israel: the Patriarchs, the people you read about in the Torah, we're going to their burial places."

And I got inside and I was very conscious that just on the other side there are people davening in a mosque. Also, knowing about the incident with Baruch Goldstein [*a Jewish settler who opened fire at the Abraham Mosque in 1994, killing twenty-nine Arabs*] was constantly on my mind. You know, I couldn't believe that a Jew could, you know . . .

You cannot condone what this man did, you know, it's just sickening to think that he went into a group of . . . So I'm thinking this the whole time. Here we are on opposite sides, praying to—for the same people, the same Patriarchs. It was difficult, it was very odd to me. There was such animosity . . .

And then after that, we're walking down the street with our guide, she's leading us, walking down the street to show us—I don't remember the name of the place—the area where the Jewish community lives. It's like a compound. And here we are, a group of Orthodox women, all of us in sheitls,* and all these eyes on us, these Arab men sitting and looking. And such anger, I've never felt. And, and I was so nervous, thinking, "Nothing's going to happen, this is broad daylight."

And I was trying to walk with confidence, but the whole time, these boys, these teenagers—not the older men, they're used to it, they see it all the time, they're religious Muslims—but these boys, they were like teenagers here, looking at us with such anger, and spitting on the ground next to our feet. And I was like, trying—I didn't know how to react, whether to look ahead and ignore them or to look in their faces.

I felt every right to be there. I *had* every right to be there. I couldn't just look the other way. But I was scared. I was terrified to look in their faces. I felt I might provoke something. So I just looked ahead, and at the surroundings. And we had security guards all around us. And I remember telling them, "Thank you!" I was so glad they were there, that I could go see these places that are very much part of our heritage.

I still think about it sometimes, seeing that look in their eyes, and wondering what they were thinking, and how that kind of anger is extremely exhausting. It requires a lot of fuel to keep it up. It's hard to stay angry.

Like when I hear German spoken, my shoulders tense. I can't stand to hear it. And I think, "Is that what they're thinking?" God forbid it should be compared similarly, that they can't stand that Jews come to Chevron. Is that what they're thinking? I don't know. It's hard to say.

These are youths. They're being told a lot of things. Children, you can tell them what you want them to believe. I'd like to think they're not being told to hate Jews. I'd like to think that Jews are not being told to hate Arabs. We should be able to live together. But it's *our* city, that's where our Matriarchs and our Patriarchs walked, that's where they're buried.

A Difficult Jew

———⟨∿⟩———

THEY SEEM TO THINK THAT I DO THIS just for the perverse or sadistic pleasure I get out of upsetting them. They don't realize I do it only with great reluctance, out of a sense of duty and obligation. And I can't even explain it to them—they refuse to engage in dialogue, to negotiate difference.

They say, "How can somebody from your background say such things? Don't you understand how we feel?" And I say, "You do me a disservice by saying that. I used to feel what you feel, and in many ways I still do, but I have come to the position where I believe you have to think with your brain, and not your kishkes.*

As a teenager growing up in England during the 1960s, Ron B. was a member of a right-wing Zionist youth group, and spent a year in Israel attending a leadership program. It was in Israel that he came to realize that Palestinian Arabs also have a legitimate right to a homeland. He now lives in the United States, where he teaches Middle Eastern history at a large state college. Ron's public expression of views has sometimes brought him into conflict with members of his local Jewish community.

In 1988 things got really serious. Shamir was in power, the Intifada had started, and you had the Jewish community here absolutely gung-ho about how to deal with it. I remember one of the Jewish students on campus . . . he was wearing a T-shirt in Hebrew, "All Arabs are shit, go to hell!" Appalling. There were some very bad scenes between Jewish students and Lebanese, Palestinian students.

And a Jewish colleague of mine and I got together and we started talking about what we could do. We organized a meeting on campus and we got several hundred people. We talked about the possibility of reconciliation, that Israel should accept the case for a two-state solution in its own best interests, that it was the only way to go, et cetera et cetera. It was a way to defuse the awful situation on campus; it was a way to reach out to Palestinian students, to Muslim students, and encourage Jewish and Palestinian students to make connections. Not necessarily to agree, but at least to find ways of talking to one another, to understand where each side was coming from.

And then a few years later on we wrote a piece called "The Jewish Case for a Palestinian State," and we came in for *massive* condemnation. And after it appeared in one of the papers here, a senior Jewish official here responded by saying that speaking up for Palestinian rights was quote "the moral equivalent of a Kurdish apologist for the mustard-gassing of his own people by Saddam Hussein." Strong stuff. I still regret I didn't sue over that . . .

And what made it worse was that people were calling me up and making phone threats. I turned on the answering machine one day and got someone saying I was dead meat and . . . And then I met someone, a judge who was also involved in Jewish community affairs at a senior level. And I told him what was going on, said, "You have a responsibility—You have an obligation to make sure that Jews do not threaten other Jews' lives over political differences."

And he looked at me and said, "You knew *exactly* what was going to happen to you if you did this, and you are now getting what you deserve." And this was someone who was a judge! A personal friend of my family's. He was actually condoning, making himself complicit in threats on my life.

It was a very nasty period. And then along came the Oslo Accords in '93, and suddenly Rabin appears in the Jewish newspaper shaking Arafat's hand. What I'd been saying suddenly becomes the official position of the Israeli government. And all of these people who'd been saying I was dreck and rubbish—Suddenly it all changes. [*parodying incredulity*] "Why didn't you tell me it was Beethoven! I love Beethoven!!" [*laughs*]

And interestingly, it was palpable the relief *they* felt. They no longer had to defend the indefensible. And it was fine for a while, well, fairly bearable . . . but then the Netanyahu government comes along. It became obvious that he was going to negate Oslo without explicitly repudiating it. He was going to stall, displace responsibility onto the other side, to negate, stall, and provoke.

And on two occasions I spent quite a bit of my own money taking out a half-page advertisement in one of the Jewish papers here — once for the Hasmonean tunnel incident [*when Israeli archaeological excavations of the Temple Mount below Muslim holy sites angered many Palestinians*] and once for the Har Homa thing [*an Israeli housing project in East Jerusalem, initiated in breach of the Oslo Accords*]—just pointing how foolish and dangerous, and counterproductive such actions were.

And then there were other things . . . the Baruch Goldstein business, which just shocked and appalled me beyond belief—and not only me of course—but then I kept shtum* for a while, but then over the last few weeks, the latest piece of scandal . . . I was asked to speak to a group of Palestinians here on campus. They said there'd be a commemoration on the fifteenth of May [*May 15, 1998, fiftieth anniversary of the founding of the State of Israel*] to remember the fiftieth anniversary of the Palestinian dispossession, the nakba, the Palestinian catastrophe. And it happened to be on a Friday. And so I went along and I said what I said, about a two-state solution, and the need for reconciliation and justice.

And the response from the Jewish community? How could I say such things? How could I be critical of Israel outside the Jewish community? How could I do it in front of what they allege was a hostile audience? And how could I do it on a Friday night!

Three-second pause.

But I do find some encouragement that according to the polls more than fifty percent of Israelis now support the idea of a Palestinian state. There are now people who recognize that what has been redemption for one people has been a tragedy for the other.

It's now impossible simply to talk in monolithic, triumphalist Biblical terms. So I do feel some encouragement, well, slight encouragement . . . It assuages some of the pain I feel. But at the same time, the very ground upon which the possibility for mutual recognition, for a two-state solution—the very ground on which that stands, the physical ground and the human ground of understanding and reconciliation—is being narrowed and shrunk and eroded. It's being devastated by this government . . . And Netanyahu is only too pleased to see antagonism replace the possibilities of reconciliation.

I feel unease about Israel, foreboding. And I feel powerless about it. I remember standing at an intersection once. My car had broken down, and I was waiting for a mechanic to come. And while I was waiting, I saw two cars approaching the intersection from opposite directions. And I could see that unless they slowed down, there was going to be a terrible crash. And they didn't slow down. And there was a godalmighty collision. And I saw it coming . . . and there was no way I could communicate to them, there was no way I could get them to hear.

It was Hegel that said, "History is a butcher's shop, history is a slaughter block." And it will continue to be until people recognize they have to allow human reason, informed reason to have a say in human affairs. So I say the things I say, and write what I write, and get the response I get from some Jews.

I'd prefer not to have to do what I do. I'm reluctant to put myself in a situation where some people feel entitled to excommunicate me, put a cherem* on me, denounce me as morally beyond the pale. It brings me great unhappiness. And apart from the harm it does me, knowing that what I say causes pain to other people — some of whom I couldn't give a shit about, between you and me — but people who I do care about, knowing it causes them bewilderment, heartache, resentment, is very painful.

And my position has made me quite isolated. I feel that isolation terribly, because I do feel myself Jewish. I have a Jewish subjectivity, that resides in Jewish talk, in the Hebrew language. I may be a difficult Jew — there are lots of difficult Jews — but I am a Jew, and that's my moral universe.

On Kibbutz

Sunday morning in Geneva, Illinois. Cory G. is twenty-seven. He gets paid, he says, for the local news articles he writes for a suburban newspaper. He gets pleasure, however, from writing short stories. His laptop purrs quietly on the kitchen table. Beside the computer, a Siamese cat is coiled in sleep. The floor around us is covered with untidy piles of Cory's latest work in progress. "It's the story of this talented writer who lives with a cat who makes it onto The New York Times *bestseller list, " Cory explains, "The cat, not the guy. The cat's story is about the horror of having to live with a failed writer."*

Cory wrote his first short story when he was on kibbutz in Israel. It was about an Israeli teenager who goes to live in Chicago. Cory has often thought about returning to Israel, but somehow he's still in the States. He has a short story on that topic as well, he says.

YOU MIGHT NOT WANT TO LIVE THERE, but you can't help but be glad it exists. You hear so much about the place and inevitably you idealize, like, I really did think at some level it was going to be dvash and chalav: a land of milk and honey, the first time. Literally. Well, almost. [*laughs*]

I know this is naive, but at some level you do think it's going to be just incredible. And of course it is. Just the fact that it exists at all is the incredible thing. And then you get there . . . it's going to be an experience . . .

The first time, I was just out of high school, and I spent the summer on kibbutz. I remember the plane coming in—it was dawn over the coast, and it had been this really long flight from the States, and I was really tired, but it was just incredible to think down there, that curve of coastline is Israel . . . This place you've heard so much about, finally, you're going to be there. And I remember it was so hot, it was like, six in the morning but it was already really hot. And like, seeing Israeli soldiers at the airport. "Hey, this is my country, Jewish soldiers, we're in charge, kinda thing." It's an amazing feeling.

And then the signs, you know, in Hebrew. This is not Biblical Hebrew, this is like, Shtei Coca Cola: Drink Coke, stuff like that. This is real. And then, the food, the smells. It's all totally different from what I expected.

MG: *And what did you expect?*

What *did* I expect? I don't know, maybe somehow you think it's going be like a Jewish neighborhood in the States, like Skokie or something, and it's not. It's Middle Eastern in many ways. Obviously. Even the people. Half the time I couldn't tell who was a Jew or who was an Arab.

So it's like home: this is the one place I can be in a Jewish homeland, and yet it's totally exotic at the same time. You know, all these dark-eyed women too, Yeminis, and Moroccans. It was like, "Wow! These are my people, and yet . . ."

So for me, looking back on it, there were lots of emotions, and some mixed ones too. I mean, you see the Western Wall, the Temple in Jerusalem, and that has to be one of the great emotional moments, whether you're religious or not, this is where it all started and and you know, for the first time in two thousand years, the Jews are back in their own land, it can't but be an emotional thing.

Then, uh, this is funny; you want to hear my story about my career in the Israeli pork industry?

MG: *You mean the "white meat" industry?*

That's what they call it! The first time I was on kibbutz I ended up in a place called Mizra, which is in the north of Israel, not far from, from Afula and from Nazareth, which is a mostly an Arab town. And anyway, I didn't know this before I went there, but Mizra was famous for its pork products. They have —well, they had—a large meat processing factory, and they had beef, and they also had pork. So there I was, first time in Israel—and I come from a kosher home—and there I was surrounded by these pig carcasses, all hanging on hooks, waiting to be processed. And as you said, it's "white steak," because you can't say [*whispers*] P - O - R - K.

So it all seemed totally surreal to be in Israel—and here I am working in the pork industry! I didn't mind, I thought, "If that's what it takes, fine."

But I did begin to feel a little odd, but for other reasons. I got to know this kibbutznik. He was older than me, around twenty-five, he'd finished the army, and Ilan worked with us in the factory, and he was just *dying* to leave the kibbutz, and he was constantly telling me how much he wanted to be in the U.S. And he was always buying these lottery tickets and every time he didn't win—which was every time, maybe every week, I forget now, it was like, total gloom!—And I couldn't believe I was hearing this. I was this, like, total Zionist, and here was this guy living the dream, and hating it. And I was more enthusiastic than ever.

And in the meantime, there we were surrounded by all these hunks of pork on hooks. [*laughs*] I don't want to read too much into it, but there did seem to be a kind of message there. A land of dreams and strange realities? Something like that. It *is* beautiful, and sometimes it's ugly, and it is real, and it's a dream too, and it is home, and it's not. It's all these things. It's hard to explain, isn't it?

Rien de Rien

I'M VERY STRAIGHTFORWARD, nothing subtle or psychological. I just
explain what it's for, what it's about, and tell 'em that the Jews in
the diaspora should be acting in partnership with those in Israel to
bring about this renewal of Jewish life, and the money's needed . . .
large budget . . . good things being done blah blah blah. Aaaaaand
would they like to contribute! [*tilts head, fakes a smile*] Simple as
that.

> *For the last fifteen years Harry P., a U. S. Treasury Department official in
> a midwestern city, has also been a volunteer fundraiser for Israel. Harry
> finished work an hour ago. I meet him in the bar of a Holiday Inn near his
> office. The pianist is playing "My Funny Valentine" to an almost deserted
> room. A waiter arrives with Harry's second Stoli on the rocks. I ask Harry
> if there's a connection between his work in the Treasury and his fundraising
> activities.*

Pure coincidence. Sure I'm in the Treasury, but I work in the area
of statistics, that kind of thing. Matter of fact, I haven't done too
well, careerwise. I got promoted early on to quite a good position,
but I've just stayed there. I make a comfortable living but I really
am miles behind my ability. Another guy I went to college with —
also Jewish — is now head of a department . . . and I'm just as smart
as he is. In fact, I got better grades than he did, and later on, he in
fact worked for me. And now he's way up there . . . [*gestures ceiling-
wards*]

You see, I have an antagonistic attitude when people tell me to do something that's slightly uh, immoral or illegal. And Andy's just that fraction more flexible. And he's done *extremely* well.

Anyway . . . the fundraising thing. I sort of stumbled into helping because they needed someone to do it. And maybe that wouldn't have happened in a bigger city. Here, if you're prepared to do the work and you've got even a moderate amount of ability, you're very welcome. In the big centers, you got to be well-connected, have a lot of money, or your family's been on the board of the temple for you know, three generations. Then you're fine, you're accepted . . . Or you're a lawyer or a physician . . .

I could've been a doctor. I had good grades. But I thought medicine was too boring. I thought math was more interesting.

Harry sings quietly.

Non, rien de rien, non, je ne regrette rien.

He laughs, coughs, and sips his vodka.

And I earn about a quarter of what I would've earned otherwise. You know, when I've been to fundraising dinners in New York or L.A. I'm sitting at a table with people worth two hundred, three hundred million dollars. Gold rings, gold cars, the works!

At one dinner, I was sitting with this guy who's one of the biggest condo developers in the country. You meet some interesting people. Like, the head here until recently was a guy who's totally self-made, but who's now a billionaire. He's in construction, he's in cable TV, he owns one of those drugstore chains—What is it? Not CVS . . . the one—doesn't matter. And he didn't ask to be elected. They asked *him* if he would like to do the job, and he did it as a favor! [*sniffs*]

So the people running these things are interesting, different sorts of people. I've met some interesting people. And . . . I've kept doing it! We have a once-a-year fundraiser here in town, which I organize and chair. I put the chairs out! [*laughs*] Just kiddin'. I get my kids to do the chairs. This year we had someone—He was involved in—[*sighs*] Well, in fact was the director of the Jewish Agency operations in the former Soviet Union. You know, hundreds of thousands of Jews transported to settle in Israel. He told us about how he did it and so on and so forth and how they still need money . . . "All very unstable . . . maybe the window of opportunity will blah blah blah . . . parallels with the Holocaust," and so on and so forth . . .

So we have the meeting, people give their pledges, and, I have to follow up and try to squeeeeeeeeze money out of the folks who don't come to the meeting. It doesn't really work. People don't want to give, they don't want to give. I don't even do it every year now. Some people clearly are not going to give.

Sometimes we get a hotshot down from Chicago, if there's a possible big donor. Personally, I think it's a mistake. One time we had someone come down, he tried to get—I don't know—five thousand out of someone who said they were interested, they were committed, they'd just been to Israel, a partner in an accounting firm, and I didn't think it was going to work. And it didn't! The guy was so taken aback at being asked for five thousand dollars, that he didn't give anything! And then finally gave fifteen hundred, which is what he would have given in the first place. Stupid, huh?

Of course, you realize I'm a volunteer? And ninety-five percent of the people who do this work are volunteers. And not only that, it can actually *cost* you money. It *has* occurred to me that I should charge them, and then donate the money back, and that way it's tax-deductible. But essentially it costs you.

He signals a passing waiter.

[*to me*] You want another margarita?

MG: *No, thanks, I'm doing fine.*

OK. [*to waiter*] Same again. With just a twist of lemon, please. Thank you.

I guess in a way I still believe in altruism. I certainly don't get a lot of personal—I don't get a lot of kudos, nor do I get much satisfaction out of it. It's no fun asking people to contribute money. But I do it because it's worthwhile . . . and somebody's got to do it. I guess I'm a little burnt-out. But you know, I never had that intense commitment. I did it because they'd run out of people to do it. But I regard myself as capable. And I'm a responsible sort of guy, and so until I find someone to take over I will have to keep on doing it. You interested? [*laughs*] Just kiddin'.

The Whole Desire
of Many Years

———— ◦◦◦ ————

*A graduate of Tel Aviv University and a former Israeli paratrooper,
Mordechai K. is now studying for a Ph.D. in development economics at
New York's Columbia University. We're in the small apartment he shares
with two other grad students. He's wearing jeans, a plain blue T-shirt,
and a small woven kipa.* *

*Mordechai was born in Ethiopia. In 1979, the village where he lived with
his parents and six older brothers and sisters was occupied by rebel
forces fighting President Mengistu's Marxist government. Like many other
Ethiopian Jews who hoped for a better life in Israel, his parents decided
the family should leave Ethiopia. Mordechai was eight years old.*

THE REBELS, THEY GAVE US PERMISSION TO LEAVE, even though they
tried to convince us to stay, because now Ethiopia going to be
free. But we were sure we have to leave. And we sell the cattle we
have, and we left the home and the fields and the land, everything.

We going to walk to Sudan with donkey or horses. In my convoy
we were three hundred people without a guide. After one week
we met some Sudani people that came to Ethiopia to hunt. And
we make a deal with them, that they will take us to Sudan.

One day they told us, "The next pool is not for one day, one day and a half. We have to carry enough water in order to reach the next pool." But it was Friday and our leaders told the guides we cannot go with you because it's Shabbos.*

The guides said, "It's desert here, complete desert. You have to move on with us. You're going to risk the children and yourself." A big argument.

But we decided to stay there and they left us there. And there is no animal, or tree, or river. Shabbos morning, around ten o'clock, ten-thirty, we finished all the water. The men began to search for water, but they couldn't find. And then around four o'clock, some guy, he saw a pile of stones, and he start to dig, and then suddenly he discovered that it was a pool. Water come gushing out.

Saturday evening, the Sudani guides, they back to see if we are still alive. And they were in shock. They say, "We travel here seventeen years, we never could imagine that it's possible to find water out here in the desert." And they say that it is by God. A miracle.

And again we made agreement with them that they will show us the way to Sudan. And it was another week, and then again argument broke out between them. There was an Ethiopian town near the border. And they told us we have to go through the town to reach Sudan. Otherwise, the way will be long. But we didn't have the governor's permission to enter the town. We have the permission of the rebels, but not the Mengistu government. And it was very risky to get into the town. And again they left us there and went into the town, and we stayed in a valley outside.

And again we finished the water, and again we start to search for water. But here there were animals, a sign there must be water. Ten men with horses and guns came to us. They were Ethiopians. And they said, "We know you are Jews and you go to Israel." And they say, "We know that you sell everything in Ethiopia and you have money . . ."

And they ask where we live in Ethiopia, and each family start to tell them. And one of the robbers, he start to shout to the others, "Don't harm them! I know this man. He is our neighbor." He was the neighbor of one.

The robbers went to the pool, they brought water to the children. And they said, "We will show you the way across the border." And so we make a deal with them. They took us to Sudan, another three days, four days. And they told us that the government of Sudan, to see three hundred people come into their country, they will want to know why we come. We said that it was because of the civil war. We did not tell them we are Jews. Sudan, as you know, is Muslim country and very dangerous.

And the Sudani government gave us help: water, flour. And we reach a place that is called Hamlait. And there we met the Israeli agents, the Mossad. And they make a list of each family, and they send it to Israel.

After one week, two week in this town, the Sudani government decided to move us to another town, that called Waled Hilo. There it was a big building of the Red Cross. They put us there. And the keis, the rabbi of the group, he told us that we cannot continue to hide our identity. We have to tell the Sudani that we are the sons of Avraham, Yiztchak, and Yaakov.* It was crazy, it was really crazy, because the Sudani are very fanatic Muslim, and you tell them you are Jewish and that it. [draws two fingers across his throat]

And there were big argument between the keis and the group. They tell him, "You mad. You can't tell them you're Jewish." And between the arguments, some Sudani, they heard this story. And the Sudani army come to see if we are really Jewish. And we told them, "This man is mad. There is no black Jewish."

And they believed the story. They say, "We know that Jewish are in Israel and they are not black." [laughs]

But they put a guard around the building, and people start to be scared. And we have to bribe the guard in order to escape to another town in Sudan called Okrev. And there the Jewish, they usually work in hard job, in labor. People they stay there months or maybe years before they go to Israel.

I spent two years in Sudan. My mother she was sick. She had cancer. And she went to Israel, before us, to hospital. And after two years I told them, "I can't stay here any more in Sudan, even if it is not my turn."

There was a big argument with the family: "People wait here many years . . . It's not your turn. What will people say?" But I decided to escape from Sudan. I heard that the Mossad, they came to smuggle people one night and I went with this group outside the city and they put us in a big cave until the cars came.

The Ethiopians, they work with the Mossad people. One guy he came with a torch, he recognized me. "What are you doing? It is not your turn." I said, "I've had enough time in Sudan, and my mother, she is alone in Israel; I have to go to Israel even if it is not my turn."

He begin to pull me out the car. And then the Mossad came, he said, "Listen, we don't have time for argument." And he close car, and we drove the whole night and next morning. And then they put us in the desert. They give us food and tell us to rest.

And the next evening, we start to move again. There were four cars, three full people and one is empty. And we have to cross a checkpoint in order to get into the next town. And there was a guard with motorcycle. And the empty car, he went first, and crossed into the city, and the guard, he chased after him so we can enter the city.

And in the middle of the night, we reached the Red Sea. And there wait for us the Israeli navy, the commando. And they put us in the boat, and they took us to the ship. It's take another week until we reach Eilat. There wait for us Israeli planes, and they took us to Ben-Gurion [*airport*]. And when we reached there, people began to cry and kiss the Land of Israel, the Holy Land, the whole desire of many years.

So Natural

Sheitl,* shaitl, depending on your dialect. I say sheitl, that's my Litvish* background. [*laughs*] Most of the women here wear sheitlach.* I think the woman that just walked in was wearing a hat. Was she? One day she'll wear a sheitl, one day she'll wear a hat. Whatever . . . There are those that just wear a sheitl, those that will wear a sheitl with a hat on top, those that will cover their hair with a scarf . . . and then you have those who wear a scarf and leave the front part of their hair exposed. There's quite a spectrum . . . Among the Chassidic women there are some that shave their heads, but our women don't.

Morning in the office of Rochl F., the director of an Orthodox kindergarten in Brooklyn, New York. In a classroom along the corridor, a ragged chorus of tiny voices sings the letters of the Hebrew alphabet. Mrs. F. is wearing a short, ash-blond—and remarkably natural-looking—wig.

The trend to wear a sheitl has really evolved here in the United States over . . . oh, I'd say the last forty or so years. When my mother came here from Europe, she didn't wear a sheitl, she wore a hat. She always wore a hat, but she did not cover all her hair. But somehow life in America evolved in a certain way that more women began wearing sheitlach.

I remember she bought her first for my brother's bar mitzvah;* we're talking thirty-five years ago. So for me it was just a given. I knew I would cover my hair when I got married. As a bride you do your sheitl shopping. You go to the sheitl lady. There's a catalog, and you choose the style. This is what I chose. [*pointing to her sheitl*] This has been my hairstyle forever—twenty-six years—though my own hair is much longer, midback. It's very fine, though, so it doesn't get in the way under the sheitl. But the color's still my own color, more or less: they oxidize over time.

MG: *And what sort of prices are we talking?*

Ranges. Human hair starts at about two hundred, two fifty. If you go into the custom market, you're talking thousands. But any wig would do, though there are styles that are uh, very inappropriate: ones that are made provocatively– You know: long, sleek, very thick . . . That would be within the *letter* of the law, but not the spirit. Unfortunately, it's not uncommon here in New York, where perhaps people have more of a sense of style.

This one I'm wearing is a blend, human and synthetic, in the two hundredish range. It was a Shabbos sheitl, but now I use it for everyday wear. I have five. They're all the same model—the New Age—but they each take the curl differently, they set differently. And the older they get, the less responsive they are to setting. You can get two or three years out of them.

We always instruct young brides never to buy a sheitl that's different from their natural hairstyle. If they're going to change style, they should wait till they're happily married. [*pointing to me*] You are the girl he's marrying.

It takes me some time to process this.

Don't appear at the wedding with a totally different style!

MG: *But if it's so much like the real thing . . . why bother?*

Well, of course in sheitl circles we can tell sheitlach very easily. You just know instinctively. But anyway, it is not contrary to Torah for a woman to look attractive. A woman *should* look attractive. I understand what you're saying though, but the sheitl is still a sheitl, a hair covering. It's a reminder. *I* know I'm wearing a sheitl, so it's a constant reminder to me that I'm a married woman. And . . . And look, did you ever hear of a man running his hands through someone's sheitl? Think of it in those terms. It might be attractive, but it's no substitute for your own hair. So it's a reminder for both: for the woman that's wearing it and for the man that's aware she's wearing it.

MG: *Assuming that he is aware . . .*

[*smiling*] Oh, he is, he is. In our circles, we know. And to us, it's so natural. It's like eating kosher food. Of course, at the beginning . . . You have to get used to it, you have to remember to cover your hair every time you leave the house. I remember my sister, shortly after she was married, she went for a walk—she had to go to the store—and a woman came over to her and said, "Breindl, your sheitl is just so beautiful. And it looks so natural!" And of course, that was because it *was*! She had totally—[*chuckles*] totally forgotten to put her sheitl on! Oh, she felt *so* bad. [*laughs*]

A Hat Like This

A chance encounter in Rome's main synagogue. Jerry Y., from Leeds, England, happened to be sitting next to me at the Yom Kippur service we both attended earlier today. Like me, he was traveling alone, so we decided to break our fasts together. It's seven in the evening and we're at a window table in a bar on Piazza Navona. In front of us two pizzas, a bottle of San Pellegrino mineral water, and a carafe of Chianti. On the chair beside Jerry, the stylish brown fedora he wore at the service. Apparently, it's a new departure for him in synagogue headwear.

THE FIRST YARMULKE* I EVER HAD . . . I suppose I was—I certainly remember having it when I was three or four. It was a little woolen number; I've still got it somewhere. It was white, divided into four sections with sort of embroidered flowers in each one. And on top, it had this little tassly thing that you could make it spin with, like a helicopter. [*mimes a twirl*] Do you think the pope does that with his? [*laughs*]

And we had these really frum* neighbors. And Mr. Horovitz always wore a big black yarmulke, the no-frills industrial type. All the time. I don't know if he went to bed with it on. But probably! I actually believed for a long time it was just a shinier part of his head. Seriously.

He swallows a mouthful of pizza and drinks.

Then anyway, when I was older I had a more serious velvet number.

This was bar mitzvah,* pre-bar mitzvah time. Gotta look grownup for your barmy, eh? I had two yarmulkes actually. One was dark blue with silver embroidery, and the other was dark blue with gold embroidery. I think they both had Yerushalayim* written on them or something. I can't remember why I had two now. Oh yeah! One belonged to my dad and one was mine, and we sort of swapped from time to time.

And it was always falling off. I had quite a lot of hair in those days, would you believe?—this was the late sixties, right?—And I spent most of my time in shul,* leaning over my seat to fish up my bloody yarmulke. Hairpin technology hadn't arrived in those days.

And in shul, it was very different to now: you had basic velvets— mostly blues and reds—the odd daring green or purple . . . then you also had the heavy duty sort of, uh, Horovitz black, and the occasional, occasional small knitwear type. But they were only worn by Israelis, or other exotics. And of course, finally: the party paper hat that you could pick up from the back if you happened to breeze into town hatless.

I mean, we used to take this very seriously—Well, old man Horovitz probably thought we were heathens for not wearing them all the time—but yeah, we took it seriously. I remember, if you didn't have a yarmulke for some reason, at a friend's house on Friday night or something, we'd sit there with napkins on our heads. Or in extreme cases, hands. [*demonstrates*] The ultimate minimalist accessory: the hand!

I refill our glasses with the remainder of the Chianti.

Mm. Thanks. And then of course in shul you had *hat* hats. Quite a lot of trilbies à la Frank Sinatra and some of the more serious-minded would have a yarmulke underneath that. Then, this being England, the odd bowler hat. Do you remember those?

MG: *I certainly do.*

My Uncle Dennis had a bowler. I mean, nobody had bowlers except Uncle Dennis and bank managers. And then the members of the board—I suppose the president and vice-president who used to sit underneath the bimah* —the guys you'd go and shake hands with after you'd been called up [for a Torah honor]—they actually used to wear top hats! This was 1968, 1969. Can you believe? The last bastion of the top hat outside Fred Astaire movies and racing at Ascot. My grandfather had one too. Kept it in a leather box in the shul.

Anyway, then for years I never wore one. Basically, I didn't go near a shul for about twenty years. I mean, I bought myself a Moroccan berber hat and one of those lacy haj hats the Muslims wear when I was in Marrakesh. Which of course are kissing—or spitting [wincing at his own pun]—cousins to yarmulkes. But this was sort of strictly weekend wear at home. I mean, I couldn't really imagine myself going to shul in them. There again . . .

And then a couple of years ago, I bought myself a new one. I was doing this rootsy-schmootzy trip to Poland and I wanted to wear one, kind of to make a statement, "I'm back, you bastards didn't get all of us" kind of thing! So I went to this Jewish gift store and I—

Well, I already decided I wanted to upgrade, get into the latest knitwear kind—the ones that were just coming into shul when I was like last going out, the ones that look like potholders, the ones the right-wingers wear. Very politically incorrect! And of course by this time, they're not yarmulkes any more, they're kipas.* Kipot, indeed. Y'know, at some point between 1969 and 1995 we've gone from yarmulkes with flowers to kipot with Uzis on them. So anyway, I got myself a sort of greenish grey item with a collection of stylized Stars of David round the border. They were out of Uzis that day. [laughs] And then I went to a chemist's and got a supply of hairpins and clips.

And I took it with me to Warsaw and wore it a couple of times, once when I went to Majdanek [concentration camp] and once when I went to the place my grandfather came from. Nobody seemed to notice one way or the other, actually, which was a bit disappointing.

Oh, yeah, I must tell you this one — Shall we get some more wine first?

MG: *Good idea.*

Let's test out the old phrase book . . . [*to a passing waiter*] Scusi, ci porta mezzo litro di rosso, per piacere? Grazie. OK. [*to me*] Yeah, maybe you could use this one in your book. I went to shul one evening, I think it was Kol Nidre.* Yeah, it was Kol Nidre . . . or Rosh haShanah* or something last year, and anyway, I wore it to shul — this was in Leeds — and the service finished quite late, and I was really tired and I drove home — don't tell the rebbe!* [*laughs*]

Yeah, anyway, I got home and — Well, I should preface this by saying that a few days before, I'd heard this scratching sound in the basement: scratch, scratch, scratch . . .

He scratches the tabletop.

And when I went to check it out, I saw this pair of gleaming eyes and a long tail, connected by a brown furry body. A rattola! Which departed at high speed when it saw me. Y'see, my basement sort of connects with some open land . . . And that was the last I saw or heard of it until I got home that night. I was really tired and I was sort of shlomped in an armchair, and I was kind of dozing, half asleep — drooling probably — when I heard it again: scratch scratch scratch. But I was so tired I just thought, "Oh, yeah, rat in the basement."

The waiter arrives with a fresh carafe.

Oh thanks. [*giving the waiter the OK sign*] Grazie! So I was sort of drifting off to sleep, when suddenly: I feel the most *agonizing* pain on the top of my head! And I realized: "Oh, fuck!" — pardon my

Hebrew—"The rat's got out the basement, it's jumped onto my head and it's sinking its claws into my scalp!" What to do?

And I had this terrible fear that if I put my hands up to grab it, it'd sink its teeth into my hands or . . . I don't know, I just couldn't—So I jumped up, thinking that maybe I could shake it off somehow.

So here I am, dancing around the room, screaming, "Aaaaaaaagh! Rataratat!!"—just as well I live alone—and shaking my head like a bucking bronco trying to, to throw its rider. And I actually fell over a chair flat on the floor during all this. I really hurt myself. [*rubs elbow*]

And the rat was still sitting tight. And the pain was *excruciating*! So I eventually put my hand up there trying to knock the bugger off: quick little swipes so it couldn't bite, and of course my hand connected with the rat.

Which turned out to be the hairpin on my yarmulke. Which had been digging into my scalp!

True story. I'm not sure what the moral is though. [*patting his fedora*] Wear a hat like this, maybe.

Now *That's* Tircha

———— ❧ ————

WHEN YOU'RE NEW TO THE JOB, you can make mistakes. There was a new mashgiach* standing over one of the kitchen staff staring at him, and the guy told him, "I've got this sharp knife, I get nervous . . . stay away from me!" Nobody likes people standing over them while they're working. That's something a mashgiach learns, to make himself invisible to talk and observe. A lot of the mashgichim—Well, unfortunately, they're using inexperienced people straight out of high school or college. The money isn't so good . . .

For the last six years Aryeh J. has worked as a mashgiach for an Orthodox kashrut authority in New Jersey. On Sunday nights he supervises the restaurant where we're talking—checking on kitchen procedures and even keeping a wary eye on wayward customers: "We once had some people arrive with McDonald's french fries! . . ." On Saturday mornings he supervises the kitchens in a private clinic, starting at six-thirty A.M., in time for the breakfast shift. The clinic is a brisk forty-five-minute walk from his home, but since it's within the distance set by rabbinic law, Aryeh is not violating the Sabbath. Apparently, it's permissible to walk up to two thousand cubits outside the city limits. A cubit, Aryeh explains, is the distance from the bottom of the elbow to the end of the middle finger.

I always look at the patient lists, and if there's an Orthodox patient, I'll go ask them if they want me to make Kiddush.* It's a touchy subject; I did get warned that it isn't my job. One of the nurses complained, objected to me visiting the wards without invitation. Could be a little anti-Semitism, I don't know . . .

There's always conflict. And on Shabbat, you're supposed to avoid tircha* . . . But most of the time it's nonstressful. Basically the kitchen runs itself, the staff are well-trained, they've all been there for years, they know what they're doing. But I do have to check the eggs when they're cracked, to look for bloodspots, and check that the milk and meat things don't get mixed up, make sure there are no insects on the vegetables, though I must say, the staff do wash 'em very well . . .

Then there's the fact that the food has to be cooked by a Jew, but Jews can't work on Shabbat, which of course includes lighting any flame. And how we get around that, we have a Yahrzeit candle* that gets lit on Friday afternoon by the mashgiach who's on duty then. And the cook is supposed to use that flame to light the gas oven on Shabbat. There is a pilot light, too, of course, which was also originally lit by a Jew, but they normally use the Yahrzeit candle. And my job is to make sure the cook uses that, that he doesn't use his own lighter or matches. Because, of course he's not Jewish.

He's Chinese. And he can be . . . a little difficult about it. And I've had some problems with him. I mean, he has a very, very caring side to him, but he also likes to talk about his sexual exploits, tells dirty jokes. [*rapidly*] I mean, he doesn't tell *me*, I'm just part of the audience: it's a small kitchen and you hear everything. It's *very* upsetting for some of the kitchen staff. He says it's all in fun, but he doesn't take into account people's feelings. The Dominican ladies complain about him. He makes, uh, unwelcome advances . . . One of them says she'll bring sexual harassment charges . . . And he's not a young guy either, he's in his sixties, he's just had a stroke.

And the worst thing is, he has no respect for religion. I never know if he isn't gonna try and light the gas with his own lighter. I caught him right in the act once, so I had to get him to turn it off. And then I asked him to turn it on again, lighting it this time from the Yahrzeit candle, which the mashgiach lit on Friday afternoon. Now *that's* tircha. I have to watch him all the time. I can never tell when he's gonna do it. But it's also avoida,* and it's a change from going to shul, a novelty, the freedom to daven* at your own pace.

But I have noticed over the last year or so that my davening has been deteriorating. Low concentration. It's much more difficult among the goyim.* And it can be very distracting in the kitchens: the staff are talking, they have the radio blaring away on a rock music station, and I have to daven in the middle of all this. In fact, there are *two* radios, because we have two kitchens, the milchik* and the fleishik,* and so you get stereo. And I can't ask 'em to switch them off or down because that's getting them to do work for me. So I either go into the lunch room, in which case I can't see what's going on, or just put up with it, block it out.

I just try not to focus on the difficulties. If you ignore them, they don't exist. A person could be in such a state of kavanah* he doesn't notice, at least in the case of the rebbei'im* big in dvekus.* There are stories . . . [*sighs*] But unfortunately that's not usually the case with me in the kitchens. [*smiles*] But the food has to be kept kosher at all times, and it's a mitzvah* to do it. So I do it.

The P Word

―――――⟨⟩―――――

Lunch with Steve R. in the window booth of a vegetarian restaurant in downtown San Diego. Steve's a film critic and writer with an interest in cooking. His rich, deep voice sounds a little unhappy at the moment— the tofu salad just wasn't right, he says, pushing his plate away. Too little oil and just a hint too much salt. Steve admits he's hard to please; he's always been extremely particular about what he eats.

I GREW UP IN AN OBSERVANT HOME. Everything was always strictly kosher. If we ate out, it was at a kosher deli, though we would occasionally go to a fish, seafood place, have flounder or something. But if we saw people at the next table with a bib on eating lobster, I mean, [*makes a face*] this was the worst thing that could possibly happen, just to *see* someone. It's like you had to cover your eyes. [*chuckles*] And so it would *never* occur to me to think about eating something nonkosher.

And later on, when I was at college, people'd maybe order hamburgers or whatever and it always looked so good and I'd just have American cheese on bread. You know, just this feeling of being an outsider, not by choice but because that's all you know. And also, if somebody were to have asked me, I really would be ashamed to say the truth: "I don't know why I'm not eating this, but I would throw up if I did, and that's the way it is!"

And that was pretty much the way things were for me right through college. And then I had some friends who invited me up to Maine for the weekend—I was living in Connecticut then—and I went with a friend, Margaret, a, a Catholic girl, and we drove up to stay with Bob and Kitty. And they cooked this incredible meal. There was fried chicken, pasta with some red sauce, and these meatballs: big ones, almost the size of a baseball. And they had this sort of pale look about them, not like a brown *Jewish* meatball. It sort of looked [*shaking his head with disgust*] . . . pallid.

So we're sitting there, and I'm pushing everything around, thinking, "Oh God, what am I gonna do? I'm hungry." So I had a little bit of spaghetti, but even the sauce didn't taste good. I don't know . . . And then Bob says the meatballs—It's his Sicilian grandmother's recipe, and nobody knows it now except him. And so, I think, "Oh God, I gotta actually taste this thing."

I take a little bite, and then Margaret says, "C'mon, Bob, tell us what's in it." And Bob says, "Oh, well . . . there's beef and veal . . . and pork."

I heard the P word and I literally turned cold. Total cold sweat. Totally numb. Lightheaded. Didn't know what the hell I was gonna do. And everybody's waiting for my reaction. "How *delicious!*" And I just very gently wobbled up from the chair, left the room, found the bathroom, locked myself in, got on my knees—I'll never forget it—leaned over the toilet bowl, and *barfed.* The whole thing came gushing out.

And Margaret's outside, knocking on the door. "Steven?! Are you OK?" I mean, whaddya *say?*

MG: "*I just gotta have that recipe!*"

Right. "Could I have some more, please?"

With an expression of mild disgust on his face, Steve distractedly scrutinizes the tofu salad.

And I guess at that point, I vowed, "I gotta resolve this somehow." So then I started eating hamburgers, cheeseburgers, even shrimp.

Did that for a while, but it never felt right. And then I stopped. And — don't tell anybody — I would not go into a restaurant and *order* shrimp but if I'm with somebody and it looked good, I would take one.

So it's not like it's a religious conviction, but I feel a certain obligation. I don't want somebody to see me eating it. I don't know, I guess I still haven't resolved it. Now I'm basically a vegetarian. I never bring meat into my house. The only times I eat meat are on holidays: Rosh haShanah,* my mother makes turkey. Or if we have a barbecue, I'll make kosher hot dogs. And chicken.

This is interesting: If my mother cooks a chicken, I can eat it. But nobody else, even if it's kosher, I couldn't. But if Mommy makes it . . . there's somethin' special about it. Is that it? I don't really know.

Why Can't It Be the Toe?

———— ❧ ————

PETER: OK. The story—One of the stories is that He created Adam circumcised. But when he was expelled from the Garden of Eden, the foreskin was put on. It's a barrier between man and God. That's why it's removed. You can't find any halachic* reason as regards health.

BETH: Peter, you want to show him the glass mohel we got from Venice? It's this gorgeous little glass figurine. We have quite a collection of mohelibilia. And when Peter became a mohel, I had a tie tack made for him, a gold one, in the shape of a clamp.

Peter proudly points to his tie tack.

And then there's the license plate he told you about. But he didn't tell you about mine. Mine's M-O-H-E-L 2.

> *Peter C. is a cantor and a mohel—a ritual circumcisor—who's been singing for twenty-five years and snipping for fifteen at the same Conservative synagogue in suburban Connecticut. In the kitchen of their garrison colonial home, his wife, Beth, is making coffee. Peter and I are doing a sound test at the table. He's wearing a white shirt and a dark blue tie with a prominent, rather oddly-shaped gold tie tack. I press "record" and ask him to go on speaking. "You ever seen a brit* close up?" he asks. "Just my own," I reply. "You want to see a video of me at work?" After the video . . .*

PETER: I don't want to say that I *perform* but I'm used to being in front of people, I'm used to singing, I'm used to speaking Hebrew. So what I try to do at a brit is to take their minds off the fact that they're witnessing a circumcision. It's a Jewish life-cycle event, one of the most important. I put the emphasis on that, through explanation: what the baby's going to experience, why he cries, interject a little humor to relax people, and the circumcision is really just a thirty-second procedure under normal circumstances. And then we name the baby. And I think if I had an epitaph I would like it to say, "He made a brit enjoyable." That's the greatest compliment I can be paid as a mohel.

He looks towards Beth and smiles.

You know what my license plate is? M-O-H-E-L. Try getting that in New Jersey or New York. Impossible! Oh, it's a great plate. People that pass me, they'll go: [*He makes a "snip snip" gesture.*]

BETH: Tell him what happened last Christmas on the highway.

PETER: Oh yeah, Christmas Day I was driving home, and I heard the traffic report on my car radio, that the tunnel is blocked up. But I just got through; it's open. So I had my cell phone and I called the station and I said, "The road is open, there's no problem." And it was Gary Leitner, the guy that does the traffic reports from a helicopter! I don't know if you've ever heard of him. Anyway, it was Christmas Day, right? Only Jews were working. So he says, "What are you doing today?"

I says, "I'm just comin' back from work."

"Work? What do ya do?"

I says, "I'm a mohel."

He says, "You're the one with the plate!" He says, "I pass you all the time when I'm in my car." He says, "That's you?"

I said, "Yeah."

And we started talking. He's from Little Neck. He's a landsman.* He told me about his education, his Jewish education, where he lives, the temple he belongs to, and I had like a half-hour conversation with him all the way back home. Unbelievable. The guy in the helicopter.

BETH: We can't go anywhere without somebody knowing him. Last year we were in Aruba. We got on this little bus to take us around the resort, and this guy's behind us: "Rabbi C——! Hi, how are you?" [*laughs*] Hey, tell him the story of the guy in the wicker chair.

PETER: Oh yeah. As you probably know, full circumcisions on adults, they have to be put under general anesthesia. I've assisted in the OR room, generally making the first cut, drawing the first drop of blood, then making the appropriate blessings, and then the urologist or whoever's performing the surgery will complete the circumcision.

But when the gentleman has already been circumcised, you can't recircumcise what's been circumcised. So I'm generally left in the room with the person alone, and I take one of those little needles that they use to prick your fingertip with, and just draw a little blood from the side of the shaft of the penis. And then I will show it to the Beth Din,* the people that are outside, the witnesses. It's exactly like drawing blood from the fingertip except it's done from the penis shaft—which by the way is less painful than the fingertip. Take my word: it's all in the mind.

So first, I explain what I'm going to do, how I'm going to do it. And you know, the first question: "Why can't it be the toe?" I explain it can't be the toe it has to be the—the organ of progeneration. But they're usually fine.

Not always though. I was doing one gentleman—I'd say he was in his late twenties, early thirties—who was very nervous. His fiancée waited outside with the rabbis. He said he got—He fainted at the sight of blood. I says, "There's only a drop, it'll be fine." And I told him, I told him to "pull your pants down and sit in this chair"—it was a wicker chair—"and I will do it."

And I could see he was a little nervous, and I says, "Don't worry, everything will be fine." So I drew the drop of blood. No problem. And I showed him the blood on the gauze pad. I says, "That's all." He takes one look, and all of a sudden he starts moaning. And he's rocking back and forth on the chair [*demonstrates*] aaaaaand he's passing gas at the same time! So you have to picture [*chuckles*] that I'm trying to keep him from falling off the chair, and he's passing gas on a wicker chair. Both ends are going off: I don't know if he's going to regurgitate, if he's going to . . . defecate.

And my feet are *below* the chair, and it's a *wicker* chair, right? I mean, *anything* was possible at this point, you know what I mean? And finally, he collapses in my arms. So I called the fiancée in. And I said, "He's fine, he's fine. He'll be fine." And so we completed the procedure.

That was probably the, uh . . . the most unusual hatafat dam* experience I've had. But it had a happy ending. About a year and a half later they had a child and they called me up to do the brit.

BETH: Great story, huh?

PETER: She's always saying to me, "You gotta write it *down*. You have to keep these memories." Some of the things that happen, it's incredible. People ask me, "So what do you do with the foreskins?" I give 'em a few jokes, but the truth is, it's part of Creation. You cannot discard the foreskin. It has to be buried. I bury mine in the front yard: scoop out a little earth, throw it in, cover it over, that's all. My son wrote an article for the local newspaper about the . . . uh . . . the penis tree in our front yard.

BETH: I got it here.

MG: *What about the neighbors?*

PETER: Oh they had no idea.

BETH: Until they read the article! They loved it. They thought it was hysterical!

She passes me the newspaper article.

You want a bagel or something?

MG: *No, I'm fine, thanks.*

PETER: Once I did a brit and the grandfather asked me, "Have you got it? Have you got the foreskin?"

I said, "Yeah."

He said, "Can I have it?"

I said, "Sure. You can have it, and you can bury it yourself." Then I did another grandchild of his. Same thing. "Can I have it?"

And what he was doing, he was freezing the foreskins, and storing them in his refrigerator! He goes to Israel regularly and he has a little area in the Mount of Olives cemetery, I believe. And this is where he buries the foreskins of his grandchildren, and the grandchildren of his friends. And so he always has a freezer full of foreskins. [*laughter*]

The World's
a Good Place

In a Jewish community center in New York City on a wet Sunday after-noon in March. From the gym across the hall, the thump-thump-miss-a-beat-whoa! of teenage boys shooting baskets. Thirteen-year-old Ben F. has been playing pool with his friend Martin. Ben comes to the club most Sundays, he tells me. He likes to swim in the center's indoor pool and "just kinda hang out." Martin leaves us to check his e-mail account on one of the room's three networked computers. Does Ben ever surf the Net here?

No, NOT REALLY, BECAUSE I DO THAT AT HOME, usually. I have my own web site, actually.

MG: *How did you learn about that?*

At camp last year, I did a course, and we learned how to design a web page, learned how to read and use HTML, things like that. It was cool.

MG: *Tell me about your web site.*

OK. It's called Ben's Den. It's an interactive site, people register their name, and they get a tour around my house and see photos of my family, stuff like that. It's pretty cool. I put up information about myself, what I'm doing, stuff that's happening at school.

And I get a couple hundred hits a month. I correspond with a few of them. There's this guy calls himself The Rat, and someone else called Wigger, and then there's Princess Leah. Like, a ton of people. And I update it regularly. Like, when I had my bar mitzvah* couple of months ago, I put in some news about that, some extracts from my speech.

MG: *Can you tell me about your bar mitzvah?*

Sure. I studied for six months, I had it. Had a big party afterwards. It was fun.

MG: *Do I have to log on to get more details?*

Only if you wanna see the photos.

MG: *So tell me . . .*

OK. I studied haAzinu [*Deuteronomy* 32]. It was about like, Moses, how like, God tells him he's gonna die, and he goes up to the mountain and uh even though he knows God's gonna have him die there, he says like, a prayer, and it's like, Moses turns into a poem.

MG: *He turns into a poem?*

Yes, it's like this beautiful poem. And that was my Torah portion.

MG: *What was the poem?*

I have absolutely no idea. I can't translate the Hebrew, I'm not *that* good. [*laughs*]

MG: *So what do you think that story is about?*

It's like about how, like, the world's a good place, and even though he's gonna die, he's like, really happy about his life.

Ben seems happy now, too. He starts to loosen up.

The whole thing was only like, an hour and a half, and like, I couldn't even keep track of the time, it took like, two minutes in my mind! [*smiles*] It was good though. I was a little nervous, but not really.

And I decided to chant my Torah portion, so that was fun. And that was like, a big learning experience. So first I learned it because I didn't know if I really wanted to chant it, but I had an extra month to learn the chant—our rabbi made a tape for me—and it turned out to be *really* good, like, it definitely complemented the service. I loved chanting it: *Ha-azinu hashama-a-yim, v'adabera al* . . . et cetera

MG: *Wonderful.*

Thank you. And then I gave a speech. Basically, just a lot of thank yous, and a couple of stories, little stories.

MG: *Stories?*

I took—Well, because my Torah portion was about learning from your elders, like Moses, my rabbi said that I should interview my family and find out some of their stories. And this was like in January. So like, on Super Bowl Sunday we always have this big party at home, and my parents invite their friends over, and like, there's my grandparents come too, and uh, the guys are all in the TV room watching the game, and the women are all in the kitchen talking. So like, I got to watch the game too, and then afterwards I asked them if they'd help me with the interview.

And my grandfather told me about the time he'd just joined the army, and then he found out that they'd dropped this A-bomb or something on Hiroshima, and y'know, how he felt about that.

MG: *How did he feel?*

Pleased that he didn't have to go to Japan. So that was one . . . And then he told me about how, like, when he was in college, he placed a bet on a horse—like, he didn't have any money—he was down to, like, his last five bucks, and so he placed a bet on this horse. And it was like, a hundred-to-one outsider. That was another story.

MG: *Did he win?*

Nope. [*sniffs*] And then he told me about how he'd watched so many movies that he wore out his VCR. And stuff like that. Like, I would never have known all that if I hadn't given that Torah portion.

MG: *And you told these stories in the synagogue as part of your speech.*

Right.

MG: *I'm sorry but I don't understand the connection between your grandpa's VCR and Moses.*

'Cause I, like, would never have asked about stuff like that, if I didn't have to, I guess.

MG: *Oh, I see . . .*

Yeah, and like, I said that I learned. I learned you should always ask people about their past, because you can learn some really neat things about them, or maybe even not so good things, but you get to know something new about them. It all depends. That's mostly what I learned. Didn't you have a bar mitzvah?

Drama Queen

Early summer. Midday in Washington Square, Greenwich Village. Alissa M., who comes from upstate New York, is an eighteen-year-old fresh-man at a nearby drama school. She's just come from a workshop where she played Nora, the wife of lawyer Torvald Helmer, in a scene from Ibsen's A Doll's House. *A Nora with spiky purple hair and an eyebrow ring. But her styrofoam coffee cup and cream cheese bagel were not in the presentation, Alissa points out.*

I'VE ALWAYS BEEN INVOLVED IN THEATER, from a really early age, and I also kind of associate my bat mitzvah* with theater as well, but mostly not in a good way. I remember it being so much work, like, just learning the different melodies, and learning to read from the Torah. And back then, I was taken up with the fact that it was taking me away from playing soccer . . . And more importantly, I was not allowed to do this show I wanted to be in. It was a school production of *Grease*, and I was very resentful of that.

MG: *Who were you going to be?*

I don't know. I never even got to audition. My parents and my rabbi laid down the law. They were like, "You need to concen-trate, you have to put all your effort into it . . ." And it was a lot of work. I had to do the Friday night service, the Saturday morning service, *and* Havdalah,* Saturday night. It was intense. And every-body was putting such pressure on me to study.

I'd come home from school, and they'd be nagging me to study— y'know, my rabbi had put my haftarah* and everything on a tape, and I would just wear my headphones and listen to it all the time.

MG: *Do you remember what it was about?*

Don't have any idea now. I don't really remember the story, but we had gone through it and kind of talked about the lessons. I had a general sense of what was going on, but in terms of the prayers and the details, I don't remember anything! [*laughs*] It was just something I was supposed to do.

It sounds stupid, but thirteen is a terrible age for a bat mitzvah. I felt like it was unfair that I had to do that, while all my friends were out having fun, and I had to go to Hebrew school like, twice a week, and I had to go to like, services on the weekend. And I looked at it at the time as one big hassle.

Looking back on it now, I realize it was probably because my dad was president of the temple, that was why there was all this pressure. Like, when I was working on my speech—because when you finish your haftarah, you have to give a speech thanking the rabbi, your parents and everybody—and I remember writing down what I wanted to say.

I wanted to thank my rabbi because he put in a lot of work; and I wanted to thank my parents—because I was really [*smiles*] excited about this party—and my sister and brothers . . . And . . . and my dad came in while I was writing it, and he's like, "Well, let's add a few things here . . ." Like how important Judaism is to me, and how I vow to continue my studies . . . Like, I would *never* have said that. And I felt that if *I* was delivering a speech, it should be what *I* was wanting to say. And it wasn't. But I gave the speech my dad wrote. And everybody was so impressed, and I remember thinking, "But that's not me . . ."

Y'know, [*with frustration*] I have gone through this whole process of being bat mitzvahed—[*concessively*] And some parts of it were fun . . . like, I had a lot of fun getting up there in front of all those people. I'm the drama queen, right? And also, knowing all the Hebrew, and performing in front of all these people—it was a big accomplishment, and I was very proud of myself. And it *did* mean something to me, but not nearly what my dad expected, and what he wanted. It was a miserable experience . . .

MG: *So if you had kids, you'd do it differently.*

I wouldn't force them. But y'know, I'm not even so sure if I'm going to raise my children Jewish. I'm not sure. I've been hearing from my grandmothers for the longest time, how important it is for me to meet a nice Jewish boy. I mean, let me decide for myself, let me find someone I *love*. . . . Maybe you should interview me again in ten years' time . . . [*biting into her bagel*]

That Gem in It

———— ✥ ————

WELL, I'M IN MY OFFICE, WHICH IS IN OUR HOUSE. I have two windows, and from one I can see trees—there is a house there, but you can't see it—and from the other window, the mountains, with snow on 'em!

And I have a lot of books around me—professional books, uh book proposals, and personal books too . . . like, you want some titles? *Tearing the Silence, The Stone Diaries*—and—I'm not making this up!—*The Art of Biblical Narrative* by Robert Alter, which was lent to me by our student rabbi. And I'm actually looking right now at our ketuba,* which is on the wall here. It's in Hebrew . . . It's a *little* far away to read, and no vowels either, so no, I can't read it. Except for my name and my husband's names and the word "Yisrael." But I do enjoy looking at it.

MG: *And how would you describe yourself?*

Oh, God! I'm . . . I'm . . . [*laughs*] I'm prematurely gray [*laughing louder*]—it makes me sound decrepit—but I'm actually in better shape than when I was younger. Since we moved out here from New York, I've really got into skiing, and you have to be in good shape for that.

A series of beeps becomes increasingly shrill.

Oh God, my battery's gonna go dead, and we're gonna be cut—

A phone interview with Karen K., a linguist and book editor who lives in near Denver, Colorado. I last saw Karen some months ago at a linguistics conference in Seattle. In the meantime, she has had a bat mitzvah.*

I'm part of that big cohort of women in their forties who didn't have a bat mitzvah when they were twelve or thirteen, because it wasn't the done thing at the time. And, and then we'd all sort of come of age in the era of feminism, and now we're saying, "Well, why *didn't* we do that?" So I found myself with a group of several other women connected with a synagogue here in town. And we would meet with our student rabbi—who's a wonderful spiritual leader—but she was only here once a month, and even then she often had other people to deal with. Like children doing their bat mitzvah.

In fact some of the best conversations I had with her were sitting in a car, driving her to and from the airport! But we had a few classes with her where we would talk about the course of a service or definitions of God, or what it meant to be an adult member of the Jewish community.

And there was a book we were supposed to learn from—I actually threw it away, because I didn't like it—And it was a course of study for adults, for bat mitzvah, and some of it—Well, it had some interesting questions that were provocative, but it started with the *deadliest* chapter on philosophy! Can you imagine? Just impenetrable if you didn't already know it.

And anyway, we sorted ourselves into groups, and this other woman and I, we'd get together in chavruta*—we called ourselves the Chavruta Chums—once a week. Sometimes it was just practicing the various blessings before and after the Torah reading, and then we started practicing our Torah and haftarah* portions.

And it was good to have the other person there as a sort of tutor or monitor. And we would also actually sit and talk about why this portion—what was particularly interesting about it. Her parsha,*

was Shabbat Shira,* and so she has an *incredible* voice, so it was just perfect for her. This is the Mi Kamocha* portion, where the Children of Israel are celebrating. They're saying, "You're just driving us out of slavery to die in the desert, but we actually have seen the power of God and God's salvation." It's just stunningly beautiful, and hearing her sing it was just a thrill!

And *I* wanted to find something that was similarly special for me, and I worried that, "Would my Torah portion have that gem in it, that point in it, to say that, 'This is my identity'?"

And what I *realized* was, that it really didn't matter what portion I found, because you find yourself reflected wherever you look deeply enough. It really is the *process* of looking, that makes it your own, not what you're looking at. I think that was my great discovery during Torah study, and that was what hooked me and made me say, "Yes, I wanna continue doing this."

So I chose a piece because it was around my birthday, and in fact the year I was born, my birthday was in fact the first day of Pesach.* So my portion was Bo [*Exodus 10–13:16*]. And in my Dvar Torah,* I talked about issues of journey and discovery, and because I'm trained in language, I talked a little bit about the sounds, and I talked about the semantics, and the larger frame of the discourse, and that sort of satisfied me as a scholar, and that gave me what I was looking for, and paralleled what my friend had done.

And then I learned so much about service leadership. I had to choose what had to be said, which prayers I would do, which the rabbi would do, which melodies, kind of personalizing it. You realize how much *work* there is involved in it.

And I, I found myself wondering what it would be like to do this as a twelve- or thirteen-year-old. "Well, it would be nice to be able to concentrate on my performance, and not have to worry about all the things that a bat mitzvah's mother has to do, which is sending out the invitations, doing the catering and all that stuff . . ."

And then all those last-minute things. On the Wednesday night—the bat mitzvah was on Saturday. On the Wednesday night, I called the rabbi up and read my haftarah portion to her over the phone. And she said, "Well, that's very good, Karen. One thing you might want to do, though, is go back and look at the, the trop* marks, because even though you're not chanting, the trop marks help because they actually mark the stress in each word."

[*with stunned surprise*] "Oh yeah?" [*laughs*]

So I had to go back and basically relearn everything. And then! We had a seder* on Friday night, with my husband, the kids, family that had flown in, a friend from Ireland, and Saturday was my bat mitzvah! So after the seder, I was up baking—unleavened chocolate nut cakes and almond bars—and then when *that* was finished, I had to word process the handouts for the service. And when that was finished, I had to go and put tzitzit* on my new talit.*

MG: *Really? I thought they all came ready-to-wear.*

Traditionally, you wind—is it called winding? I forget what the verb is— It's like macramé, you tie your own, and they come with a set of instructions. So, I'd been up for twenty hours already, and now I'm winding tzitzit onto my talit.

MG: *I didn't know that, either. So it's a custom to tie tzitzit onto the talit the night before a bat mitzvah?*

No, no. I just hadn't gotten around to it earlier. I mean, I could've used one of my husband's or his father's, but having one of my own seemed appropriate.

And then next day, you go up and you do it, and it was great. I was proud of myself that I'd acquitted myself well on the bimah,* I couldn't wait to read the Torah again, and I was pleased to have had the chance to share the moment with lots of different people, family and friends, for lots of different reasons. And listen . . . it's very nice to, to be in the spotlight. There's rarely an occasion when you have such an opportunity for such a long time all by yourself. I mean, when you get married, you have to share it with another person. When you have a *baby* you have to share it with another person.

MG: *I guess you've generally got the funeral all to yourself.*

Yeah, but I imagine they're not so much fun. And now I feel completely empowered to contribute. In fact, I sometimes lead the services.

[*a sudden burst of delighted memory*] Oh, but this is perhaps my favorite story. During the actual service, my husband, holding my younger son—he was about three and a half—was standing on one side of the ark, and my older son, who was seven, was on the other side of the ark. They'd opened the ark, for the blessing that the, the rabbi gave for me, Yevarechecha.* And this was a very private moment. It's sort of sotto voce. And during that time, the cantor was singing something else with the rest of the congregation, so no one could really hear what was being said to me, but obviously it was something very ceremonial: she had her hands on my shoulders, she stood close to me . . . And afterwards, my older son—on the other side of the ark—said in a voice loud enough for at least the first couple of rows, said, "Mommy, are you a rabbi now?" I said, "No, honey, not yet!"

Four Funerals
and a Wedding

―――――――∽∾―――――――

Cleveland, Ohio. A line of early morning customers snakes back from the cashier's counter through the espresso bar and out into the atrium of this shopping mall. Fortunately, we beat the rush and have a couple of stools by the window and a ledge for our cappuccinos. My breakfast companion, Andrew H., takes a bite out of his blueberry muffin, brushes a crumb from his tweed sport coat, and checks his watch. Another twenty minutes and he'll have to open up his jewelry store across the atrium. In what I take to be an aggrieved manner, Andrew's very prominent Adam's apple regularly rises and falls above the Windsor knot of his Liberty of London tie.

COUSIN OF MINE BECAME VERY RELIGIOUS, and she married this very Orthodox—well, Conservative to Orthodox fellow whose family is very traditional. I went to the wedding in New York: a lot of Israeli dancing and folk songs, and all this kind of stuff. And there was a whole bunch of these Conservadox Jews there. And I didn't know the Jewish dances, but I just followed along and had a good time. But I got a comment out of that, like, "God, I was surprised *you* got so into it."

[*aggrieved*] I mean, why wouldn't I? I was kinda involved in the group, and they're like, "Who is this guy?"

I mean, I think those Orthodox groups deserve a lot of credit for preserving the traditions and everything. But I think over time, people tend to converge on what's quote-unquote normal, or what the mainstream does, and maybe that's a good thing too. I don't like this exclusionary attitude.

And I'm not saying I know all the rules—I'm not an expert—but I know a lot of the rules, I know a lot of the customs, but for some people, it's like if you're not going to synagogue every week, and you're not doing this and that—"Oh, you're not practicing? Oh, you're not Jewish enough! Tsk. Tsk."

I think the Jewish tent should be big enough for everybody. And often, I'm not sure that's the case: "You don't do it our way, you're wrong," that kinda thing. Like, my family—they're in this perpetual mourning thing—You heard of that film *Four Weddings and a Funeral,* in my family it's four funerals and a wedding. Like my grandmother on Yom Kippur, she'd bring out the memorial candles, not just like, for the immediate family . . . for *every* aunt and uncle you can imagine! Y'know, it was a tray this big [*demonstrates with hands a yard apart*] literally. And she would put herself through such agony of mourning with prayers for the dead . . .

He finishes the muffin and wipes his hands on a paper napkin.

My mother's family all have a plot not far from here actually, and it's kind of like [*smiles*] our holy burial ground really. And my grandmother is now buried there too. She passed away last spring.

And the interesting thing is my mother wanted the unveiling the Labor Day weekend. It was actually only about five months after she passed away. [*Traditionally, a gravestone unveiling ceremony occurs about twelve months after a death.*] But my mother wanted it then because everyone would be back in Cleveland for Labor Day. That was like the second departure from tradition. First was when my grandmother passed away, my mother and my uncle decided the funeral would be four and a half, almost five days after she died, instead of right after. Y'know, because my sister had to come home, from New York, and my brother in Boulder thought maybe he was coming in, so my folks thought, "Let's leave enough time so everyone can get here."

And y'know, they caught some flak for it from some of the cousins: [*kvetching*] "Y'know, you really should do it within three days at most, better, you should do it *immediately*," and all of this stuff. Everyone has to be more Jewish than the next person . . .

His Adam's apple shoots up.

And also *presuming* — Another cousin told my mother, "You know she has to be bathed? And cleaned? and, and wrapped, and . . ." And my mother was like, "What, you think I just fell off a turnip truck? You think I don't know this stuff?"

See, when my grandfather died, these old men took the body, did with it, buried it — bing bing gone — and my mom and her brother, my mom especially, was not connected with it. And so I think, this time, I think she and my uncle decided that this time they weren't going to let whoever it was, take their mother till they were ready. But they certainly made sure it was done in an Orthodox fashion — the shrouds, the pottery, the sand — I mean, they didn't do it themselves, but they had the women from the burial society come in.

And they were *extremely* offended by these cousins . . . And then same thing with the Shiva.* They didn't sit Shiva — Well, they had two, two nights [*traditionally seven*]. I mean, no matter how liberal they are about religious matters, they weren't gonna not do something. But y'know, same reaction, "You only doing *two*? You know you should be doin' seven?"

I dunno. I guess it is good to have some ritual, I guess you don't wanna screw it up. I mean, what if you didn't do that thing right, and now your grandmother's sittin' in purgatory somewhere, because you [*laughs*] screwed up with the ceremony?

So anyway, they decided to have the unveiling on Labor Day, but our rabbi was away and my folks really didn't want just any rabbi to do it. So they said, "Why don't you and Steve do it?" That's my brother. I'm like, "Y'know, I think there's gotta be someone more qualified than me!" [laughs] I didn't wanna do it!

But when I did the research—it was interesting—the first thing I did was go to the Bible, and I was flipping through, and I happened to come across the death of Jacob. And that became like my first thing, like he'd made his children promise to bring him back from Egypt, so this great procession came back to Israel. And I drew that as a parallel for that unveiling ceremony. How we laid my grandmother in, with all the patriarchs and matriarchs of our family, like her father, and mother, and my grandfather and . . . y'know, just like Jacob's children had done.

So my brother and I did the research. I mean, it was a little awkward at first, you think you have to be a rabbi, but you don't. And if people are gonna say, "You should say this, and you shouldn't say that," you can tell 'em, "You do it your way for your grandmother, and I'll do it my way for mine."

But I did check with this other cousin, who's a rabbi-in-training—he had the books—and I pulled together some different passages. But I didn't want to say Kaddish.* I don't know why . . . It sounded very official . . . My mother wasn't crazy about it either because she associates that with sadness, and didn't want that. But my brother really thought that it was appropriate, so we decided to do it. And then my cousin sent us some stuff but it was old and dry.

In the temple I grew up in, you find the driest thing you can, and that's the one you read. But my brother found some poems . . . And my grandmother happened to have written a letter before she died, about what she felt about her soul, and her existence, and all that. And I thought that would be interesting to read, kind of as . . . well, I guess what *she* would've said if she'd been there, "Not to worry about me, I have this sense that, y'know, I'm going home, and continuing to do good work . . ." and all that.

So it was a quick thing. My brother and I, we read the Kaddish in, in Hebrew, but we alternated in reading it, 'cause that's a thing I always have a problem with: when people read in Hebrew, and no one knows what it means, and everyone's standing there like this: [*squinting with incomprehension*]

So he read one line in Hebrew, and I'd read it in English. And that was interesting too. Before we did it, I went over the Kaddish with my mother, in the English translation, and she was like, "God, I never knew what it actually said." She thought it was like the death chant, and it's not at all. It's really a song of praise. So that's kinda like, what you learn in watered-down Judaism is not what it really is.

So anyway, we did this. And I think we did a good job, and it was in the tradition, but it was like, it was meaningful for us, because we made it meaningful.

Kaddish

St. Louis, Missouri. Leah M. is a clinical psychologist. She's in the front room of the ground-floor apartment where she both lives and works. I'm in the armchair normally reserved for clients. Opposite me, Leah's face is in shadow. The afternoon sun, striped by a venetian blind, falls on the far side of the room. Six months ago, Leah's father died at the age of eighty-eight. Leah, her brother, and sister flew to Arizona for the funeral.

HE AND MY MOTHER HAD BEEN MARRIED SIXTY-TWO YEARS. She has Alzheimer's, so she couldn't remember that Dad had gone. So when we were there, we would sit with her in the garden and she would look around and say, "Where's Dad?" And one of us would say, "He died." And she would say, [*dreamily*] "Did he?"

And, of course, she was *there* when he died, she was there when they took his body away, but she just . . . I'm sure it was a combination of Alzheimer's and denial . . .

He was cremated. That's against the Jewish religion, but that's—that was my father. He was very much his own person. So after we cremated—After the cremation, we scattered his ashes, and I flew home. That was on the Friday.

I walked into the house here—I live alone here—covered the mirrors, lit a seven-day candle, and went to the synagogue on the Saturday morning. And I hadn't been a regular attender, but I really felt the need to go then. I told some people what was going on, and that I expected to go there every morning and come back to my house to sit [Shiva*].

And that evening, somebody called me from the synagogue: "Would you like us to come to you?" I couldn't believe it. But they came, and there was a minyan* every day. It's very time-consuming, it's very early in the morning, seven, seven-fifteen. I just couldn't imagine that people could be so generous.

And on the Monday they brought a Torah. So I sat there—well, I stood when they raised the Torah—and I couldn't believe that there was a Torah in my house, and that it was for my father. And I said to myself, "God must really love my father, to provide this kind of Shiva. And, I guess God really loves me to provide me with the support that I was getting."

Everybody brought food; it was so much in the Jewish tradition, and was completely unexpected. Neither of my siblings wanted to sit Shiva. My sister said she was sure my father didn't want that, but when we talked about it, I said, "Well, I'm going to, because it's for me. Whether Dad would've wanted it or not, I have to do this for me."

So I had the opportunity to just sit in my house, and not have to do anything, and just be there. And people came and went and I was just there with the depth of brokenness that I was feeling—I was astonished how broken I felt—that my father was gone from the world.

One of the strangest things was that my mind was gone. I did not have a mind, in the sense that when I started seeing clients again—the day after I stopped sitting Shiva—it was very hard, very hard for me to concentrate, to be present. It took many, many weeks, maybe a couple of months before I could consider that I had a mind to work with.

It was just going within a deep place in myself, and being able to be there without distractions, and I felt kind of sorry for my brother and sister that they didn't allow themselves to . . . I think they just didn't realize the potential there is in sitting Shiva, of having an experience of oneself.

MG: *Did you talk with them about your experience?*

I didn't. It's very sad, it's a great sadness to me, that there's so much of myself that I can't bring to my family but that's . . . how it is.

For the past six months Leah has attended synagogue twice a day to recite Kaddish.* She intends to continue until she has completed the traditional eleven months of mourning.

I feel like I'm a train, running on these two tracks of morning service and evening service, and when I go to shul,* I can stay on these tracks. And it's not something you can do alone. It has to be done in a minyan. There's a response from the community, you're being witnessed. The whole point of the Kaddish—at the least the major point I think of—what one does is support the soul returning to God. It elevates the soul of the person who died, and when there's a group, a community of people witnessing that intention, I believe it increases the lifting. [*smiles*]

I'm not sure if that's true from the point of view of the rabbis, but it's true for me. There's something about the call and response. It's a very . . . Beautiful is not an adequate word. It's very rich, it has a powerful resonance, and when I was a child, I went to synagogue a little bit. There's a lot of resonance with my childhood.

Another thing that's happened is that I'm feeling more whole and more strong than I have possibly in my whole life, maybe since I was a child. There's something about not having a father . . . I mean, for a long time he never really was much of a father in the course of my life. The relationship was painful in a lot of ways. But when he died—and it took me a while to figure this out . . . what died was the hope that he *might* be the father I wanted him to be.

Once I got that, that he was gone, and never going to be a father for me in this world, something happened: there was a kind of shift in which I said to myself, "OK, well, I gotta be my own father, have to take care of myself in the way that I would've wanted him to." Which is sort of where I am now . . .

Also, when I think about it . . . Well, uh . . . I wasn't gonna say this . . . It's a little . . .

Leaning forward, she looks towards the window. In the street, a car door slams.

As I said, he didn't want anyone to say Kaddish for him. There was a lot of alcohol, and uh, self-destruction in his life and . . . we had a difficult relationship. [*deep inbreath*] And here I am saying Kaddish for him, sending him back to God, when he was going in completely the opposite direction. It's kind of revenge in a way . . .

She leans back in her chair and looks straight at me.

That must sound pretty weird but it's what I feel, too.

Suffering

———— ❧ ————

Carla F. grew up in Slovakia. During World War II, along with her parents and younger sister, she was deported by the Nazis, first to Sered concentration camp and then to Auschwitz. On arrival there, her father was shot on the railroad platform; her mother was sent to the gas chamber. After a month in Auschwitz, Carla, who was eighteen years old, and her sister, aged fourteen, were transferred to a smaller camp, where they worked in a textile mill.

Today, Carla lives in a Jewish retirement community near the Jersey shore. For the past few days she has not been well. She's sitting on a sofa, her head propped on cushions. She speaks slowly and precisely, without apparent emotion, as if she is recalling the words themselves, not the events they describe. For long periods her eyes are closed.

IT WAS SNOWING. It was the morning of the eighth of May nineteen hundred and forty-five. It was quiet. We did not hear them shout, "*Aufstehen.*" We didn't know what happened. Then there was a knock on the door. Nobody answered. So in walked a German soldier—an old man—and he said, "*Häftlinge.* Prisoners. Get up."

We were not used to such nice conversation so we didn't move. He said, "The SS and the Jewish kapos* left last night and I'm in charge now to see that things go the usual way. The war is coming to an end today at midnight, and then there is the danger that the German army on the retreat will shoot you all."

So we got up.

Her eyes open, meeting mine.

Some Czech girls went into the kitchen to look for food. They found a lot of empty cans. You must remember that everything was done by the Polish kapos. Wherever there was anything to be gained, there were Polish kapos. And there was a bag of potatoes. You can imagine the quality: black and rotten. There was a decision to be made. Shall everybody have two potatoes, or shall we cook the lot up?

We were standing there in the parade ground. We were so used to be standing there in fives, and we were waiting for the Germans to come and shoot us. Nobody had the faintest idea to run away or hide or anything. We were there as we were coached all these months.

And then suddenly the gate—which was always locked—opened from the outside and three soldiers came in riding on three little horses. I thought, "That's it . . . I didn't survive. I never wrote my book. They're going to massacre us now. I'm going to be the first one. Let them shoot me first."

So I walked out of the line. I came closer to the soldiers and saw these Mongolian-looking guys, and I looked at their caps, and there was a hammer and sickle and a red star, and I realized that this was the Russian Army. And they had in a pouch a revolver and blossoming lilac. I said, "*Kak pazhevayet Tovarishch Stalin* [*How is Comrade Stalin*]?"

They started to cry. I couldn't understand. You see we didn't realize how we looked. We were used to seeing each other, but this was the first camp which they liberated and we broke their hearts. They said, "*Germania kaput. Poyezhai damoi.* Go home."

And then suddenly, from the distance and louder and louder, in Greek, and Czech, and in German, and Hungarian, and in Slovak, and in Romanian people sang the song of the Third International.

She hums a few bars.

I only knew it in Hebrew — we learned it in HaShomer haTzair* — but I sang it too. These crying soldiers and this jubilation of freedom was, I think, the greatest moment of my life.

Three-second pause. In a nearby apartment a washing machine enters a spin cycle. Carla clears her throat.

I looked for my sister, she was in a terrible state, and I had to carry her, and with three girls which I was friendly with, we left the camp.

And then came the trauma: Where do we go? To the left? To the middle? To the right? Which way is home? So we went to a nice little villa, the first one we saw. We went to the lounge room. Lots of books. I put my sister on the bed and I went to the bookshelf and I picked out *Vom Winde Verweht, Gone with the Wind.* I lay on the floor because I was so used to hard bunks; it took me a long time to get used to a mattress.

And then I realized: No matter what is coming, I survived. I can read, I enjoy reading, I haven't forgotten it. I will go back to school and I will study and I will write my book about my life. And to me, with this *Gone with the Wind* the war was finished.

MG: *So you were finally free in this abandoned house.*

When we went in, we thought it was deserted. But in the kitchen there was a woman hanging from the light fitting. Whether they hung her or she hung herself I do not know.

MG: [*incredulously*] *And she was hanging there while you were reading* Gone with the Wind?

Am I going to resurrect her? After you have seen hundreds, thousands of bodies, what is one more?

219

A week later, I visit Carla again. She's much brighter. At Macy's yesterday, she treated herself to a navy blue chenille cardigan, which she proudly models for me. It's a mild day and so we sit in the courtyard outside her apartment. On a bench across the lawn, an elderly man reads The New York Times *with a magnifying glass. A jet heading in to Newark airport passes low overhead.*

You are a nice man. You are not snobbish. You are not looking down at me as the old lady from the Jewish home. You make me feel young because you don't have this attitude: "This poor old lady . . ." I'm a sort of pariah here. I don't feel I belong here. I have nothing in common with the people here, being not a member of the community, not to belong to any shul.*

I went to a Jewish school the other week, talking to a group of children about the Holocaust. They picked me up by car and there were five of us. These four women talked about a bar mitzvah* with a hundred and fifty people that one of them went to. I felt miles apart from them. I didn't say one single word all the way to the college.

But I related very well to the children. They called me afterwards, and said how they missed me and how interesting it was, what I had to tell them, and how different I was from the other ladies. I wasn't in the mood to ask them how I was different to the others. I should've asked them . . .

So being amongst Jews is very difficult for me. But being Jewish amongst non-Jews is pleasurable. I like the goyim.* They haven't got the hang-ups Jewish people have. They don't have the same aspirations like career and money and living in the right neighborhoods and the children in private schools. They might have even more money than the Jews but they are not so snobbish about it.

MG: *So despite everything they did to you in the war, you still feel—*

[*vehemently*] "They" were the Jewish kapos in the camp. That were "they." The SS didn't do anything to me. It's the Jewish kapos which made my memories so painful. They spoke Yiddish. They didn't speak German, they spoke Yiddish.

You see, I have lived by choice in many different countries: India, China, Africa. Places where there are no Jews. I feel comfortable. I miss the non-Jewish contact now, living here. I miss it, that they don't talk about the Holocaust, they don't talk about synagogues, they don't talk about hairdressers. They are different people.

[*smiling broadly*] I like being the Jewish mama in a non-Jewish environment. I like that role. I can be different. I like being different. I can tell them Jewish jokes. To them, I can talk about the Holocaust. They are impressed at my survival, are impressed what I went through. Jewish people here are not, because they went through the same thing. They even try to outdo me: they say, "I was in Auschwitz since 1942, you only came in 1944. You don't know what suffering is."

What Am I Gonna
Do About It?

———— ✈ ————

Sydney, Australia. His hair is stylishly waved, his well-cut shirt and slacks crisply pressed. A gold chain hangs on his wrist. Harry F. was born in Rotterdam in 1922. During the German occupation of Holland in World War II he was deported to Auschwitz, where he spent three years in a labor camp. A bulging album lies on the glass-topped coffee table in front of us. It contains photographs, press cuttings, letters, documents, as well as scores of typewritten sheets, the periods like tiny bullet holes through the pages. In the background, the rhythmic tearing sound of highway traffic just beyond the patio wall.

THIS IS MY BOOK. I started it during the night when I could not sleep. I dream every night of the camps, of the misery, men chasing me. It's the one thing I just can't help. I can do hypnotherapy; I can help other people, but I can't help myself.

I live on stress. One doctor explained to me that I'm so well *because* of stress. It's the opposite of what you may have heard. It puts more fire into me. So I have been reading a few things and researching. How would people know about the stars and the universe if they don't read? Most of it, though, is my own story. I also have written some biography of other survivors. I found a book at a fête. I thought, "What a shame that this book is lost to the world."

I have put some of his stories into the book too. I also put quite a bit of Dutch in it: things what happened, speeches of the Queen's representatives to encourage the people of the Netherlands.

I have now five hundred and fifty-six pages and more than two hundred fifty photos.

He pushes the album towards me, pointing to a magazine clipping.

I have an article here about Hitler, that Jewish were the most un-intelligent people, that they never achieved nothing.

He turns the page.

And here I have a picture of hell. I want to have it sketched with the Germans burning, and you see people in striped uniform walking through the pearl gates of heaven. People may laugh, say, "Harry is insane, how can he say this after all the things he has been through, after his parents have been murdered?"

Did you read about *Computers in Heaven*? Every little thing that a person does, the good deeds and the bad deeds, will be registered in those computers. People say, "Harry's meshuga,"* but they don't have the feeling for it.

There is hundred of pages here about my story . . . My escape from the cattle train . . . Here is the piece of paper the Germans gave me as a free passport. They didn't know I was a Jew. It's a long story.

He continues flipping the pages, pointing to photographs and documents.

Here is Roosevelt, Churchill, Stalin: the people who helped us to achieve our freedom. And that's my father's bakery. That's the Chief Rabbi of Holland, many, many years ago. A great-grandfather of my mother.

That's a friend of mine who was looking after my bike while I was away in the camps. He sold my bike for bread.

Is he describing an act of desperation, or betrayal, or both? He looks at me intently, waiting for my response.

Here is a school teacher in Amsterdam. He was a midget. They stripped the skin off him in Matthausen and made him into a skeleton.

This is a postcard I sent on the sixteenth of September 1942. My birthday. I translate it to you. "I'm on my bed. I'm thinking of home. Oh, my dear God, please let me come back to my family again."

That was in the camp.

Here is death march. I can see myself walking there with thousands, thousands people. You can see the cold, snow. People were laying all around being shot. I put this picture in for the time being, but it has to be altered; it was a different death march. I was twenty-three days without food. A miracle gave me food. A miracle made me stay alive when a German pointed his rifle at me.

He turns to another page.

That's when I came to Paris. They wanted me to guard German prisoners. The commandant, he was giving me a rifle, he saw my tattoo. He said, "I can't let you guard them, you might kill them."

My number was one hundred seventy-seven thousand, hundred and forty-seven. I had it removed on the ship when I came out. A doctor, he said, "It's hot climate where you're going. Most of the time you wear short sleeves. People always asking you, 'What is it?' You explain . . . It's no good for you mind. I want to take it away."

I said, "No, I want to keep it."

He said, "Come on, Harry, I got a needle, I want to cut it out."

He did a bad job. *He pushes back his shirt sleeve.* You can still see part of the last number, the seven.

He turns the page.

That's me in Jerusalem laying tefilin.* I'm still a good Jew. [*laughs*]

Here's the Israeli army. That's my wife, Marilyn. Nearly seventeen years younger. She looks after me like a wife and a mother.

That's my sister's son who died of AIDS . . .

That's where I saw my mother for the last time . . .

That's the memorial from Westerbork*. . .

My friends from school . . .

The Queen, whom I met personally.

This is me in the Jewish Museum. I talk to the students who come. It's not like a guide talking about paintings. You tell your story and sometimes they start to twitch their face and cry. Sometimes I'm worried I tell them too much. Sometimes I'd like to stop. But the guides who experienced it have to tell it.

I donated a chair on the second floor. Every time I go to the museum at a quiet time, I sit there and watch the video. Every ten seconds a photo appears on the screen of a murdered person. Every ten seconds. Picture comes . . . ten seconds . . . picture fades . . . another picture comes. They have no grave, only a photo. I see my mother, my father, my brother, his wife, the whole family. I see my mother coming for ten seconds on this video. I say, "Please, Momma, don't go away . . ." I want to keep her. You know what I mean?

Another page.

That's Ben Kingsley. I met him when *Schindler's List* came out.

Here's me at a fundraiser last year for the Jewish Welfare and the Holocaust Association. [*smiling with pleasure*] I was there with about five hundred people. It gives me such a good feeling to be among Jewish people. Eighty-five percent I did not know, but I feel at home.

He looks up and turns towards me.

Sixteen years I have been working on my book. I have already taken out about hundred and fifty pages; it became too many pages. When it come to the publisher they will probably take out more anyhow. I haven't been able to get anybody helping me with grammar, with editing.

I talked with Thomas Keneally [*author of* Schindler's Ark, *the novel on which the Spielberg film is based*] about a year ago when they had a reception after *Schindler's List* come out. I said, "Could you possibly advise me on a publisher or editor?" He said, "Harry—" He looked at my name tag. He said, "Harry, it's not easy to find a good editor." I said, "Don't tell me that you need an editor, too!" He said, "Oh, yes. I'm a writer, not an editor."

But I haven't been able to find anybody. I sent it to one publisher, they returned it after a week and a half. Too difficult for them to do editing of a book they didn't know nothing about. They have been publishing books about country walks, nature. Completely something different.

The lady, she said to me, "We wouldn't do it justice. I couldn't think your way. You must have the neshuma* to edit that book."

This is Elie Wiesel. He read my story. I showed him my escape story at eleven o'clock at night. The next day I got a letter in the box. The next day! I don't know how it was possible. It was written on paper from the Hilton. He must've gone back to the hotel, he was reading my story, and he thought, "I must write this man a letter."

He was encouraging me to finish. He wrote, "If I'm still available when it is finished, I will . . ."

Then I had another lady, she rang me two months ago. I showed her the book at the museum. She said, "Harry, I've seen your book; it's very good. It needs very, very little work done on it. But it needs editing, grammar." Because Dutch speaking back-to-front. [*smiles*]

She said, "I will do it. But you realize that I charge fifty dollars an hour?"

I said, "What's gonna happen if you do fifty hours? I haven't got money for that. I'm a pensioner."

She said, "Well, then we just have to let it go."

So it's stalemate. I was going to have it printed myself. I took it to the bookbinder. He said, "Well, I can do the binding, but some of the writing is too close to the edge. And the photos are a problem."

He begins to turn the pages more quickly.

That's the death certificate of my mother. Fifty-five years old. They gave it to me in 1947.

This was my wife for many years, the girl I married and divorced.

That was my best friend Jack that he died some months ago.

This is Mark Tannen who teaches about the Holocaust at the university. I saw him on the train last week. He said, "What you doing with your book, Harry? I will do my utmost to help."

People say they do something but they don't. People letting me down. What am I gonna do about it? I already have a book cover and a title: *The Devil's Greed.*

He shows me a letter-size illustration of Hitler as half man, half devil.

In my opinion, Hitler was the devil. He created this terrible hurt in the world. He was so greedy he swallowed up the world. The cover cost me four hundred dollars. Do you like the idea? Of course, it will be smaller in the final version.

It still hurts what terrible things Hitler has done to us. The way he had made animals out of us. I have seen people with knives they made themselves, trying to cut pieces of human flesh off dead bodies. Standing at roll call for hours. We were not allowed to go to the lavatories. Slime was running down your legs like animals.

When we had to walk to work, we weren't allowed to stop. While we were walking we had to let our water go. If it wouldn't have been so sad it would've been laughable, all these people opening their pants and pishing while they were walking: there a man, there another, there one, pishing on the highway while they were walking.

Harry closes the album.

I was reading my book once, what I had written before. My wife was away that morning. She went into the city to get her nails done or something. She came back, and I was sitting here in tears. She said, "What's happened?" I said, "It's so sad." She said, "But you're writing it yourself." I said, "I can't believe it, that this happened to me."

Der Kleine Salzmann

Fred Salzmann grew up in Berlin. A few days before the outbreak of World War II, Fred left Germany to study at an ORT school in England. He was sixteen. His grandmother, parents, and younger brother remained in Berlin and were murdered by the Nazis. Ironically, Fred, along with other German Jews in Britain, was interned as an enemy alien. After the war, Fred settled in the United States. Since his retirement, he and his wife have lived in Palm Beach in a condo overlooking the ocean. His grey hair has a razor-sharp parting; his thin mustache is perfectly clipped. He's wearing cream slacks and a pale lemon shirt.

THE JEWS IN GERMANY WERE THERE FOR GENERATIONS, they had assimilated this German culture, they absorbed some of the beauty — I say the *beauty* — of German culture. I was educated in that milieu, that's where my roots lie, a mixture of German and Jewish. In the public school we were shown — I forget the year, '34, '35, '36 — a film: *Hitler Junge Quex*. It was a Nazi propaganda film for Hitler Youth, to glamorize it. And it did.

It had the effect that I, who had to go with the class to the cinema, loved to join the Hitler Youth. The Germans were so clean with their shirts, and they showed the Communists so dirty. Why should not a German boy join? It seemed a normal thing to do. I couldn't join, of course. I had arguments with my father because I wanted to. He thought I was crazy. [*chuckles*]

It's not a popular thing to be Jewish, nor is it a popular thing to be

229

German, but that's what I am, and I happen to love it. But the relation to everything German is very mixed. German Jewish refugees often deny the German part of their background. It's understandable.

My Uncle Max, my father's younger brother, survived the war. He was a bank manager at the Dresdener Bank in the branch at Potsdamer Platz.

Through his connections he was able to get away very late, and get a position at a Jewish bank in London. He had the same customers in London that he had in Berlin: the immigrants were his clients. He was a very clever man and I always looked up to him. My mother always used to say, "Uncle Max comes, take your hands out of your pockets. Stand still!" [*laughs fondly*] He was very German in that way.

He wrote me a letter after the war: "There are refugees here in London that have such little character that they are able to return and set foot on German soil."

I took note of what my uncle said. But I felt like that anyway. When we knew what was happening during the war, we wished that Germany would disappear from the face of the earth. But that's not what happened, and good or bad, we can't turn the clock back. Today, I do not feel the same. Today, I have mixed feelings about it. I'm on both sides. I'm with concentration camp survivors, I represent them here on committees, I share their attitudes: "Don't forget and don't forgive."

But *who* not to forgive? I hate the war criminals and the Nazi ideologues and the people who still today would proclaim the same ideas. And if I personally would see one, I would become aggressive. Physically. But that does not extend to people who have nothing to do with it. What have the children to do with it?

And I have been back to Germany, in 1973, and again in 1989, invited by the Burgermeister of the city of Berlin, along with others of

my schoolmates, the hundred boys who left in August 1939. It was
the last transport that crossed the border into Holland and then
went to England. And these boys were invited back fifty years later.

I had a hire car the first time. And I remember the distances as so
big, big . . . But when I went now with the car, this is nothing! So
small. I come to my old house. The West was not much destroyed,
and what was destroyed was built up again and looked the same as
before. I came to my house, Karlsruhestrasse nummer drei [*number three Karlsruhestrasse*]: an apartment block, four stories, two
apartments on each floor. Then there's the backyard—a *Hof*—
and more apartments. The poorer people live in the back. The
better class live in the front. That's how it is. That's how it was, I
don't know today.

So we parked—I was there with my wife—and I opened the door
of the block. Even from the smell I would've known that house!
You wouldn't believe it. We walked up the stairs and there's the
wooden figures carved in the banister. When I was little I looked
at it all, and now I see it again. *Mein Gott!* This is strange! I recognized these little figures. You could pass it, you wouldn't notice it.
But I remembered.

Then you go up the next floor, and there's a window with . . . what
you call it? Stained glass. And we used to open it a little bit and
there used to be an organ grinder man comes once a week.

He hums a tune and smiles.

And there was the monkey sitting on the organ, and you used to
throw ten pfennig—ten pennies—down. And then he would take
off his hat and say thank you. [*dreamily*] All these memories. It
was beautiful.

And so I came to the second floor. That was our floor. There's the
main door: nice, beautiful door, wood panel and all. And there's
the bell, still the same brass bell. And there's the nameplate, not
the same name, but it still looks the same. We stood there for a

minute. [*swallows*] I rang the bell.

A man opens the door, an elderly man, about my age, fifty, I would say. I said, "Hello, *mein Name ist Salzmann*. This is my wife. I come from America. Fifty years ago, I was born in this apartment, *in dieser Wohnung*."

The man said, "*Kommen Sie herein*." Come in. Should I jump at him? He didn't do anything to me personally, I don't know to anyone else. But he said, "Come in." He could say, "So? What has it do to with me? Very nice to see you, *sei gesundt*." He could've said that. But he said, "Come in, please."

So we come in. And then I dried up completely. Couldn't say anything.

His eyes are moist with tears.

There was new wallpaper, new carpet, everything new. But I didn't see that new, I seen the old one, the old paper and carpet. I said to my wife, "Here was my grandmother's room. And here was my parents' bedroom, and here was my brother and I . . . we slept here. Here was this and here was that . . ."

The man stood next to me. He could see I was upset. I gave him my card: "Elite Fashions." That was my company, and I was managing director. It looks good in Germany. [*chuckles*] Everybody says, "Managing director? Very nice!"

Then I said to him, "Tell me. There was here in the back a Mr. Fischer. He was an electrician. He used to come to fix the light." "Mr. Fischer? Ja. He lives in the front now. Go and say hello to him."

"Alright. Thank you. Nice to meet you," and so on. What else should I say? Finish.

So we went down the steps, knock at the door. "Who's there?" I have to say it in German: "Wer ist da?"

"Salzmann."

An old man opens the door. And when he opens the door, I say, "My name is Fred—Fritz Salzmann, and I was your neighbor before the war. We lived on the second floor." "Ach!" he said, "you must be the grandson of Mrs. Kolonymus." [*delightedly*] It's a difficult name to remember.

I said, "*Ja, es stimmt.* Right." Then he turns round, calls back: "Mutti! *Der kleine Salzmann ist hier!* [*Momma! Little Salzmann's here!*]" [*a long, delighted laugh*]

Der kleine Salzmann. [*chuckles*] He was so friendly, even if he was not Jewish. I remember how he once came to repair the bell. We were having dinner. We sat there, nobody said a word. "*Man spricht nicht.*" We don't talk anything when a goy* comes to the house. That's how it was. And he invited us in. The wife was there, spread out on the couch like the Queen of Sheba, she's not very well. "Yes," she said. "The war was terrible. The Americans, the bombs everywhere. We were lucky this house was not destroyed. Hitler got us into trouble. And the Jews, it's *terrible* what happened to the Jews."

Now they're saying this, but what did they say then? And of *course* they suffered quite extensively. But who started it? They brought it on themselves. So I didn't want to hear this. Maybe that's my limitation, I don't know . . .

Mr. Holocaust

Alan Jacobs, who's forty-eight, was the founding director of the Sydney Jewish Museum, an institution that focuses on the Jewish experience of the Holocaust. He resigned a few months ago. When I arrive at his North Bondi, Sydney, Australia, apartment for our mid-morning interview, Alan's only just got up, greeting me with dripping hair and a bathtowel wrapped around his waist. A few minutes later, he joins me in his living room, wearing jeans and a red T-shirt. A large yellow star is emblazoned across the chest.

IT's AMAZING. They plucked me out of obscurity. [*laughs*] I'm not trying to sell myself short but . . . there was no one else after the job! No. [*becoming serious*] When I saw the ad, I just knew it was for me. I was absolutely convinced. It was a fait accompli . . . I had the job. Without [*laughs*] even applying for it. And I called 'em up, I wanted it . . . I really surprised myself, because I'd never been that persistent.

It was funny, actually. I had this Nazi answering machine message which went something like, uh, "Ve heff vays of makink you leaff your name, your number, und dein messitch after ze BEEP!!" Pretty stupid, but the museum's benefactor, a Hungarian Holocaust survivor himself, rang me up, and I wasn't home, and he got this message. [*laughs*] And he loved it! I'm convinced that I got the job because of the answering machine. But later on he asked me to change it. It was inappropriate.

234

We also had an answering machine in the museum. And I thought, "I can't put a Nazi on." So I had a Hungarian voice instead: [*laughs, slaps thigh*] "Ze Joo-wish Moo-zeum iss klo-zed. Plizz to liff missitch." He didn't like that. I was told to, y'know . . . [*deep inbreath and long sigh*]

I need humor. It's something that's very important in my life. And Holocaust and humor's something that really fascinates me. I remember when there was a documentary on TV about Jewish comedians—children of survivors—and their Holocaust humor. And the next day, one of the survivors was saying to me—outraged—"How can they do this?" And I was trying to explain to him, it's not about laughing at the Holocaust, it's about why these people need to laugh. He couldn't understand that.

I was very interested in the Holocaust—that's what drove me to the job—but it was uncomfortable being Mr. Holocaust twenty-four hours a day. And it's a morbid place to be. Obviously had some sort of psychological effect on me. So I had black humor. That was basically my way of dealing with it. Y'know, there we were doing some solemn Yom haShoah* ceremony and all I wanted to do was get up and crack jokes. And I couldn't. It was very disconcerting. I'm serious. [*laughs*]

I was there from the beginning, right? So we were discussing for example what the guides should wear, right? Camp uniform. No. [*tries to suppress laughter*] Can't help myself sometimes! You should have heard the sessions when we were discussing the gift shop: your own personalized Zyklon B cannister. [*hoots with laughter, slaps his thigh*]

I remember Deb Filler [*the comedian*] saying that the first night in Auschwitz, her father laughed the whole night because there were all these people in the bunk, and for one to turn over, they all had to turn. And they were just laughing, y'know. And I'm sure it was a defense mechanism or survival mechanism. That's something I'd like to explore, a bit later. I mean later in life. Not this morning!

But uh, it reminds me of this great—I mean, one of the great Holocaust stories in terms of reactions of Jews to attempts to broaden the perspective of the Holocaust. Tom Conti played the part of a Jewish writer in a miniseries. Frederic Raphael, *The Glittering Prizes*. And the Tom Conti character went to the Cricklewood Jewish Historical Society or something, [*chuckles*] and he's talking about the memories of Auschwitz.

And his line was basically, "We shouldn't just have sympathy for the Jews, we should also have sympathy for the Gypsies, for example." And he was going on about the Gypsies, "The Gypsies suffered, the Gypsies were exterminated."

And they heard him out, and at the end this little Jewish guy got up, and he said, "Mr. Speaker, for you I heff a kvestion. Kenn you name me tvelf famous Gypsies?"

I mean, it's always disturbed me why the Jews have—why the survivors have a lack of lack of understanding, or identity with other people in the Holocaust. I understand that victims of trauma are obsessed with their own traumas. I can deal with it on a personal basis, but in an institutional setting . . .

Most of the people who worked in the museum, and most of the volunteers, were Holocaust survivors. It was like being in the Holocaust twenty-four hours a day. [*self-parodyingly*] "There must be more to life than Holocaust!"

And I knew that for the museum to be a success, it has to get to the younger generation, and for that to happen, you have to contemporize the Holocaust, relate it to what's happening today. And that was a huge frustration because the board of management and the survivors wouldn't go along with this.

I think basically they saw it not just as a museum but as a shrine as well. I mean, you could have a problem with that, but I chose not to. The association of survivors insisted that the males wear yarmulkes.* I did have a problem with that. My response was, "I'm not a religious Jew." Like, if I go to synagogue, fine, but not there. I didn't perceive it as a shrine. I understand their perceptions, but for me it was a museum. I fought that and won.

But eventually, I had to get out. I chose to leave. Well, I guess I would've been pushed out eventually; the board of management and I didn't see eye to eye. And also, eventually there was an anesthetization. You walk through a museum, and you see things that once had a very powerful impact on you having absolutely—well, minimal impact, becoming familiar, just part of the furniture.

And then I started having health problems, just through sheer frustration, basically. I found myself really hating the place towards the end. So I knew I had to get out. But it still took me a long time to let go. I mean, I was still hanging around, going to the library. I volunteered to help out at Yom haShoah. And then it sort of hit me: "What am I doing here?"

And from about April until just recently—I went to that thing on Kristallnacht*—I just didn't go to the museum. There's nothing worse than the old director hanging around like some old retiree.

It's been a difficult year psychologically: you're director of the Jewish museum, my father's proud of me, I'd become a macher.* It's hard to replace that buzz you get through macherism, y'know, "I'm going on TV, talking as a Jew!" At the same time, I was disturbed about having a professional Jewish tag. I just had to act the Jew all the time. And only part of me is Jewish. A very big part of me, but it's not all of me. And it totally consumed me.

I still—Obviously, the job meant a lot to me. I don't get asked to Jewish professional lunches anymore. [smiles] It's a double-edged sword. But there are other things I want to get into. This year I went to Vietnam. And I've got an absolutely new love, a new obsession: Vietnam. Which is another part of my past. [points to his T-shirt] I've put on the yellow star, I wear it proudly. The Vietnamese star. And you thought it was Jewish? [laughs]

Hidden Violence

———⟨∿⟩———

A February afternoon in Blackpool, England. Low clouds blanket the sea. Drizzle turns to rain. At a tramstop, a solitary figure hunches into his anorak. A tram arrives and comes to a stop with a hiss of airbrakes. Above the empty promenade, slung between two lampposts, a giant cartoon lion silently roars.

Lawrence Miller turns away from the window and sits down behind his desk in the manager's office of this hotel on the Golden Mile. He's in his early forties, a short, stocky man with fashionably long hair in a pony tail. A native of Newcastle-on-Tyne, he has more than a hint of a geordie accent. In the bar directly below us, Dolly Parton's "Stand By Your Man" is playing on the jukebox.

IF I'D NEVER EXPERIENCED ANTI-SEMITISM, I'd probably barely acknowledge myself as a Jew today. My sense of being Jewish comes from that. I first ran into it at boarding school. The school was Anglican. Very reputable. I went to church three times a week: Tuesdays, Thursdays, and Sundays, had theological teachings twice a week. The Jew was almost always depicted negatively.

Oddly, it took years for me to start feeling uncomfortable about it. And then I finally realized that they were saying these things about my father, my mother, about me. And the Holocaust wasn't discussed either. If it was mentioned at all, it was as a footnote to the war. And my reaction was to move further away from it all, to be less Jewish, not that I was very Jewish in the first place. I didn't want to know about it, I had a feeling of distaste. Not a violent one, I just didn't want to deal with it.

Then I had my bar mitzvah* and it was thrust in my face. And at that time there was a lot of bullying. It was never recognized by the school, because it reflects badly. It's a hidden violence. And it just so happened that among the large population of boys, there were two or three who were real anti-Semites. Sure, some of the boys had stereotypes about Jews and money, and Jews and noses. But other than that . . . Then I met these anti-Semites. I couldn't get away from them. They bullied me, pushed me around, or simply threatened me, which can be as bad as physical violence.

A couple of times they stripped me naked, rubbed boot polish on my testicles . . . This happened to others too, sure. But with me, it had anti-Semitism as well. It took on a virulence that wasn't there with the others. The others were let off after a period of time. But with me, it kept going on for more than two years. And there was a silence at the school. I couldn't go and complain. And even if I'd had a word for anti-Semitism—and at the time I didn't—it would've been dismissed. It would've been redefined. They wouldn't have admitted anything that made the school look bad.

I left school early. I changed my name as a result of my school experience. I didn't want it to happen again.

MG: *What was your name?*

Goldstein. The name change was very important in my life. It brought a tremendous relief. I changed my name in 1971, and thirty years later I don't regret it. I feel sorry that I had to do it because of my father; the loss of the name is a kind of extinguishment of a person. But it brought relief to me. Unless I chose to tell someone I was a Jew, they didn't know.

And for years I had no more contact with anti-Semitism. And when I did, it wasn't directed at me, which was quite a different experience, of course. I was involved in left-wing politics in the seventies and eighties, and there I saw a lot of anti-Semitism. People tend to think of anti-Semitism as the Nazi variety: people get beaten up, windows get broken, swastikas get painted. But here it was ideological anti-Semitism, which revolved around Israel and Zionism. Zionism became a surrogate for the Jew.

The vehemence against Zionists! You could read the texts and replace the word "Zionist" with "Jew," and you'd see it was disguised anti-Semitism. Not in all cases, of course. There are legitimate arguments against Zionism. But I'm talking about something else. But I never discussed it. I told very few people I was a Jew. Most people just didn't know.

And then my father died in 1989. I invited some of my friends to the funeral, still thinking I was fairly safe. And of course, when they came to the service, they realized he was a Jew. They didn't know him, but I showed them a photograph, and straightaway one of them—who happened to be one of my best friends—said, "Oh, he looks like a Jew." And of course, he *didn't* . . .

And then this friend said that *I* looked like a Jew! Now these people weren't dummies, they were mostly university educated. And he was trying to say it in a benign way I suppose, but what he'd done was—An entire conceptual framework descended on me, in which he could no longer see me any other way. I watched this happen. I could see it happen.

All of a sudden, this thing that had never been talked about before became a topic of conversation, of problematic conversation. The Jew at this point in history is something exotic. In the first instance it's benign attention; there's no hostility. But everyone looks at you. You feel uneasy with the stares. Then the question of Israel comes in. Zionism becomes a surrogate for anti-Semitism. The Holocaust is now considered as propaganda, something to justify Israel's oppression of the Palestinians.

And after my father died, I began to experience feelings of guilt.

He'd wanted me to go to Israel with him and I never went. He'd asked me, not once, but a number of times, and I never went. So in 1990 I went, first to Israel, then to Poland — my father was from Warsaw — to see the camps, to do the same search he'd done a decade earlier.

I invited my friends to see me off at the airport. And that's where the crunch came. I've still got a photo of the group. I was expecting to be given a good send-off. But for them it was like I was going to the most evil state on earth. And this was the state that came out of the Holocaust. That altered my attitude towards them. I no longer see any of those people any more.

In Israel the main thing I did was hang around Yad vaShem.* I wasn't interested in Israel as a country, as a people, anything. I didn't even like it. It was just another country. Nothing attracted me except Yad vaShem.

I spent three months there. It was traumatic. In one part of Yad vaShem is the Hall of Names, a hall with several million names in books. It's all on microfiche. I told the woman there that my father's name was Goldstein, and she went through the microfiche and she went on and on and on and on . . . All these Goldsteins. I couldn't believe it. Many of them had photographs. The murder of all these people like my parents, like you and me.

It was a defining moment for me. I still don't have any positive feelings about being a Jew. I still feel negatively defined. I don't have a real lot of interest in religion. It's not plausible. What is plausible is the Holocaust. That, I understand. It's had a major effect on my psyche, and it still does.

Sort of Jewish

July in Philadelphia. Elaine B. is a photographer and writer. She has copper-colored hair and blue eyes—a Scottish face, I'm tempted to say. Or is that just because she told me she was born in Nova Scotia? We're in her fifth-floor office. Across the street, and making up half the view, a windowless wall of purple and brown bricks. When we met over lunch with mutual friends a few days earlier, I mentioned that I was working on an interview project about Jewish identity. Her ex-husband, she told me, was Jewish. Did that qualify her to be interviewed?

WHEN SOMETHING HAPPENED AT THAT LUNCH and you said you were Jewish, I had this feeling like, "I know you," y'know, "You're somebody who I can talk with." There are other things too, of course. I'm sure there are a lot of Jewish people I wouldn't necessarily feel that way about. But—

Elaine's phone rings. She seems uncertain whether to answer it. It rings again and then stops.

And yet I wouldn't expect the reverse to be true. Because you wouldn't know that about me. You wouldn't . . . And I wouldn't be able to say to you I'm Jewish. So you wouldn't . . .

I remember Phil always used to tell me that he *knew* when someone was Jewish. He just knew. I don't know if he did. [*laughs*] But he thought that he did. And it really mattered to him. It mattered a lot. And I guess it began to matter to me too.

I was brought up without much religion, although we did some-times go to church on Easter. Things like that. But not even al-ways. My grandparents came to visit, we'd go to church on Easter. So when I got married to Phil, my parents had no objection at all to this. They had no personal discomfort with it.

The only thing I remember very clearly was my father saying to me—not that I didn't know, but he felt that he needed to reinforce this—that there's a lot of discrimination against Jews. And that by doing this, my kids would be Jewish, and they might be subject to discrimination. And he really wasn't trying to talk me out of it. He just really wanted me to go into this with my eyes open, I guess.

And my husband's parents were terribly unhappy when we got married. They just . . . Especially his mother. Phil's mother was just so upset. Crying, hysterical, and all of these things, to prevent it. They did a lot to try to prevent it from happening.

And then we got married and things kind of—I converted actu-ally. But it was a very uh, superficial sort of conversion, I would say. It wasn't about religion. And the rabbi who I worked with knew that. He was a Reform rabbi. And he knew I was really doing it for the family and that it wasn't a religious conversion.

Anyway, so then—But this made Phil's parents happy. But for years, though, I really did feel like an outsider. It took me an awfully long time to feel that I belonged at all. And I didn't even belong in any full-fledged sort of way. But sort of belonged. I had a right to be there, after a while.

When we had two kids, and they first started school—They started going to Hebrew school. And after various ins and outs in trying to find the right school, my elder son was bar mitzvahed.* And this actually turned out to be quite an emotional experience for me. And even a wonderful experience. I thought it was a wonderful thing that happened for him. And as I began to understand what it was all about, it seemed so significant.

The thing that really stuck with me though, that really stuck out for me about it, was the idea of community. Of joining a community. That that was what this was about. And living here in a big city with all these things happening, one doesn't have a lot of community, a lot of the time. So when Peter was bar mitzvahed it was sort of Quakerlike. There were two things that happened that were amazing. One was that I was called up to do an aliyah.* And after that, after I said it, the rabbi—who was a woman—put her arm around me and said that I had been bar mitzvahed. Bat mitzvahed. That this was now my bat mitzvah as well. Which was kind of amazing. And that was much more emotional and real than when I had done this, what I would call semi-conversion.

I think it was because my son was part of this community. And it *was* a community. And then at the end of the ceremony—which took forever, [*laughs*] it took about three hours—people got up and said things to Peter. Individually. People in the audience. Whoever was there in the congregation, could just stand up and say whatever they wanted. And my son, who was a very quiet, shy kid, and had had some troubles in school, y'know, his life wasn't an easy life . . . And people got up and said the most wonderful things to him. And about him. It was *incredibly* moving.

One of the people was my mother. It was as if—It was as if the two cultures had finally come together. At least for that moment. We had the party afterwards. And it was at our house, and that was very nice. I guess it was my way of being me in this basically very Jewish tradition. And I know it was a little bit different than other people did theirs. It was just the way I do things. I guess.

And uh, yeah, I think that was a turning point in many ways. Both for me and for everybody. It was strange. To finally become—to feel that I became accepted. It took so many years to be accepted. And I often will tell people that my kids are Jewish. I remember when I was married to Phil, it was easier to say, "I'm part Jewish." In a funny way, I am, in part. I felt like I was. And now it isn't so true anymore because we're not married.

I never became religiously involved in Judaism. But I was very involved with my husband's family. Very close to them. And that part of his life meant a lot to me. It's a funny thing though. Because people don't really think you're Jewish if you're not born into Judaism.

Five seconds pass.

And I never thought that I really was. I just felt that I had this connection that was . . . that was special, that was different than other people's. I think it will be a part of my life all of my life. Well, it depends. It will depend a lot on whom my kids marry, and how they choose to live their lives.

Actually, the first year Phil and I were separated. I think it was just the first year. Oh, no [*smiling at the memory*] uh, the se—It must've been the second or third year afterwards—it was December. And all of a sudden I decided it was Chanukah. So . . . I created one of our traditional Chanukah dinners. Which was another thing that I had really loved. And we had always done it at my house and invited friends. It was just a really wonderful kind of evening time together. So I went through the whole thing. I guess I even made a brisket, which was traditional in Phil's family, and the potato latkes, and the whole thing. So I had this whole thing all done. We were all sitting down for dinner: Ellis—that's my husband—myself and my two boys. Aaaaand uh, after a little while [*smiles*] my son looked at me and said, "But this isn't Chanukah, Mom. Chanukah's *next* week!" [*laughs*]

I was a whole week ahead of time! I just had it completely off. But it was nice anyway. It was just . . . But it felt to me as if, "Oh! Of *course* I wouldn't know. This just shows that I'm not Jewish. And of course I would be a dope and not get this right." It was just kind of like, "Don't even try!" I shouldn't even try to do it, you know? So in fact I haven't done it since.

Her awkward smile fades.

This is . . . [*sighs*] I'm feeling all emotional. [*Her eyes well up with tears.*] Does this happen a lot? I suppose it does.

She takes a deep breath and clears her throat.

There's still a connection for me. It's really interesting that there really still is. Just yesterday, Ellis and I went to a guy's house to purchase a piano. Ellis had gone to see it, and he wanted me to come and see it. And he said, "This guy's really very interesting." He was Russian. And he was—He collected pianos. And he's an engineer. And he's a martial arts teacher. And he's really kind of an *interesting* person. And so that was really why I went, 'cause I thought, "This is going to be an interesting guy." [*laughs*] uh, 'cause I'm not very musical, and it really didn't matter if I heard the piano.

So we went—And I wondered beforehand if he might be Jewish. Because a lot of Russians *are* Jewish here. And I couldn't tell. I couldn't tell. But I was very interested in knowing. And I wanted to say to him—I wanted to know, and I wanted to tell him that I have a Jewish connection. 'cause I felt that something different would happen between us if he knew that. If he felt that. 'cause I felt that there was a sort of distance and so forth. I didn't know if it was a Russian demeanor or what it was. But I just had the feeling that you know, sometimes people just go: [*indicating surprise and pleasure*] "Oooh! . . ." You feel more comfortable. And I—I almost—I started to say something. But he didn't quite pick it up, and I decided to let it go.

It seemed a little odd. But that wanting to let somebody know that I have a connection with Jews, with Judaism, that people don't perceive by seeing me. Because I don't look the slightest bit Jewish, [*laughs*] right? Whatever that means. But I didn't know how to let him know. Comfortably. And I couldn't just ask him if he was Jewish. I didn't feel like just asking him if he was Jewish. But I really felt that it would have been a different—Something would've happened.

Primary Colors

———— ◡◠◡ ————

A winter's evening in Nick M.'s design studio on the second floor of a converted warehouse. Apart from the pool of light we're sitting in, the rest of the large high-ceilinged room is dimly lit, its far corners almost completely in shadow. On the desk behind Nick, colored geometric shapes contract and expand in the glow of a desktop screensaver. Left ankle resting on his right knee, Nick leans back in his chair and yawns. A tall man in his early forties, Nick's wearing black jeans and a black turtleneck sweater. A silver Star of David hangs from a necklace he wears on the outside of his sweater. I ask him how people react to it.

WELL, LATELY, PEOPLE DON'T REACT THAT OFTEN. Most people are fairly cool about it. Sometimes, they'll say things like, "So when did you convert?" And how I deal with that depends on my mood. Sometimes I don't answer at all. Once I said, "I've been Episcopalian six months now." [*smiles*] And I've also heard, "You're wearing what *appears* to be a Star of David . . . um . . . uh . . ." Obviously, I want people to see that I am black *and* I am Jewish.

MG: *How did you come to convert?*

Well, I grew up in Brooklyn, with, with a lot of Jewish friends, and by the time I was finished with high school, if I was with people who were black, or if I was with people who were Jewish, or the people I knew who were overlaps, I just felt at home. And over the years, I'd learned a lot about Judaism, just from being with Jewish friends, and in their homes, and so, it was kind of funny, because somewhere in college, at Brown, people in my house started teasing me, because when I was living in this co-op, there were like three or four people who were the sages, the sources of information about, not so hard halachic* things, or just stuff about the holidays. And I was one of them! [*laughs*]

And in a lot of intellectual ways, it also made perfect sense, because I knew that America—that the foundations of America were like, Indian burial mounds, and African backs. I knew that the Bill of Rights, the Declaration of Independence, had nothing to do with indigenous people, or me. And intellectually, I wanted to reject as much as possible of what had been shoved down our throats. But then also spiritually, I found that the stuff I was learning made sense.

Also, coincidentally, I was falling in love with a Jewish woman. Which has also been a constant . . . like, my first girlfriend in the summer after tenth grade was Jewish. And that sort of started, well, setting the jello. And there's one South African, who I was madly in love with, who I thought I'd marry, and I think she thought the same for a while, but it didn't work. We—we're still very close friends. I mean, she just called me a few days ago. But anyway, with her, like, her first language was Yiddish and her second language was like, Xhosa!

I don't know what it is. I like Jewish ethnic looks in general, but I particularly like them when they're darker Jewish ethnic looks. I want thick, curly dark hair, big dark eyes, you know, at least tan if not darker.

MG: *Why do you think you're so attracted to that one particular look?*

A lot of it is the girls I knew growing up. I was around a lot of colored girls. Some of them were black girls, of the entire spectrum, from as white as you to darker than me. I suspect that part of the thing is I've got this mixture in my head; I've got this image in my head of every favorite girl and woman I've ever known.

But also there's an aspect to the look—or looks—which just says "home," which says "familiarity," which is resonance. I don't know . . . Also, I feel at home among small bunches of black friends and acquaintances, and small bunches of Jewish friends, and small bunches of both. I just like being around, uh, well-informed, well-identified people who are black and Jewish, or Jewish and somewhat perspicacious, who know that in a very real way that the Jewish world is more than the German, Polish, Lithuanian, Russian bit that is presented as being the Jewish norm in the U.S.

And then it's just the United Nations thing: I like the confetti parties, I like the confetti rooms, I like being in a place where almost everyone *doesn't* have basic European or American functions. And so while I don't qualify as a separatist, I'm very particularist. I don't care to spend my time out in Des Moines. And I feel a little uncomfortable saying it, because I know that, particularly in today's climate, there are only too many people who are willing to say, "REVERSE RACIST!" But the fact is, that while a lot of people might be all right when you get them one-on-one, when you start getting bunches of them, they're just a bunch of fucking Americans, and I don't want to waste my time.

I think that this is one of the ways that Judaism attracted me, and Jews were attracted to me: I have affection for the Other and I like being around Others. And for me the two primary Others are African and Jewish, and in trying to make my social life, that's what I do.

And after that, I started thinking, then eventually I started grabbing some books about mixed marriages. You see, I had gotten to the point where I was mostly paying attention to Jewish women, to the point where I was thinking, "Well, if I ever get married, most likely it'll be someone who's Jewish." And then I started getting some books about conversion, and eventually I took classes with a Conservative rabbi. I did the two or so years of classes, which for me weren't very much work because I already knew seventy-five percent of what was in class.

It's funny, I was at dinner at a restaurant with Aviva the other week and, and a black guy, whose flavor of blackness I wasn't able to determine, walked in with this woman who might or might not be Jewish. I was pretty sure she was, and Aviva was pretty sure she wasn't. And this couple was sitting at the table next to ours. So Aviva and I had been saying something related to Shabbat, and I said, "Well, blah blah this and that, but it was two hours *after* havdalah* [and hence not desecrating the Sabbath], so it was OK. And the woman at the next table turned, just enough like, to prove it. "OK, that proves it!" [*delighted laughter*]

MG: *As someone who belongs to both communities, how do you feel about the tensions that exist between African-Americans and Jews?*

Obviously there are some problems between non-Jewish blacks and Jewish whites. But I think, by and large, when you get the idiots out of the way, we do fine. I see more Jewish-looking white faces smiling at me when I walk down the street than Anglo-looking white faces. And I see plenty of mixed couples where the white person looks like they might be Jewish. I know that I've heard fewer anti-Jewish remarks from black goyim* than I have from white goyim.

Now some people don't believe me when I say that. But, it's like they're informed only by TV, the political commentary they've been getting from people like Norman Podhoretz. Sure, as American Jews move to the suburbs —which a Latin friend of mine calls Blancolandia— they turn white, and the things that I've been saying become less true. They become just like other immigrants, becoming racist, and finding that black people fall short of the mark. They know less and less about being Jewish, less and less about the history of Jewish politics and almost nothing about black people. What I say is, some Jews are Jewish, some Jews are white.

But on the other side of things, the black kids I work with certainly know I'm Jewish, and certainly do not have a problem with that, and they're close to being the norm, whatever that happens to be.

They're living in mostly black neighborhoods, and they are very identified, and uh . . . it's fine.

But unfortunately, one of the main problems with this country is that Americans don't know history. They've got no grasp of nuance, and they have no imagination. So like after the OJ trial, most blacks say either, "He's innocent," or "I don't give a shit if he's innocent or not, I'm glad he got off." And white America goes, "BAAAAAH!! What's wrong with you? And words like that *prove* that you have no responsibility and can't be full-fledged citizens, and, it's just like Thomas Jefferson was always saying, and Jefferson was *right*."

I would say, "Imagine this. Dreyfus has just been acquitted. And every French Jew is jumping up and down and yelling and screaming in jubilation, and all the French goyim are saying, "What the fuck is wrong with you?" And Jewish whites, when I say this say, "No, it's not like that." I say, "What's the difference?" I say, "Just imagine, Leo Frank just got acquitted. Or the lynching began and he was rescued." And they still don't get it; they say, "Well, you're wrong, it's not like that."

I say, "How is it not like that? A group of people who grow up with the assumption that they will not receive justice see a situation where even if justice wasn't perhaps possible, that the justice system did what it was supposed to do." I try to avoid talking about it on Shabbat unless it's with people who know me really well because I'm so angry with this country, and you know, you're not supposed to ruin Shabbat, it's supposed to be a joyful day.

His tone becomes reflective.

I don't expect much to change. There'll be non-Jewish black people who know as little about Jews, Judaism, and Jews in America as most whites know about us, as people of color in this country, and there'll be a bunch of Jewish white people who are also totally uninformed. I don't see this country as gaining in depth, so I don't expect much to change.

You Wanna Keep
This Relationship?

⌘

I HOPE THEY GET MORE ASIAN BLOOD. Jewish people has many blood mix already, but not with Asian before. I think mixed blood is a good thing. It's more . . . more . . . less problem, y'know? Like, if all races mixed, how can you be racist? It's my idea.

> *Akira M. comes from Tokyo. He's a thirty-four-year-old actor who looks uncannily like an Asian Jeff Bridges. Akira met his American wife, Marcelle, while she was working in the Tokyo office of an international accounting firm. They've been married for two years. Six months ago, the couple came to the United States and now live in the Philadelphia Jewish neighborhood where Marcelle grew up. Her father is a cantor at a nearby Modern Orthodox synagogue.*

> *It's ten in the evening. Akira's shift at the soba bar where he works as a cook has just finished. He's just joined me in a booth, bringing two steaming bowls of buckwheat noodles. I ask him how he met Marcelle.*

We met in Tokyo night club. I couldn't speak much English, she couldn't speak much Japanese. I don't remember . . . maybe she asked me, or I asked her, just: "Dance with me." Then after that she said to me, next week it's her birthday, "Come to party," or something. And then normal way to make a relationship . . . [*laughs self-consciously*]

She told me a lot, but I could understand maybe a half, a quarter. Then after a few weeks, she asked me, "You wanna keep this relationship?"

"Yeah, I wanna keep it." Then she said, "All right, if you say that, you have to convert to Judaism." [*shrugs*] For me that question was: "What does she mean?"

I think my first contact with Judaism is in movie, when I was five or six years old: *The Ten Commandments*. Charlton Heston played Moshe. You know that scene from the Red Sea split? That is first contact. [*laughs*] But, for me it was, uh … Western people is Western people. I can't see who is Catholic, who is Wasps, who is Jews, who is Israel. Everyone, we call *gaijin san*, foreigner people, y'know?

So I said, "Yeah, sure. I don't mind." I didn't get so seriously at that time. At first, I got some books about Jewish history because it's easy for me to interest, to touch the history? Then after that, I've been to synagogue in Tokyo one Shabbat evening. Reform synagogue. Slowly, slowly, I was getting involved with Judaism. After six months or something that I been going to synagogue that must be Purim or Chanukah or something, then I tried to convert in Japan. I went to the rabbi's lecture to convert. And I also met there some Japanese women, they convert to Judaism because their husband is Jewish, Americans or Israelis. But basically, they not gonna believe God. It's like their duty or something. Or even they believe something, it's so far from concept of Judaism, like Jesus Christ. It's like pretending. I think their way is very light. Maybe for them, it's enough. For me, it's very serious thing. It's more deep.

Of course, when Marcelle told her parents, then they must be shocked their daughter get married with a Japanese guy. And especially her father, he's a religious, so it was very heavy thing for him. Yes, of course. But we explain I'm going to convert. Her mother also wants her she gets married with Jewish guy so . . . so . . . so my conversion's also for them. [*rapidly*] But basically my thing. It's my business. It's not for their business.

But we realized it's not gonna work, Reform conversion in Tokyo, because this community here is kind of traditional. So I find some private tutor. He's from Israel. He's super strong religious. He's not Chassidim or such type, but Israeli . . . like crazy! For example, he show me the Shabbat dinner or something. Suddenly, he become angry. [*laughs*] "Don't touch anything!" Because I'm not a Jew.

MG: *What couldn't you touch?*

Anything. Some wine, bread, or candles. Of course, I understand. I'm not gonna touch them. But even he didn't wanna shake my hand.

MG: *This was your teacher?*

Yes. [*laughs*] Because I'm goyim. He says, "You are not Jewish yet." He wanted to keep kosher everything in his house.

MG: *How did that make you feel?*

I'm student, he's master. Teacher master: I think it's a very Japanese idea. If teacher say something, student must follow his word.

So I study, and last December we come here for first time. I meet Marcelle father at airport. He was very nice. We shook hands. Not like tutor. [*laughs*] A small thing, but makes me feel relieved. And then I started Orthodox conversion. I'm studying with Rabbi Wolf. Very practical: morning prayer, evening prayer, and what is Tanach,* and what is Midrash,* and what is Talmud.* Kind of practical or knowledge things. I really wanna be a Jew, y'know what I mean? Because maybe next year, we're gonna have a kid, a baby. Then I wanna be a good Jewish father. Maybe for you it's strange. Of course, if mother is Jewish, the kid's Jewish. But maybe they're gonna leave from Judaism or Jewish, because of the father. I don't want that.

I believe Judaism is a religion, real religion, original religion. Christianity's only a cult from Judaism. And in Japan we also have an original religion. We call Shinto. You know Shinto? I think Shinto is very similar to Judaism. I think. It's very close to kashrut.* I also got a book from Israeli guy. It's called *Japanese Is a Lost —*

One of Lost Tribes. [*pensively*] hmmmmmmm . . .

In the beginning, sure, it's like political, family political stuff, but now it's my thing. Maybe I got involved so deeply already.

MG: *Do you attend synagogue services?*

uh, I want to go, but just now my job situation is—uh, doesn't let me go. I have to work Friday night, Saturday morning. But in the future if I stay here, I will ask to boss—I'm going to say just honestly, "I want to be a Jewish, so I have to keep commandments." I hope he understand. Maybe he's not gonna understand so well. But maybe I will work Sunday or something. Our economic situation is not so good right now.

MG: *Do you eat kosher?*

Well, basically, Marcelle and me, we're almost vegetarian. Usually, we're eating tofu and such thing and fish and uh, seafood.

MG: *Do you think you'll manage to stop eating seafood?*

[*rapid inbreath*] Aaaah! I don't know. It's very hard thing to stop. I *hope* I can stop. [*laughs*] For Japanese, it's kind of heavy thing. Of course, I'm not gonna eat pork or anything, but especially seafood is . . . like, from when I was small I keep eating.

MG: *Tell me, is there anything you really don't like about Judaism?*

Uh . . . a bit, how can I say? A bit macho. Like, men are better than women. And I don't like the concept you can't touch with your wife when your wife has period. It's uh, . . . I can't understand the concept, because Judaism is really, y'know, respect love, love of family, love of husband and wife. But that things I don't understand. And I'm not gonna follow it.

MG: *I suppose you've mentioned this to Rabbi Wolf?*

No! [*laughs*] I can't tell. [*blushes*] Maybe in future, after conversion. Now it's not possible. Maybe . . . I wanna talk with you again after my conversion. Maybe more . . . just now it's very . . . kind of . . . uh . . . Y'know what I mean?

Climbing the Mountain

———⌇———

Miriam Samra comes from Churachandpur in the Indian state of Manipur. She is a member of the Bene Menashe community, who claim descent from Manasseh, one of the Lost Tribes of Israel. Although Miriam's family practiced Judaism from her childhood, the Bene Menashe are not recognized as Jews unless they undergo formal conversion. Miriam went through giur—conversion—in Bombay in 1988. Five years later, when she moved to Israel, she was distressed to discover that her conversion was not recognized there.

Her husband, Myer, is an Iraqi-born anthropologist. The couple met in Israel in 1994, while Myer was researching the integration of the Bene Menashe into Israeli society. Miriam and Myer now live in Sydney, Australia.

MYER: The British took control of Manipur and Mizoram in 1891. And in 1894 the missionaries were allowed in to work among the hill tribes in Manipur, so Christianity took hold. And amongst the Chiu-Kuki congerie of tribes, you had the beginning of a sense of identification with the Israelites, the people of the Bible. Basically, the group themselves are relatively recent immigrants to the area. And they have a tradition taking them back through Burma to a part of China, and they've connected that up to the wanderings of the lost tribes in Assyria, crossing from Afghanistan then into China.

And so by the 1930s people were already seeing parallels between their own pre-Christian traditions and the Bible, and by around 1952 you had a guy in Mizoram, called Mela Chala, having a vision to say they are Israelites, and they have to return to Israel, to return to the practices of Judaism. But they didn't actually know what that implied. They didn't know whether Jerusalem was here on earth, or in heaven.

And so they sent out expeditions, looking for contacts. And found out that there *was* an Israel, and a Jerusalem, and made contact eventually with the Jewish communities in India, in particular with the Jews of Bombay. But these early groups were basically still followers of Jesus, as well as trying to follow the Sabbath and the festivals et cetera et cetera. But in the early seventies, some people began to call themselves Jews rather than Israelites, relating themselves to the early Jews who still had a belief in Jesus.

And they were very shocked to find that other Jews didn't. And then there was a crisis in the community. 1975 really is the time when you have a complete break between people who see themselves as Jews but still acknowledge Jesus as the Messiah, and another group who reject Jesus and continue in, I guess, a Jewish direction. And Miriam's family were one of the first to do so.

MIRIAM: I was a child. All I remember is that Mr. T. Daniel [*T. Daniel and Miriam's father, Joseph Jacob, had written a book asserting the tribe's Israelite origins*] went to Bombay and brought back a Sefer Torah.* And that was in Sukkot.* I still remember people dance and from that time I start to begin using Baruch, baruch Atah.*

MYER: Miriam's contact with born Jews, as they call them, didn't begin until 1988 when she went for giur in Bombay.

MIRIAM: After the conversion they say to me, "You want to say to your rabbi [*Rabbi Eliyahu Avichail, whose group, Amishav, searches for the Lost Tribes*] something?" I say, "Why not?" Then they give me a pen and I took the pen and write this to the rabbi. He was then in Israel. I still remember what did I say in the letter. I wrote not "Dear Rabbi." I wrote "Uncle." [*laughs*] "Uncle Rabbi."

[*laughs*] Then I said, "Now you know that you are not the only Jews. I too become a Jews now. So now I too can do what you can do." He wrote me a thanking letter and said, "I hope I will meet soon in Israel." I still keep the letter.

After the giur I asked the rabbi in Bombay, "What can we eat?" The rabbi said, "The only thing you have to do to be be kosher is stop eating meat," because we didn't have a shochet.* So when I come back home in 1988 I started to be a vegetarian. No meat at all.

I come to face a lot of problems with my friends. Being a teacher, every month the principal used to kill three, four chicken for the staff, specially. What the rabbi told me is, "If you want to eat, you must kill by yourself." So for me to kill a chicken I can't. [*laughs*] I just tell the principal, "So I will not eat."

Two times the principal's wife is quite happy. But on the third time she start to grumble at me, like a queen, like a Brahmin! I just went to my room and start crying to God. Whenever I had to face something because of my conversion I used to cry to God. "Why you don't want to take me to the land where I can enjoy with my fellow Jews?"

Miriam eventually traveled to Israel in 1993.

I—I was not in a good impression when I arrive in Israel. Because when I was in Manipur I was thinking that when I reach Israel people will be good and holy, and there will be no fighting. "Meeting a Jews, how much proud I am!"

But once we reached there, it become worse! Every news on TV we got a stab, killing, like that. I was surprised to see that there was non-Jews also. My thought was that in Jerusalem, which is a holy city, there will be only Jews. That was my thinking. But there were a lot of Thais, Filipinos we have seen. We went to the Kotel* and we saw lots of people like us. All these Filipinos.

And I was surprised to see a woman who was dressed not modest y'know. I was shocked to see those things in the Kotel. My impression was down. Depressing.

Also, they look at us like we are strangers. For us, we think that this is a homely land so we proud to be around. But they treat us like strangers and they will not take what we cook, because they said we non-Jew. Once I've been converted in Bombay, so I think I'm a Jews. But when I come down to Israel, they said it's not allowed for Jews to switch on and off the light on Shabbat but *we* can do. So I come to know that I am like a non-Jews, until and unless we got giur in Israel.

I was so depressed. I was so depressed . . . If I am living like a non-Jews then I better go back home. In Manipur I have a strong faith as a Jews and hold on my Jewsness. I follow halacha,* I follow the Shabbat, and I do everything what I can like the Jews. But now I've been treated so.

After that [*sighs*] I lost all faith, so to say. And I don't want to study, and I don't want to do anything, and just what I want to do is go back home. Because I have not been treated like a Jews. I shown my certificate of giur but they didn't accept that.

Then Rabbi Avichail gets to know about that and after six months I got giur. And after I got giur again I start to be very strong again. At that time only, I come to love, I come to be as nature again. In the yeshivah when we are giur, we become a Jews, we can take part like a Jews, we are no longer kept apart. We are not the only converts. They are from America, from New Zealand and from Switzerland, and from Britain. Compared to those we are not the less in religious way. We are not the less than others. We are strictly observant.

I'm proud, even though the beginning was such a terrible experience. I don't think any more I come from here and here, I just follow what the Jews follow. People may not call me a Jews but I have my faith in myself. And I am satisfied and content with what I am.

In 1996 Miriam and Myer moved to Sydney.

It's very nice here compared to Israel. Somehow in Israel people see differences in face, but here I enjoy a lot. I've been welcome as a Jews, which is my life. So I feel content. I've not been questioned, "Who are you?" "When did you become Jews?" "Are you a Jews?" I'm relieved from that questioning.

MYER: I think the fact that Sydney is more racially diverse is helpful, whereas in Israel, there is a racial and religious divide with the guest workers. So it *is* easier here. Everyone's been quite friendly to Miriam, she's been participating in shiurim* everywhere.

MIRIAM: Oh, I keep myself busy every day. Monday I go to Chassidic Women's Group, Tuesday, I went to Sephardi shiur where we study Ethics of the Fathers, and Wednesday I went to class, which we study about all the halacha,* halacha about what women will do according to the Jews. And Thursday I went to Hebrew class. And Friday, Friday is the busiest day for women, for preparation for Shabbat. That's only free day I have! [*laughs*] I enjoy a lot.

On Shabbat we normally go to Sephardi synagogue. I—I like it. I don't allow them to disturb me. If we are looking at people then surely people will talk to us, and so we have concentrate on my prayers, and people cannot disturb.

MYER: Yeah, on Yom Kippur I think it was, one woman came to greet Miriam and Miriam continued with her prayers and didn't look at her.

MIRIAM: Because I'm reading Slichot.* But later I said, "I'm sorry, I cannot talk to you during the prayer because if I take away my eyes to talk to you, then I lost my prayer. Very sorry." She was quite happy. [*laughs*] That is life.

The worst part is finished. That is just like climbing the mountain, but now we are among the people, we are a Jews now. I'm proud to be being Jews. We are high in spiritual level; we are above all, we can say, not in worldly pleasures, which is going to finish in no time, but in spirituality, in the world to come. That much I can know about my experience.

Doing the Right Thing

Being Jewish has not been easy for Gidon Druery.

IN THE LAST SIX MONTHS OR SO, I've come to realize that I think I need to talk things out, and maybe professionally. Because the way of coping, the strategies I've been using, are damaging to myself and to others. I can remember many times being in real pain, and blaming Tamara for things. It was Tamara's fault basically, "I didn't choose to convert. It's something she thrust upon me," that sort of garbage, right? That doesn't help. Blame's not a good tactic. Doesn't solve my problems, doesn't make me feel better. If anything, it removes me from trying to solve the problem, just leaves me depressed and withdrawn and sulking. Which is pointless.

> *Phillip Druery met his wife, Tamara, when they were both teachers at a Sydney Jewish day school. Before they married, Phillip underwent an Orthodox conversion, taking the name Gidon. The couple now have two children and a son from Gidon's first marriage. Two years ago, Gidon became the principal of Mandelbaum House, a Jewish residential college of the University of Sydney. We're talking in his office.*

When Tamara's parents found out I was seeing their daughter, there was this very sort of formal interview. We actually went to a restaurant. Basically, her father said, "Whatever ideas you have, forget them!" And I was not invited into their home at all. My wife's grandparents in fact were the ones who initiated contact. They wanted to find out a bit more about me, and whether conversion was a possibility. They sort of laid the groundwork, I suppose. They were the first people to accept me. I mean, I was already teaching in the community, so there was that acceptance as a person, but not as a Jew. And their next step was to convince my in-laws to invite me into their house.

But I remember that first dinner with my wife's sister, Tamara's sister, not speaking to me, her brother speaking to me in a very uncomfortable way, and her parents desperately trying to feel happy about the situation.

And later on, after the conversion, I can remember one of my wife's cousins making a statement to the effect that really, their criterion about whether I was Jewish or not had to do with my level of observance. So then there's the quesion of, "Well, at what point will I satisfy your criteria?"

I guess that's part of the dilemma. It's a question of, "To what extent am I accepted?" I suspect in fact my reason for taking on the task of running a Jewish college here has really been a matter of somehow making a mark, and hence proving that "You've gotta accept me now," something like that.

I'm not sure it's made any difference to my in-laws though. I would've expected them to ring me up and congratulate me when I got the job. But their reaction was quite strange. It was like . . . they were perplexed: "Why was this job given to Gidon?" It's like, "There are all sorts of people in the community who could've filled this position. Why Gidon? Who's he?"

But you know, to what extent do *I* accept myself as a Jew? How fake am I in my conversion? There was an enormous amount of pressure to convert. And of course, people, when they hear I'm the principal of a Jewish college, make all sorts of assumptions: number one, that I must have been born Jewish, and number two, that I must be a fairly religious person. And that's a little uncomfortable, you know. I sometimes wonder if I'm supposed to be.

Have I made the mark? Am I seen to be doing the right things? Am I presenting the Jewish faith in the right light? I'm actually a spokesman for it in a way. I'm an ambassador in a certain sense.

But I often feel, "Hang on, don't ask me, 'cause I'm not an authority." And yet, there are many Jews I come across, and I feel as if I know much more about Judaism than they do. When one converts, one learns a lot. So it's quite right that I'm an authority but I guess it comes back to the question of what's emotional and what's intellectual. I guess I don't feel emotionally I'm an authority.

On Sunday, somebody who wasn't Jewish said to me, he said, "Your name is an interesting name. 'Gidon' says that you're Jewish, 'Druery' says that you're Irish, and I can't put the two together."

I said, "Perhaps you're right." That's all. "Perhaps you're right."

Gidon lightly taps his lower teeth against his upper lip.

The other aspect that has made this process so much more difficult is what happens to your family, that is my non-Jewish family. I was born into a fairly religious Christian family. My parents are churchgoers, and that's the most important thing in their lives. They're Evangelicals, so it's sort of fundamental Christianity as well, that's another aspect of it. Certainly, I wasn't happy with that version of Christianity myself, so there isn't a sense of a lost faith or anything like that, but it has made life a lot more uncomfortable for them as well. "What did we do wrong? Our son, born into a good Christian family, should convert to Judaism?"

And certainly, the relationship between us is not so comfortable either. I've tried to include them in things to whatever extent I can, and often end up feeling, "This was a big mistake."

My son having a bar mitzvah.* Obviously, you have to invite— Well, it was a meaningful event for us, and I felt that they needed to be included in what was happening to their grandson. But I'm not entirely sure whether it wasn't a personal statement by me . . .

[*softly*] This is all very cloudy. I thought my father would behave, at least to the extent of saying congratulations, but his only comment on it after the—the shul* service was, "It's a pity it's in Hebrew."

There was nothing personal in the comment at all. It's was like, "Let's not talk about this, let's talk about it as if it's just something out there." My mother went at one stage to introduce herself to the rabbi, and to go and shake hands. Of course, he didn't shake hands with her, being an Orthodox rabbi, and her response to that was to burst into tears.

And now, I don't know if I can include them in Jewish events. I feel it's too upsetting for them. It's likely to make them upset or feel excluded. It's certainly going to produce anxiety in me. I don't think that's ever going to settle down. I don't think there's anything I can do or say that's going to convince anyone one way or another. [*very softly*] What am I trying to say? There are two things I want to tell you. I can't—I'm not objective about what any of this means, but let me just tell you what the events were because I think it does throw light on things, on some of the conflicts.

My sister was married last year. And one of the circumstances— She chose to have her wedding on Kol Nidre,* not knowing . . . that that was what it was going to be. And that put me in a bind. What was I going to do? See, I mean her fiancé called me and said, "Look, you've got to make a choice. You've got to forget religion for once and really choose family. You really should be here."

I didn't appreciate him saying that, but in fact he was right. Well, not right, but there was the choice. What was I going to do? I don't think I would feel comfortable with people in the community knowing that on Yom Kippur I was going doing something else. I certainly wouldn't want the college board of management to know that. But I have a sister who's being married, and this is a very important event in her life, and I wanted to be a part of it. So there was a lot of conflict in me which went on for many weeks. I remember my sister calling me and saying, "I think you believe that we chose to put the wedding on Yom Kippur in order for you not to be there." [*sighs*] So I had to deal with those things. So, anyway, what I did, I decided to go to the wedding. And I thought, "Well, how can I be — How can I cover my tracks so it's not too bad?"

So I went to the wedding, and then afterwards I went to a synagogue which was within walking distance of college. One of the board of management was there, I actually sat next to him. No problems. And afterwards, I thought, "Well, what was all the hassle about?" I mean, if someone had seen me at the wedding, there might have been problems. But most of it was just constructed in my head. And it was the right thing to do. I made the right decision.

What was strange though, was at no point did I think of my wife going to the wedding. And she didn't. And afterwards, because it seemed so easy to do, there was a lot of resentment in me. "Why didn't she come? This was so easy." And of course for her there was not even a question of risk to be considered.

This is why I feel my parents have been taken away. Because there isn't two sides to it. It's like Judaism to some extent feels like it's uncompromising. No one in the Jewish community is going to make allowances for my family. I have to go *their* way. I guess that's what this story's about.

Sometimes though, I feel I can't continue to live this pretense. I can't satisfy everybody, I've got to make some choices. It comes back to me making some choices for myself. But I haven't got there yet. I don't know if I can necessarily resolve all the conflicts. But I can perhaps come to live more comfortably with the choices I've made. I don't know.

A Thousand-Miles-
an-Hour Man

At a fashionable sidewalk café off Atlanta's Peachtree Avenue with Matt B., who runs a Jewish dinner-dating service. In contrast to the traditional image of the shadchan—Jewish matchmaker—often portrayed as an aging, down-at-heel schemer, thirty-four-year-old Matt is a golden-haired picture of casual elegance in a Tommy Hilfiger polo shirt, cream slacks, and gleaming cherry pennyloafers. But he seems distracted and a little agitated, repeatedly scanning the street, as if he's looking for someone. The smooth flow of talk, however, is unaffected.

MATCHMAKING OF COURSE IS THE THIRD OLDEST PROFESSION in the history of our people. Did you know that?

MG: *I didn't.*

Do you know what the oldest is?

MG: *It's the one that you don't need a shadchan for, right?*

No, no. That's the *second* oldest. That's the second oldest. The oldest is taxi driving.

MG: *Taxi driving?*

Right. How else would all the girls get to their clients if they didn't have taxis? [*laughs*] No. Seriously. I started about five or six years

266

ago. I was married, and we were putting on a dinner every Friday night, and inviting friends of ours for dinner. Many of them were single. It just happened that sometimes people would meet and . . .

A waiter refills our water glasses.

Thanks. And it just went from there. And it went out of control! To a dinner for forty people with two professional chefs cooking Thai or Chinese cuisine. Kosher, of course.

And we've generated lots of marriages. And a lot of relationships, and a lot of friendships. You just show up at seven-thirty, pay thirty-five bucks, we'll seat you next to a suitable lady or gentleman and you just, ah, let magic take its course.

He waves to a couple strolling on the other side of the street.

[*to me*] Two friends of mine there.

[*shouting*] Hi! Good to see ya! How ya doin'? All *right!!*

[*to me*] I know a lot of people, y'know. [*resuming a more authoritative tone*] If someone does marry out, I hope they're happy. But I would prefer to see people marry in the faith. In Hebrew there's a prayer. It's only a couple of words, three words, and it's sung in every synagogue when we lift the Torah in our hands. We say, "*Eitz chayim hi*: This [*sic*] is the Tree of Life." Now every time a Jewish family is formed in a Jewish marriage, it's as if the Tree of Life grows more branches. And every time someone marries *out* of our faith, then it's like you snap a branch off the tree. Not only do you injure the tree, you, uh—The tree will ultimately die.

Every time I think of the Holocaust, it gives me a burning desire to do something. Six million. I don't know anybody who's ever driven six million miles. I don't know whether any ship has ever sailed six million miles, any plane has ever flown six million miles. Six million is unbelievable. A regime killed six million of our people. And yet it only happened fifty years ago. A blink of an eyelid. And for this reason and more: the Spanish Inquisition, pogroms in Czarist

Russia . . . the . . . the rise and fall of ancient Rome . . . ancient Egypt, from *all* the history of our people I'm out there doing it. I do what I can. And what I can do is do something for Jewish continuity.

There are—Excuse me. Renee! Hi! How *are* you?

He leaves the table to talk to a tall tanned woman in her early thirties.

Five minutes later.

So yeah, my best achievement record is forty-seven people for dinner, and five engagements resulting. One couple broke up since, but the other four got to the line.

[*putting his hand over the tape recorder*] Hey, just hold it. Here's a client. Hello. Hi.

A *woman passes by with a quick smile.*

Of course, I'm not the only one doing it. Everyone's doing it. I just happen to do it a little more publicly. [*to another passerby*] Hello. [*laughs*] I feel like I'm a goldfish in a goldfish bowl. I've ignored about ten people I know that've walked past.

MG: *You know a lot of people. You're a busy guy. What do you do to relax?*

Relax? I'm a thousand-miles-an-hour man. I've got a million and one things to do. I've gotta go here, go there, do this, write this, fix this, fax that. The woman that I was talking to just now. You saw her. I told her that I've got a guy that I want her to meet. When we're through here, I've gotta make some calls to fix her up.

MG: *OK. I won't keep you long. By the way, are you still married? Something you said before made me think—*

I'm not spoken for. I had a four-year lease with no options to renew. But we're on good terms.

MG: *You must have a lot of opportunities to meet people.*

If it happens . . . if something falls into my lap—no pun intended—so be it. But if I met someone and it precluded me from working on Jewish continuity, I wouldn't be in the relationship for more than a day.

OK. I gotta go make that call. If you wanna talk more, call me. If you wanna do more, different angle, different approach, call me.

Too Good-Looking

A warm evening in late June. From the square below, the scent of lime trees wafts up to the balcony of Nadia H.'s fifth-floor flat in Bayswater, London. Nadia's wearing a black T-shirt and blue jeans. Her fair hair is tied in a pony tail. Between us on the seat of the glider, a glass bowl containing a freshly-cut mango.

My first boyfriend was Jewish, and someone I'm seeing now is Jewish, but sort of like in fifteen years or something, since I was sixteen, seventeen, no one else has been.

She spears a mango cube with a toothpick.

I don't think I would've gone out with a Jewish guy two or three years ago. I haven't been very impressed with the Jewish men I've met. They seem very conservative, the way they see the world, their values and attitudes. They don't match with mine. I know I'll end up having an argument. Or it's boring. They're not risk takers. I've always been very attracted to physical men. I think I've . . . matured a little bit because I've moved beyond that. Have some more mango.

Both of us skewer cubes.

Just didn't find that Jewish men were very physical. Israeli men are. But they're not . . . very stable emotionally. Well, that's just my experience. And Jewish men don't like *me*. If I go out with — I have a very close friend of mine, Tanya, who's blonde — not

Jewish—and if we meet in a group, the Jewish guys all go for her! She's just had an affair with a Jewish guy. And I explained it to her: it's upward social mobility for these guys. They're attracted to Waspy blondes. And she likes *them*. Thinks they're sensitive, intelligent, good in bed.

But . . . my experience is very limited . . .

She pauses to think.

Mm . . . I actually *have* had another relationship with a Jewish guy, now I come to think about it. Someone I met through work. He's a guy called . . . uh . . .

MG: *I always change the names in the final version.*

No, no. I'd *like* to name him. He's called George Varga. And he's sort of a very self-important, pompous solicitor. And he's from a Czech background, and Jewish. But he used to spend his time denying that he was Czech *or* Jewish. And used to hate the fact that I would bring it up all the time. And he always said that being involved with Jewish women was disastrous. And certainly our relationship was a disaster, but that was because he was so . . . so fucked up, basically. The relationship was very one-sided. He was much more attracted to me than I was to him. He was very neurotic.

MG: *And what do you think he thought about you?*

Oh, I didn't do anything that would constitute sort of zany or off-the-wall behavior. And anyway, he was very uncomfortable about being Jewish. Had a huge chip on his shoulder. Almost anti-Semitic in his views. If there was something not quite right with the relationship, he'd say, "Oh, it's because you're Jewish." You know, he'd rather be involved with an Anglo. Really fucked up.

I'll tell you something else that happened recently: I went to a singles' group. The thing is, up until a year ago, I wouldn't be seen dead at those things. No way, it's just too nerdy for words. Going to a singles party, number one, and number two, going to a singles party full of *Jews?* My absolute worst nightmare.

But I went to one, a dinner party thing. And you know what? I quite enjoyed it, so—The guy I'm seeing now, I actually met there. So it is possible to meet someone you're attracted to. But it was interesting what the reactions were. A couple of guys said to me, "When you walked in the door, I felt, 'She couldn't be Jewish.' You're just too good-looking to be Jewish."

It's interesting the low self-esteem that Jews have about being Jewish, and looks and things like that. It's crazy stuff. And another guy, a Jewish guy who went out with Tanya said to her, "I really like your arse. Jewish women have big arses." I thought, "What a fucking moron!" "How *dare* he say that!" I mean, he's got a big arse himself. [*laughs*] I actually confronted him about it a year or two later. He was very embarrassed. He said, "Well, they *do.*" I said, "Well, I haven't, thank you very much." And anyway, big arses can be sexy, can't they? So he's another guy that's hung up about being Jewish or with Jewish women.

A distant car alarm whistles.

Anyway . . . So where did you grow up?

MG: *Manchester.*

Oh, really? My friend Warren Glass lived in Manchester I think. You don't know him? No. Or the Margolises?

MG: *Teddy and Jonathan?*

No. Tony and Pam.

MG: *No. But I mean, I haven't lived there for ages.*

Oh, right. And, uh, . . . your background's Russian, is it?

MG: *Well, all my great-grandparents were from that part of the world.*

But your hair. I mean, you must be originally from Spain. I mean, your family. You're dark, and you've got, like some Israelis, sort of curly hair. So you must be like, directly descended from the Jews who were expelled from Spain. It's attractive. I think men and women with hair like that is an attractive look. Sort of Israeli, isn't it? Sort of Sephardi. It has that Sephardi look. Yes . . . Can I get you something else to drink or something?

The Full Circle

———— ✧ ————

Monday morning, Skokie, Illinois. In Cecile Y.'s kitchen. Water's boiling.

OK. We've got chamomile, lemon, red zinger, or . . . decaff, caffeinated, instant, filter—

MG: *Majorly caffeinated filter, thanks.*

Cup or mug?

MG: *Mug, please.*

You want, "Happy Birthday"? "Computersaurus"? "Has anyone seen my sanity"? Or just plain?

> *Cecile grew up in Skokie, a Jewish neighborhood on Chicago's north side. As a teenager in the early 1980s, she hated living there. Her relationships with Jewish boys were always so difficult. For one thing, she could never understand why her dates weren't interested in sex. Now she's older and wiser . . .*

Being gay in the Jewish community was like . . . it's a big stigma. I had three boyfriends that were gay. Julian came out when he was twenty. He had this Rocky Horror birthday party, and we all put on wigs, three-inch lipstick and eyeliner, dressed up in high heels and fishnet stockings. It was an amazing party. And he told his parents that night. And they were devastated. But at least he told them.

My other friend Richard was way, way down in the back of the closet. I went out with Richard for nine months when I was twenty. I tried to like, to get him into bed. I was really crazy about him. I'd met him at camp. He was a really nice Jewish guy. I knew his parents, they were good friends of my parents. And I used to think, "What is *wrong* with me?" I said to him, I said, "Richard!" We have been dating for nine months. You are one of the sweetest guys I've ever met: you're cute, you're polite, you're intelligent, you're cultured, you take me to good restaurants, you take me to nice movies." I said, "What is it? I DON'T EVEN GET A GOODNIGHT KISS OUTA YOU!!!"

And he said, [*whispers*] "I just can't handle that kinda thing."

And then, I found out, about two years later. I met a Jewish girl he'd dated for about a year. And I said to her, "What's with Richard? I dated him for nine months, you dated him for a year, Diane. Tell me . . ."

And she said, "Oh, didn't you know he's gay?"

And I said, "So, it's not me . . ." [*theatrically wiping a hand across her forehead*] Pheeeee-ooooo! Relief! [*laughs*] I'm normal!

Y'know, I thought, "Is it that I'm totally unattractive to men?" Then I found out he was gay. Thank God! Y'know what I mean? But he was such a great guy. And when his parents finally found out, I think it destroyed them. He kept that secret for so many years. And eventually, the only way he could get away with being gay was to go and live somewhere on the West Coast. It's sad, but that was all part of the claustrophobia, and the gossip in the Jewish community. Maybe it's better now, I don't know.

After graduating from college, Cecile moved to Portland, Oregon, where she taught elementary school. A few weeks after arriving, she met Bill. He wasn't Jewish. But he was straight. Seventeen years later, Cecile still considers their relationship the most exciting she's ever had.

Oh, he was like a prince. He had those very goyishe* looks. The high cheekbones, gorgeous hair, greeny eyes. Tall and sexy, and cute, and shy, and just plain drop-dead go-o-o-o-rgeous! And what made it even more exciting was that he was forbidden fruit. I'm not supposed to be doing this! It was one big adrenalin hit.

> Cecile's adrenalin hit lasted for three years until she discovered that Bill was involved with someone else. Six months later, Cecile and Bill finally broke up. The following year, she returned to Skokie and the Jewish social scene she had once found so claustrophobic.

I had four marriage proposals in the space of six months.

Why am I so popular, Michael? Four marriage proposals from four extremely nice Jewish guys. One had his own computer company, one was an opthalmologist, another was in advertising. Very well established, really great Jewish guys. Two of them were quite serious relationships . . . Well, all of them could have been serious.

Like, the opthalmologist was crazy about me. We were having dinner in this restaurant —at this really neat Greek place in the Loop— and he brought out this ring, this beautiful, expensive engagement ring, and he said, "Cecile—" And he was like, a genius, too: he'd graduated top of his class at Harvard Med School. And he said, "Can I make it any clearer than this? I really want to marry you."

And I said, "I—I can't take this ring off of you." I said, "Eliot, I just can't marry you." I mean, we hadn't even been to bed together! I couldn't face the idea. I mean, the thought of him physically made me gag.

I said, "I just can't marry you, I'm still in love with Bill." Which was also true. And he was devastated; he'd even taken me to Philly to meet his parents.

But it was different with Arthur. I decided the night I met Arthur that I was going to marry him. I thought, "He's a good guy. He's responsible, he's a realtor, got his own company too. As people, we get on well. Like, even if I had no physical relationship, even if he was just my friend, I would never have a bad word for him. I could live with this guy for fifty years."

So after six weeks or so, I said, "Arthur, we're gettin' married." [*gulping*] "We are?" I said, "Yep." And he said, "Done deal." I said, " Are you in love with me?" He said, "Yeah. I'm meshuga* about you. Completely."

He said, "Are you in love with *me?*"

And I said, "Nope, not really." I said, "Arthur, I don't know if I'll ever be in love with you, I don't know if I'll ever be in love with anybody again."

Because I'd told him about Bill. I'm very straightforward with people. Everything that's on this tape you could tell Arthur, he'd say, "Yeah, yeah, I know all that stuff."

And we've been married now for fifteen years. We've just had our fifteenth anniversary. And we still get on very well. And believe me, Arthur is very boring, traditional, predictable, but he's also a very good person. And he loves me. I'm forty pounds overweight, and he loves me; I can treat him like absolute garbage—I mean, I wouldn't—and he'd love me; behave like a total bitch—which I don't most of the time—and he loves me! Even if I scream at him, and tell him he's an idiot and an asshole, he loves me!

And he's a good provider and a wonderful father. He cares about our kids' Jewish education. He's a decent, good man. He's polite to everybody, he treats my mother better than she deserves . . . I mean, he's a good person. All my friends are jealous, all of them. And he's Jewish! With Arthur and me, it's the same neshuma,* the same soul.

If there's something on the news about Israel, or the Jewish community, suddenly we're both focused. When I was with Bill, he used to say, "What do you care about what's happening in Israel?

You're not Israeli." With Arthur, I don't have to make excuses. I don't have to be reserved and quiet, and white bread. If I want to be loud and bombastic and emotional and whatever . . . I can. I can be me, one hundred percent me.

Arthur actually said to me once, he said, "If Bill showed up tomorrow, would you go off to a motel some place with him?" I said, "I sure would!" He said, "Gee, I like your honesty."

Michael, I did the full circle, grew up with it all, got sick of it, got away from it, then realized that what—I—am—is—what—I—am.

So Many Different Customs

A summer Sunday morning in Bob and Etta P.'s apartment in Phoenix, Arizona. Etta teaches English in a Jewish day school. Bob is a tax accountant. They're both twenty-five years old. Outside the window, the cascading branches of a willow tree. Inside, curves also predominate. Clockwise around the circular dining table: Bob with his skullcap, horn-rimmed glasses, and frequent broad smiles; Etta, with rollercoaster eyebrows, a paisley-pattern dress, arms folded in a figure of eight; baby Joshua, asleep in his basinet on the floor. Etta and Bob met when they were eighteen-year-old counselors at a Bnai Brith summer camp. They were married three years later.

ETTA: We'd always wanted an open-air wedding, so we had it in the park next to the shul.* It was just amazing. Like, when I arrive, everyone's singing; these friends of Bob's were singing—"Sunrise, Sunset"—but without the words; we thought that would be too kitsch! And then they bring Bob dancing towards me . . . And everyone does a different shtick: a carriage to push us round on, a maypole, glitter, balloons, Donald Duck costumes, sunflowers hats . . . Ah, no. [*laughs*] No, the sunflower hats were at my friend Michelle's wedding . . . Getting 'em mixed up!

And it's all dancing. You come into the service dancing, you dance in the middle of it, you dance afterwards.

279

BOB: You're in training for six weeks.

ETTA: Then there's the jump rope. They tie napkins together, and make a rope and then the bride and groom jump rope together. The rabbi did it too. Then everybody put their arms together and Bob threw himself into their arms, and they tossed him in the air . . .

BOB: And caught me.

ETTA: And then the rabbi did it too —

BOB: And my father —

ETTA: Everyone gets totally involved; it's not just the young people, the parents, the rabbi —

BOB: Like he was standing on the table, at one point, conducting the band. And everyone's clapping, and he's like —

ETTA: And he's fifty-five years old! And he's launching himself off the table [*mimes an arms-akimbo leap*] —

BOB: And people caught him.

MG: *This is the rabbi?*

BOB: No, this is my father.

ETTA: Well, the rabbi did it too . . . The rabbi was really into it. He was balancing a bottle on his head. It wasn't formal at all, just very, very heimishe.* But the most emotional thing is before the chuppah.* The fathers bless the bride. And then Bob took the veil down.

MG: *The veil?*

BOB: Right. I'm danced down to the bride by my friends, and Etta's sitting there with all her friends, on a big chair, like a kinda throne, and I have to pull the veil down — to check she's the right one, make sure they haven't done a switch. [*winks*]

ETTA: That was like, *really* emotional. We hadn't seen each other for a week.

MG: [*smiling*] *You had an argument?*

ETTA: [*laughs*] No, no, no. This is the custom. We'd spoken on the phone every night—every day, for like, five million hours, but we hadn't actually *seen* each other. And the guys are dancing him up, and you haven't seen each other for a week, and the buildup is really intense . . .

My grandmother was sitting next to me, crying her eyes out. And then Bob pulls the veil down. And he said to me—

BOB: [*in a stage whisper*] "Do we really have to go through with this?"

ETTA: [*vexed*] This is not him! This is not him. He's just saying that for the tape.

BOB: [*with an exaggerated shrug*] I was nervous. Lot of people, big moment. What's wrong with that?

ETTA: And then there are the Seven Blessings; and we had seven different people to say them, and then there's the chuppah. Some customs, the two mothers walk the bride to the chuppah, and the two fathers walk the groom. Which I didn't want. But Bob's parents—[*she colors*] Well, we won't get into that . . . There was a bit of family politics . . . I mean, there are so many different customs.

BOB: And as I was walking to the chuppah, my friends were singing "B'lavi, mishkan evni: In my heart, I will build a sanctuary." And the girls [*his forehead corrugates*] . . .

ETTA: I can't remember either. We'd have to see the video. I just remember Mom standing on the train of my dress. [*smiles*] And then as soon as I come up, I walked around Bob seven times . . . But I wasn't counting—I was just out of it—and one of rabbis said I'd done seven, and the other said, "Nope. She needs to do one more."

BOB: And the dress is so long, it gets wrapped around the groom. Unless someone's there to carry it.

ETTA: And so my mother and mother-in-law were walking round behind me holding the train. So I went round one more time.

BOB: And her mother's like, walking round me seven times, hissing in my ear, "So you're gonna look after my daughter, right?" It was pretty scary.

ETTA: She's not scary. [concerned] Do you really think she's scary? You talking about . . .

BOB: [smiling] No, I'm just kiddin'. Just a mother-in-law joke. Jewish mother-in-law joke. And, uh . . . the ring has to be worth the value of an ancient coin called a pruta. Which apparently isn't worth much.

ETTA: It's not supposed to be ostentatious.

BOB: And the rabbi says, "Is this your ring?" and "Is it worth a pruta?" I said, "It is."

MG: [I look at the gold band on Etta's finger.] He didn't ask to see the receipt?

BOB: Fortunately not.

ETTA: And he actually puts it on this finger [indicating a bare forefinger], but I changed it later on. And after that we were holding hands, we didn't let go after that . . . [smiles] And I'm forgetting of course, the blessing on the wine, and the reading of the ketuba,* and then the rabbi talks, and you give your speech, break the glass [commemorating the destruction of the Temple in Jerusalem]. Then everyone shouts, "Mazel tov!"

And they start singing again. Well . . . our friends do; some of my dad's family aren't so frum* and don't know the songs. And then at the end, we danced away, and we spent time just the two of us, in this room in the shul. It's a custom, you're supposed to have food together in this special room.

BOB: We'd both been fasting to that point. There's a custom that your wedding day is like Yom Kippur.*

ETTA: [laughing] But they knocked on the door about two seconds after we got in, because we were behind schedule. I was actually late arriving. It was my bridesmaids' fault, because they were so nervous and kept having to go to the bathroom. And then afterwards they had to have their cigarettes. So I was late. And my father was outside platzing* because you have the whole schedule with the photographers, and the signing of the civil stuff.

And then after that we danced, and then there was dinner, and speeches, and more dancing.

BOB: Yeah. We didn't get away till around one in the morning, and then we stayed at the Hilton. Arranged to check out around three the next afternoon, and then at six we had the first of the dinners.

ETTA: It's the Sheva Brachot.* What happens is that each evening for a week friends host you to dinner. And it's a great idea: 'cause you don't get any sense of anticlimax. And every night they did a different theme. Like the first night was Tex-Mex, then it was Chinese, then . . . What did Ron and Vivian do?

BOB: I don't remember. Indian?

MG: *What were you doing during the daytime?*

ETTA: Unwrapping presents, getting our apartment organized.

BOB: Getting our furniture in, setting up bank accounts, basic administration.

ETTA: [with delight] And like, being there, and saying, "It's ours. This is really ours!"

BOB: And then we flew down to Acapulco.

ETTA: And that was also like, amazing with a capital A. We arrived with all these boxes of kosher food. Like, we had a week's supply of bread! And the guy at customs, he said, "You no like Mexican food?"

BOB: [*laughing*] "You no like tortillas?"

ETTA: It was a total riot!

Every Step Along the Way

<hr />

Tom P. and Brian U. are both in their late thirties. Tom runs a marketing company; Brian is a physician. They've been married for two years. It's eight P.M. and David, their fourteen-month-old son, is already in bed. During the course of our hour-and-a half-long conversation, their answering machine records eight phone calls. One is from Tom's mother, who is a member of a local Conservative synagogue. Tom and Brian are also members but still ocassionally attend the gay and lesbian congregation where they first met.

TOM: My sister was past president, and Brian had been a service leader, and very, very involved for ten years or more. And Jean— My sister Jean had been encouraging me to come: "Come and meet somebody nice!" And so I went. And going to temple on a Friday night means you get dressed, and so I got dressed, you know, appropriately. And was alone in that. [*laughs*] You know, there were people there with no shoes on. Which was a revelation. [*smiles*]

And we were sitting a couple of seats away but didn't see each other. Auditorium-style seating. But Brian has a beautiful singing voice. And I said, "Gee, there's a beautiful singing voice somewhere over there." And then after services there's a Kiddush* and people mingle—I'm sorry, an Oneg Shabbat*—and people mingle around.

And I was standing by a group of people, not really knowing anybody, just listening in, and Brian came over. He and my sister had known each other for many years. And he and Ruth, my sister-in-law, had been friends for about ten years or more. And he was coming over, and was so tired that he didn't say anything, just came over and leaned against the wall.

He turns to Brian and smiles.

BRIAN: Just immobile . . .

TOM: Friday night after work is hardly the best time to meet. But we did meet. And we went out for coffee. And that was the beginning of this happy relationship.

BRIAN: That's right. Five years ago.

The answering machine message beeps for the third time in fifteen minutes. It's Tom's mother asking how David is.

TOM: [*smiles*] Every day, same time, unless she's here, of course. I'll call her later. So yeah, it was five years ago this January.

MG: *And eventually you decided to get married.*

TOM: So uh, yeah, it felt completely right to both of us. It seemed just the next logical step. We put together—Brian writes beautiful services, and worked very hard on this with a wonderful rabbi, Rabbi Rachel Green. We had spoken to a few rabbis, but we really connected with her.

BRIAN: Actually the majority of rabbis wouldn't take on, wouldn't preside, from an Orthodox rabbi to one Conservative rabbi.

TOM: The rabbi at our local synagogue didn't even attend our wedding, though invited. We invited them for social reasons because, uh, his wife particularly has been a big part of my parents' life, and it just felt right to invite them.

We didn't ask him to officiate, knowing that it might present a conflict. But Rabbi Levine chose not to attend. And he didn't talk to us about it, right up to the very end when he said, [*disapprovingly*] "that his very attendance could be interpreted as condoning our marriage, which the Rabbinical Assembly [*organization of Conservative rabbis*] wouldn't approve of." But his wife attended. She was her own person, distinctly.

BRIAN: Interestingly, one Reform rabbi said he had no problem presiding at a *gay* Jewish ceremony, but would not at an interfaith ceremony—

In his room, David whimpers softly.

We took the basic outline of the wedding ceremony, took some material, reinterpreted some material, got ideas from an outline of gay Jewish ceremonies written by the rabbi of Sha'ar Zahav,* the San Francisco gay synagogue, got some ideas from a gay Orthodox friend we have, and put together a ceremony with vows that . . .

Probably the vows were the single hardest part, because it made us put down on paper what we expect from each other, and what we hope from each other. And that was a hard negotiation, because it wasn't only looking backward on where we've come from, it was looking forwards, and it was not simple.

TOM: Brian wrote seven benedictions, which were beautiful. And they rhymed. Or they had a—a meter to them.

BRIAN: They were based on the Sheva Brachot.* But the ones that simply weren't appropriate, that brought up images of husband and wife, we rewrote.

TOM: And they were read, under the chuppah* by our grandparents, our parents, siblings. Very beautiful.

BRIAN: It was awe-inspring. And people had told us, "Well, you don't have to have a rabbi, you can just run your own service." But having experienced it, and having watched it on video—

TOM: We certainly could not have done it.

BRIAN: Could not have managed it. It was too emotional, it was too heavy, it was too intense and—

TOM: Overwhelming. And the rabbi, midway through the service, said to take a moment and turn around, and look at our guests who had assembled. And it was a very beautiful day; it was at our cottage in Vermont; the sun was pouring through the trees, and we were lakeside, and the guests were . . . all teary.

BRIAN: And we had lost sight of them. Because we were under the chuppah and . . .

TOM: Yes. 'Cause when you're under the chuppah you don't really remember anything. It's all going on but you're oblivious to it. And uh, that was really significant. And she was wise to do that. 'Cause that's the strongest image I have of that day.

BRIAN: That's one of the strongest images here.

He gets up to pass me an album of wedding photos.

That's when the rabbi asked us to turn around to see everyone's response. It was very moving.

TOM: It was an extraordinary day.

BRIAN: The other thing is, Jewish wedding ceremonies don't talk about children, although everything about Judaism alludes to Creation and procreation. And David was in the making at the ceremony. And in fact was present in utero. So . . .

MG: *You knew this at the time?*

BRIAN: Yes.

TOM: Yeah. It was new information that we didn't share with our guests, excluding like, my parents, because we didn't want one to detract from the other in either direction. We waited till after the wedding, and then we let it be known, what was happening. It was very exciting.

BRIAN: We had actually looked at adopting in the six to twelve months beforehand and had found an adoption agency in California that we were happy with. But in around March, February or March, decided we're not going any further now, because if things go further, if an actual mother becomes available and a baby, then the ceremony's gonna take second, take a second place. And we decided not to let that happen.

And then of course the opportunity to get David came along and we weren't gonna let that go. So in retrospect it was very meaningful that he was there.

TOM: When David was born we received dozens and dozens and dozens of congratulations and donations, through the temple, in his honor, in our honors. In all the combinations. It was very public. It's not a secret. We were at the delivery. I cut the cord. That was very exciting.

BRIAN: I took the pictures, until I started crying.

TOM: Mm. And of course right away we had to plan a bris.*

BRIAN: And the mohel* had no issue with it. And it wasn't the first he's done.

TOM: Well, it was the first of—of men.

BRIAN: Yeah. But not the first of—

TOM: He had done a baby born to a lesbian couple.

BRIAN: But this was a baby born of Jewish birth parents to be raised as a Jew.

TOM: His only question was, "Are both the birth parents Jewish?" Otherwise he would have to perform an additional—

BRIAN: Well, just the mother. "Is the *mother* Jewish?"

TOM: Right.

BRIAN: Otherwise he'd have had to perform some sort of conversion. Which actually makes David quite unique. In that to find Jewish babies for adoption is exceedingly rare, and makes David all the more valuable, special.

MG: *From what I saw of him earlier he seems like a great kid. Very friendly.*

TOM: He likes company. He lights up. He'll try to catch your eye and smile.

BRIAN: He has an amazing amount of charisma. He—he'll be in a supermarket, and he looks at people and follows them till they meet his gaze. And then he smiles at them. [*smiling himself*] And what can you do but engage him? And so a group gathers around the shopping cart. You're off picking tomatoes, and you come back and there are four women!

TOM: And four months after David was born, my sister and her partner, Ruth, had a daughter. So there are two first-cousins four months apart. So my parents have two new grandchildren. Which is very exciting.

BRIAN: There's actually a little baby explosion in the community right now.

TOM: Yes. We have lots of friends with kids.

BRIAN: That's right. Some of them adopted from China. And some born through artificial insemination.

TOM: And one couple coparenting. A gay man and a lesbian woman. Lisa is now four? Five?

BRIAN: Six.

TOM: Six. And she spends most of the time with her mom, and two days of the week with her dad. Sleeps over. And you know, it works. And then we have Jewish friends—lesbian couples—who have had children, who have adopted children. We have one friend who had a child as a woman, and then went for a sex change and became a man. And that child, we have a close relationship with. And he's really OK. He's weathered this transition really well. A delightful, incredibly bright kid. Really smart boy.

In his room, David starts to cry.

TOM: He slept beautifully the last three nights. I mean, he wakes up in the middle of the night, cries, but within five minutes he's back asleep. But he never wakes this early in the evening; it's always like three, four o'clock in the morning. But that's what happens. He had a runny nose today. When he gets sick he doesn't sleep as well, he doesn't breathe as well.

David's crying gets louder. Tom goes to check on him.

BRIAN: In many, many ways this is a very exciting time. We can experience things now and live in ways we couldn't fifty years ago. But it's also very hard. Even though many people have come out, it's still a very difficult process, for which one has no training. And even if there are precedents, they're too abstract and too distant. One still has to go through a painful, personal process.

And then if you want to have a gay ceremony, well, there are no precedents out there; you have to create them. And if you want to make it Jewish, you also have to create them yourself. And if you want to have a child, and create a Jewish environment, there are even fewer precedents, and you have to create one. Every step along the way . . .

You go into it with a lot of energy, and a lot of hope, but it can be very tiring. You wish something just came easier: "Hey, let's do it!" And "Yeah, I can get a book, and it talks about fifteen hundred different ways of doing it, or fifteen hundred different experiences that people went through just like us . . ." But it's just not out there.

So it puts us in the position of role models. You're not just doing something for yourself, but also for the next person who may not feel permitted to do it, or that he or she has the right to do it, because no one has ever told them they could. And so a lot of gay people feel that they're second-class citizens because they don't have life-cycle events, and they don't know anybody who's had children. So even though it's very nice to live in 1999, it's nice to fantasize what it'll be like to live in 2049, fifty years from now. You know, you could focus your energies on other things, and all this will be a nonissue.

Getting a Get

She's been weeding the rose beds in the garden of her detached home in Hale Barns, near Manchester, England. "My husband used to do all the gardening," she tells me over a cup of tea on the patio. "And then he insisted on hiring a gardener, but I rather enjoy doing it myself." The roses are a mass of yellows, mauves, and pinks. Six years ago, Pat M., who was then thirty-seven, obtained a civil divorce after sixteen years of marriage. Two years later, her ex-husband requested a get—a Jewish divorce—since he wanted to remarry under Jewish law. Pat agreed, thinking the ritual would have little emotional significance for her.

I WAS A BIT IRRITATED WITH HARVEY because I felt I'd done enough for him. We'd been through enough. As far as I was concerned it was settled, having gone through the courts. We'd had a financial settlement, a child support agreement, the whole number. I was irritated but—I really didn't feel in a position to be—to be irritated about it. I could've said, "Nope, I'm not going to cooperate," but I mean . . . I just don't do that sort of thing. I'm a peacekeeper. And there's my kids as well involved in all of this, so I decided, "All right, let's do it."

He said to me that I would have to ring up one of the rabbis who wanted to talk to me. And when I rang him up, he tried to tell me what would happen, that there would be three rabbis, a scribe, and a couple of Kohens* or Levis* and it would be at the Beth

Din.* He assured me a few times that "there was *no* way that I would be humiliated."

This made me wonder a bit. "What is it about this ceremony that is humiliating to women?" I believe that traditionally there is a lot—a lot of humiliation. Apparently, women have been spat on, and all sorts of things. I've been spat on as a woman in Jerusalem by these black hats. I was walking down the street and I was . . . spat on.

And at the same time, when Harvey asked me, I thought, "Oh well, let's go and see what happens." I was a bit sort of blasé about it too. I thought, "I expect dignity and respect, and if I don't get it, I'll simply walk out."

The point is that I wasn't expecting it to be any sort of a—a meaningful process for me at all. It was a bit of an imposition by other people, namely men. I didn't feel that it was going to have any meaning for me at all. I arranged to meet Harvey at the place—the Beth Din office in the synagogue. It was the ecclesiastical court. That's what it is. It's about claims to property. The whole point of the get is that I can make no claims to any of Harvey's property. That's the whole point of it, I think.

They asked whether we'd gone through the civil courts—yes—and whether we'd had a child settlement—yes—they asked me if I was pregnant. I said I wasn't. There seemed to be some concern that there might be a child who could then claim his property later. They had to have absolute proof that no claims would be made by me, or any of my children, to his, his property.

We were taken into a room and there were these three rabbis. I don't remember their names. There were two Levis . . . Kohens? Who do you usually need? Levis? I'm not sure. I was told, "There are the two Levis." These two little old men. There was a scribe as well. Really. An old fellow whose job it is to write with a quill on papyrus.

First we had to identify ourselves. Harvey, son of so-and-so, grandson of so-and-so, to establish his line. My line was through my father. Pat, daughter of Isaac, son of so-and-so. It went through my father, not my mother.

And the scribe had a really really important role. The process was that Harvey had to sell the scribe his own quill and papyrus. [*shaking her head*] No, not papy– parchment! Parchment. So that it could never be said that it was written on someone else's, that it was Harvey's. Of course, it was symbolic because he never had a parchment, did he?

OK, so once they'd established we were who we were, that there was child settlement, and the whole thing had gone through the civil courts, they proceeded with the get. They gave us various things to say to each other. Basically, Harvey had to ask the scribe to use his quill and parchment to write a promise . . . that Harvey released me from any bond to him. A promise to release me from the marriage. [*smiling tone*] Which sounded kind of nice. I wanted to be released. I mean, I *was* released, but there was something beginning to . . . to go on at an emotional level at this point.

When we'd done all that, the scribe took all our details, and we had to go into this other—another room and wait for him for about an hour. He wrote this thing in Hebrew with the quill on the parchment. That is the get, the promise. The unspoken text is that I will not make any claim on his property. But he also promises to let me go. And that was kind of—kind of appealing to me. Just to have that transaction out there was beginning to feel interesting.

After the get was written out, we both came back into the room. And by then, things were really starting to tap into me on an emotional level. I don't remember exactly what was said. We had to repeat certain things, something about Harvey saying, "I hereby release you from this marriage," and me saying that I accepted that. Then they folded this parchment up nine times till it was about three by four inches. They took a scalpel, they slashed it twice like a cross, almost all the way through.

To me that had an *incredible* impact. To me that was the severing of the bond that Harvey and I had had for all those years. It's a very potent gesture, isn't it? I began to feel it emotionally. Harvey had to take the parchment and I had to stand with my open hands beneath his hands, and he had to drop it into my hands, without touching me. So he dropped it and I had to close my hands over it like that. I was told what to do — tuck it under my arm and then walk out the door. I had to come back [*laughs*] but symbolically, it was my acceptance of what he was giving me. I came back and gave it back to them.

And then they said to me — and this was the most incredible part of it for me — one of the rabbis said to me, "You've now been given the get to signify your independence. You will please leave this place without your husband." They said, "We wish you luck in your new life." That was like, so powerful. I just picked up my stuff and left. I felt amazing.

There was something packed into that — that ritual . . . well-tried and tested emotional stuff, designed over time to satisfy certain needs. Not about property or ownership but about breaking bonds. The emotional freeing that the whole ceremony entailed . . . The being told to walk out was a recognition from the whole patriarchal structure that my divorce was sanctioned. It was OK for me to get divorced. It was OK.

It was the first time that anyone had said that to me. Also I had recognized the fact that I wanted to free myself and move on, on my own. I was getting an underlining of that from the rabbis, the last people in the world I would ever have thought would give me that sanction. And I didn't even know that I needed it.

To be honest, I think that going out independently is all new stuff. I'm sure they used to stone women, [*laughs*] make 'em crawl out the door in rags or something. But I was given a lot of recognition that this divorce had happened, and that my life was going on. And it actually did free me of a lot of my own guilt about the divorce, about wanting to be out of the marriage. It really freed me. I felt light. It changed my whole attitude toward rituals.

Torn into Bits

On the runway at Chicago's O'Hare airport, the passenger in the window seat inquires whether I'll be staying in London or traveling further. She's returning home, she tells me, after a short visit to see her daughter and grandchildren in Denver; has to be back at work on Monday morning, she adds with a groan. Turns out that she's a commissioning editor at a well-known British publishing house. As the 747 becomes airborne, I mention, casually as I can, that I just happen to be working on a manuscript. "On the topic of . . . ?" "Judaism, Jewishness. I ask people to share stories of personal experience." "Want to interview me?" she asks. Somewhere over Labrador, Audrey C. tells me about her Jewish divorce. She laughs a good deal, but the laughter, as she says herself, is hollow.

I GOT DIVORCED FROM MY FIRST HUSBAND IN 1980, after twenty-three years. And it wasn't a horrible, bitter divorce, it was fairly amicable and civilized, and we didn't have lawyers, and we split everything fifty-fifty: there was no need for lawyers to be involved.

And a couple of years later my ex-husband wanted to remarry. He was engaged to a woman who was Jewish and who wanted to get married in shul.* Now in order for them to do that—which they never did, by the way, they broke off the engagement—but they needed a get* so that they could be married in shul.

So Mark called me and said that he needed a get. And I said, "Fine. What do I have to do?" And he said he would do it all.

298

There was a certain amount of money to be paid, which he was paying, and I would be required to go along to a particular place at a particular time.

And there were thirteen rabbis present, I think. Maybe seven. I've forgotten, but it was an inordinate, *extraordinary* number of rabbis present. Seven? A lot of rabbis anyway. And we had to wait in the waiting room, and we sat and talked quite happily. And Mark was called first.

I don't remember the details because my memory's not good about detail, but he was called first and I had to wait until I was called to join him.

Sitting in the presence of all these rabbis kind of made me feel a bit—It was a bit awesome and threatening and black and dark and a bit sinister, and it made me feel that it was *wrong*, that there had been a wrong done. I felt they were looking at me like I was bad.

Maybe it's all in my head, I don't know, I'm only telling you how I felt. And there was a sofer, a scribe, and he had to write down when we were married, and where, and my mother's name, and Hebrew names. And then, when it was all written, we had to stand, and I had to hold my hands together, palms up in front of me . . . [*demonstrates*]

And this piece of paper that had been written so carefully was then torn into bits, and dropped over my hands. So . . . I felt that was really a very humiliating thing . . . That was my past history being torn into shreds and dropped on me. I . . . I still laugh about it but I hated that.

And then we were not allowed to exit together, we had to go out through different doors. And that was the end of it. So I didn't like it. I felt OK until they ripped up these shreds of what had been me, and dropped it in little strips. It was humiliating, it was sad. It was horrible. My marriage wasn't just . . . a thing to be ripped up. My marriage had resulted in a family, a wonderful family, and although we were no longer married, it didn't mean we didn't count for each other. We were still important to each other. Without that marriage and that love we wouldn't have been who we were, and we wouldn't have had what we had, and it was all too valuable to rip it into shreds.

Even now I find myself feeling upset by that . . . that ripping up. You can't tear a part of yourself or part of your life up, and say that no longer exists. We still cared for each other, we still do now. And even if we didn't, you don't rip that whole past and say, "This is now finished, so drop it and catch these little bits." I found that quite ugly.

I found the civil divorce much more dignified. The judge said to me, "Do you agree with what's written down here, and do you understand it?" And I said, "Yes, I understand it. It's been done with my agreement." And that was that, and Mark and I left together and had lunch.

Maybe I'm Wrong

───────◦◦◦───────

Cricklewood, London, England. Joanne B. is sixty years old. She's a re-
tired dentist. Joanne and her husband, Harold, a retired engineer, have
been married for thirty-eight years. They have four children: Shlomo,
Leah, David, and Richard. It's a Wednesday evening. Harold is attending
a meeting of his Masonic lodge. Joanne is unloading the heavily laden
tea trolley she's just wheeled into the dining room. From trolley to table,
she transfers a teapot; matching cups and saucers; a sponge cake, as-
sorted pastries and biscuits; two forks; two knives, two teaspoons; sugar
bowl; sugar tongs; milk jug; plate of lemons; lemon squeezer, tea strainer,
toothpicks. Joanne, who became quite annoyed when I tried to help
unload the trolley, finally sits down and is just about to pour the tea
when she realizes she has forgotten the napkins. The atmosphere re-
mains a little tense throughout the interview. As she talks about her
children's different lifestyles, Joanne's voice sounds tired and strained.

WE ARE WHAT I WOULD CALL A KOSHER HOME, but to Shlomo and his
family . . . [*twisting around and nodding towards a photo on the
cabinet of a bearded man, his wife, and six children*] it isn't sufficiently strict. They have a book of guidelines and they do not go
out of that. I mean, I would read a label on a packet of biscuits,
and if it says "pure vegetable oil," for me, that's fine. Shlomo has
to have a hechsher* from a . . . [*sighs*] one of the certification
authorities before they'll touch it.

And uh, they will not drink ordinary milk. *My* kosher list says all

301

milk is fine. But it's not good enough for them. They need chalav Yisrael,* which is watched from the minute it leaves the cow until it . . . which costs them double. And the same with all dairy products. Has to be made with chalav Yisrael.

So I cannot invite those children in for some bread and cheese. I mean, I can get chalav Yisrael cheese, but once it's been opened, they won't eat it the next time in case a knife has touched it which has been in contact with non-chalav Yisrael. And I can't keep that up. Not with the rest of my family who are not all that interested.

When Shlomo and Rivka or the kids come round, we have a cupboard where they keep their own plates and their own cutlery. And I stock it with tins of salmon, sardines, kippers, that sort of thing . . . Everything I have in there is for them.

Originally I was extremely resentful and, and hurt. But I've realized that if I didn't accept their way, I'd lose them. And I'm not prepared to do that. Leah, who's the next one . . .

She points to a photograph of a ruddy-cheeked teenager with braids and bands.

It's an old photo, I'm just getting a new one framed. Leah and her husband are what they call shomer Shabbos. They keep Shabbos, they eat kosher food, and they'll eat out. But they will eat vegetarian out. They certainly wouldn't touch any meat. And they certainly don't have any shellfish, or anything like that. But to Shlomo they're lax. To themselves, they're not.

David and Carol, I'm not sure. They live a long way from us. I think they blow which way the wind blows. But that—It's their responsibility, it's their decision. And they don't hurt anyone.

And Richard, my youngest, is a complete heathen. He doesn't give a damn about anything. He's twenty-three years old. I can't tell him what he can eat and what he can't eat. Providing, of course, he doesn't bring it into the house. And anyway, most of the time he's round at his girlfriend's.

MG: *Does she keep kosher?*

No. [*sighs forlornly*] Simone is a very, very nice girl. She's *extremely* nice. She's very intelligent, she's very goodhearted. I find the only thing wrong with her is she's not Jewish. And I'm sorry, Michael, but I need a Jewish daughter-in-law. And I need my grandchildren to be Jewish.

There'd be so much antagonism from everybody in our family circle. For instance, Shlomo said halachically* we could not invite Simone and Ricky home for a yom tov.*

She sees my puzzlement.

I don't know why. You're just not allowed to. It must be in the, [*sighs*] the halachas* somewhere. I don't know. I haven't read them. There's an answer for everything there.

MG: *Do you ever invite them here?*

Oh yes, but [*her face coloring*] it's always uncomfortable. Especially if Harold's here. He doesn't want it. He's polite. But there's a difference between being polite and being welcoming.

MG: *Have you talked to Simone about this?*

I don't wish to . . . I don't want her to feel that I'm asking her to convert, because I would go . . . *berserk* if someone asked Ricky to convert. And nobody's got a right to ask anybody. And [*clears throat*] I think Ricky mentioned it once. She's completely uninterested. Which is fine. And if she did wish to convert, it would have to be done in an Orthodox shul.* They're the only conversions which are acceptable. And that takes three years, and it's a very hard course. You've got to be extremely dedicated. And I don't—It's just not on the . . . And what would it do to her parents? I'd hate to think.

MG: *Do you know them?*

No. And I don't want to. I mean, what would it do to them?

Joanne looks through the French windows. A thrush alights on the lawn.

She's much nicer than any of the Yiddisheh girls he's ever been interested in. With them the measure of the man was how much money you've got in the bank. [*sighs*] But it's not just his brother that would object. *I* would object. There would be a distinct uncomfortableness all the time. And I really don't think that children of such a union really know where they are.

Maybe I've been reading too many Maisie Mosco novels. She's written a few books about mixed marriages. And not one of them has worked. I don't know if it's a bad thing, but I haven't seen too many successful mixed marriages. I really haven't. But who knows, maybe we only hear about the ones that break up. But there's an awful lot of them.

Joanne turns back towards the French doors. Her mouth is so tightly shut that her lips have vanished.

She's a lovely girl. She is *so* nice. She's so genuine. She's so warm. And she's the soul of kindness. But something tells me it's not right.

MG: *Can you try to—*

[*sharply*] I'm sorry, I *can't* explain. [*clears throat*] But I think the Jewish people have had too much persecution, humiliation, to risk bringing it into the family. Because there always will be conflict. It may be very miniscule to start off with, but it will—I'm convinced that it will build up later. And one day there'll be a confrontation. "You're a Jew! I shouldn't've married you!"

I'm sure that will happen. It may take twenty years, but it will happen. It'll happen. And then the children will suffer. Maybe I'm wrong . . . [*forcing a smile*] Maybe I've read too many books.

Outa Left Field

On the surface, Francis Z. would seem to have little in common with Woody Allen. He's a six-foot-five-inch twenty-nine-year-old Denver-based financial consultant who weighs in at "a cheeseburger over two hundred and twenty pounds." A former college linebacker, Francis plays squash twice a week and jogs five miles every day to and from his office. He also finds it hard to tell me whether he prefers skydiving to speleology. Nevertheless, when I pose the usual question to him, his answer is immediate.

WHAT DOES BEING JEWISH MEAN TO ME? Guilt and anxiety. I think there's a lot of things in life that we can pretty easily dismiss, at least over time, but with Judaism, even the smallest things . . . Like, you have to give to a Jewish organization, or you have to do one ritual or another—*That* doesn't go away. And if you try to push it away, it can create a lot of anxiety.

I mean, I'm still single, but even if I married someone who wasn't Jewish, I would still want to raise my kids Jewish. Which may be a little selfish, I mean, the other person has their tradition too. But there is a *tremendous* pressure to pass it on, and a tremendous *anxiety* about not doing it. My dad has worked out this computerized family tree—and he's got it back to like, the mid-seventeen hundreds in Turkey and Italy. You see it and you're thinking, "God! There is this *huge* tradition."

MG: *So can you tell me a story that includes the words "I," "Jewish," "recently," and "anxiety"?*

Let me think . . .

His nose wiggles.

Yes! OK. I recently met this fellow who's very active in the UJA.*
I'd seen him on a couple of occasions, once at a UJA dinner at his
home, and once at some other UJA function, but we'd hardly had
a lot of contact, I certainly didn't know him well. But he has an
investment bank, and when I needed to talk to an investment
banker about a new project I was working on, I remembered this
fellow out of this Rolodex in my head.

MG: *Did you think that the Jewish connection might be helpful in
business terms?*

I mean, it wasn't like, "Oh, this guy's Jewish, he's gonna help me
out . . ." He just happened to be Jewish. Maybe there is some extra
camaraderie—there probably is—however, I know enough that I
wouldn't hang my hat on it! You know, in finance, people are
gonna do a deal; people will try to maximize their own monetary
utility, pretty quickly beyond anything else. I don't think anyone's
gonna give you too much of a break. Though sometimes, I tell ya,
I think everyone wishes for a fairy godmother or godfather giving
you a leg up. But it ain't gonna happen.

So I went to see this guy in his office, and we talked about the deal
for about forty-five minutes, and then we were sort of wrapping
up, and . . . completely out of the blue, he asked me who I was
dating, "And is she Jewish or not?" Completely outa left field! And
I was at first a little taken aback: "Who in a business meeting would
ask this?"

And he said, "It's very important to me that young Jewish people
marry other Jews. It would be a shame if the tradition ended with
you."

And I'm like, "Well,—I don't have any particular plans for marriage right now. I guess I'll have to see how all that works out." But
I thought, "Hey! How . . . intrusive! This guy doesn't even *know*

me!" . . . I'm trying to think of other awkward questions that come out of the blue, like, "How much money do you have?" "What's that weird thing growing outa your face?" [*laughs*] I mean . . . Jesus!

He exhales, shakes his head, and smiles awkwardly.

Thing is, I *am* dating someone who isn't Jewish. So yes, it certainly hit a raw nerve. But the weird thing was, I suddenly thought, as I was walking out, "My God! It *could* all end with me, I could kill it all, y'know?" [*laughs*].

So it's just a tremendous source of pressure. I mean, even for someone like me who doesn't subscribe to the ritual, or the beliefs, yet there's a sense that there's something that has to be perpetuated, carried on. But then, perpetuating what? Like, I don't speak Hebrew, I kind of remember a little—and that's more than most of my friends. I don't speak Ladino—just a word here and there—I don't go to synagogue, I don't eat kosher, so what is left to carry on? It's something I think about a lot. And I don't know what the answer is.

That's What Dave Says

A family cookout on the patio of Dave and Estelle C.'s ranch-style home in Cleveland, Ohio. A bottle of Heineken in one hand and a fork in the other, Dave is barbecuing hot dogs, hamburgers, and ears of corn on the gas grill. Estelle's relaxing on a lounge chair, a glass of iced tea by her side. Shrieking with delight, nine-year-old Todd and his twin sister, Julie, are playing at the far end of the family's large inground pool. I ask Dave and Estelle to talk about their experience of being in a "mixed marriage."

ESTELLE: Our son is not circumcised. It all sounded quite reasonable at first. At first, Dave said that he can't believe that it is not a deeply traumatic experience, right? That's what Dave says. And because he's very well-read, and I know he thinks deeply about things, when he says something like that I think about it, OK? So that was the first thing. But being Jewish . . . I mean, if you're Jewish you just automatically circumcise your sons.

DAVE: [*preparing barbecue plates for the children*] That's not actually true. If you're secular Jewish, and you relate to a secular tradition, you're in the forefront of the movement *against* circumcision. And that's a fact.

From a side table bowl, Dave scoops potato salad onto the children's plates.

Anyways, I never took it as seriously as you did. You always read me as being stronger on that point. I just thought that if one is rational about it, one takes the advice of doctors and physiologists. And some of them would say that it's a bad idea. It deprives the child—It deprives the male of a source of pleasure, that means it's a bit like a partial clitoridectomy.

ESTELLE: [*unenthusiastically*] Yes, I know.

DAVE: [*assertively*] It is, it is. So it's a kind of rational, humane attitude that is I think compatible with being fully Jewish. You can be fully Jewish and decide that your child's not gonna be circumcised. There's any number of kids of whom that's true.

ESTELLE: I haven't encountered any.

DAVE: We'll get the statistics. I guarantee you that it's true.

Dave calls the children over to collect their food. Returning to the far end of the pool, they sit on the side, plates on knees, Cokes beside them, their feet dangling in the water.

ESTELLE: So anyway, at first Dave said, "Let's not do it when he's just born. If you really want to have it done, let's do it when he can have an anesthetic," right? And so I called all these people that did circumcisions, and they said, "You can't have an anesthetic till the child's one year old." So the eight days passed, and because I'm not religious, it was really very easy for it to go, and I was sort of counting on doing it when Todd was one.

And then I met this woman, a friend of mine, who actually couldn't have children, and she adopted a boy, but then she got pregnant. And so she had this adopted boy and her own son, her own natural son, circumcised at the same time. But the adopted child was a year old, under anesthetic, and the other did it at eight days. And she said that the child it was done to at eight days just got over it . . . cried for a moment, and got over it in a second, whereas the one that it was done to at a year actually regressed! He was beginning to walk and he sort of regressed into this, this sort of limping crawl.

And when I heard that, I thought, "Oh, I can't do that to Todd." So my son is not circumcised. And for years, when I was changing his diaper in front of other Jewish friends, I'd sort of hide. I was really deeply embarrassed about this. Now, I don't mind. It doesn't bother me, I guess, although I'm a little concerned for Todd, later on. I have a feeling that already it's a bit of a problem for him amongst Jewish children. I think it is.

Food's ready. Dave invites us to serve ourselves. We sit down to eat at a redwood picnic table.

ESTELLE: [*filling our glasses with white Zinfandel*] One day, when he's old enough, he can decide for himself. I mean, that's the idea. It's been a big issue for me, a really big issue. Because, rationally, I think Dave's right. It's a really barbaric thing to do. But emotionally, if you're Jewish, you just don't question it.

DAVE: That's just not true. It's not true. In many communities you do question it. And you stand up for rationality.

MG: [*to Estelle*] *What do your parents think?*

DAVE: Tell the truth now.

ESTELLE: [*smiles*] The truth. Well, my mother was *delighted*, because when I told her it was now the trend not to circumcise kids, she was blissed out, because having gone through the Holocaust—they're from Vienna, and people in those days—non-Jews weren't circumcised, so you could always spot a Jew by his penis. So Mom thought that in terms of protecting her grandchildren it was a very sensible thing. My father, though, was a bit upset about it. But he was OK in the end.

DAVE: What he said to me was that he was all in favor.

ESTELLE: All in favor?

DAVE: Yeah. On the basis that Todd couldn't be identified.

ESTELLE: [*pensively*] Mmm. And then there's . . . the question of Todd's bar mitzvah.* I don't know if he'll have one, 'cause it'd be so very weird for us to do it, because it's so alienating, we're so out of touch. [*responding to Dave's frown*] Oh yeah! You are too. I mean, how many bar mitzvahs have you been to?

DAVE: As many as you have.

ESTELLE: [*shrugging and laughing*] I guess, to consider it as a rite of passage is the way I would approach it. But then the question becomes, how big of a thing do we make it? And I don't know how they're going to bar mitzvah him without—[*laughs*] without his penis!

DAVE: I'm telling you: it *won't* be a problem.

ESTELLE: I tell you it will be. The Russians who come here and want to get—I don't know, whatever they get—they have to get circumcised.

DAVE: It's not going to be a problem. This has been a nonissue for decades in the radical wing of the Hebrew congregations in New York and the West Coast.

ESTELLE: Well, it's not a nonissue here.

DAVE: Well, we can make it that. We'll get him approved by some rabbi in New York, or whatever it takes. That's not going to be a problem. And anyway, you think they're going to check? Believe me. I'm—

ESTELLE: OK, OK! It's not a big deal. If they don't let him have a bar mitzvah because of it, tough . . .

DAVE: And I'm the gentile here, and I'm circumcised, you know, so . . . weird. [*smiles*]

A Little Tradition

Friday evening. In the loft of his family home in Denver, Colorado, fifteen-year-old Misha Y. is picking out some heavy metal tracks on his electric guitar and shooting the breeze with me and his twelve-year-old friend, Parker. Born in Moscow, Misha moved to the United States with his parents when he was five. Both boys are wearing baseball caps, T-shirts, and jeans. Parker's T-shirt has a Broncos' logo, Misha's a giant skull with fangs. This year, the first night of Chanukah falls on Christmas Eve, a couple of weeks from now. I ask the boys what they'll be doing to celebrate the holiday. Misha responds first, absent-mindedly strumming his guitar as he speaks.

MISHA: We're gonna have a tree because we like how it looks, but I guess since we're more Jewish than not, it's gonna be a New Year's tree, 'cause in Russia New Year's is a really big holiday. They don't really have Christmas, they have New Year's.

My grandmother won't have one because she's more . . . she's the only one in the family that like, takes Judaism a little seriously. She actually sometimes goes to temple. On special occasions. She won't get mad or anything about us having a tree, but, um . . . if we were like, real Jewish Orthodox, we . . . we wouldn't, of course. No question about it, we're not really religious. We have pork and everything, like we're not supposed to.

PARKER: That's kinda how my family is, too. We used to be like, practicing Judaism, like, I'd go to Sunday school, we'd go to temple every Friday for the Sabbath, but we don't do much now, the last few years. We still celebrate the holidays though. We also celebrate some of the Christian holidays because of my mother being Christian. And her whole side of the family celebrates it with us, and my dad and his side of the family take part in it also. So we're really . . . we've integrated both of the religions. We celebrate both as a joint religion, we believe that both are equally right.

MISHA: My dad's past ancestors were like, Russian Orthodox Catholics or something, but obviously we don't have anything against the other religions, everything's fine for us. And now I'm pretty much being raised up Jewish, I guess. For Jewish New Year, for Yom K—No. Rosh haShanah*—The one where you eat the apple and stuff? We got together this year at my grandmother's house. We didn't have it in a real Jewish traditional way, we just had dinner, we had Russian food. It's just kinda a little tradition with us. Like also the Passover holiday we sometimes get together. It's sometimes important for everybody to look back. 'Course, you don't know if it's true, this Passover stuff. Nobody knows.

MG: *Tell me about it.*

MISHA: You don't know it?

MG: *Yeah. But it's always nice to hear an old story told again.*

MISHA: Well, uh, it happened in, uh, Egypt, aaaaand uh, the king, the Pharaoh, he took all the Jews into working labor—Oh God! I'm guessin' here—probably all day with the minimum amount of food and not payin' them, and treatin' them really bad and all that and, um . . . uh . . . uh . . . Help me, Parker.

PARKER: OK. The story kinda began when the queen had a son, and it was Moses.

MISHA: Was she Jewish?

PARKER: Yeah. . . . I think so.

MISHA: Oh . . .

PARKER: And because she wasn't supposed to . . . they sent him in a basket down the river, and he was found by . . . I can't remember who . . . And they brought him up, and uh, he began to side with the Jews, and then he tried many times to free them from Pharaoh.

And it came—The last time that he tried, he went to the Pharaoh and he said, "If you don't free all of the Jews I'm gonna have God send ten plagues on you."

MISHA: Right. I know a couple of 'em: there was one, it was like, raining snakes or somethin'.

PARKER: Raining pests or insects.

MISHA: Yeah. So the guy said, "No, I'm still gonna have 'em work." So it rained pests for uh . . .

PARKER: A day or two.

MISHA: Yeah. Anyway, eventually Pharaoh really decided to let them go when they said that God was gonna kill his firstborn son, but Pharaoh broke his promise, and he chased the Jewish people, and it was over the Red Sea, and for the Jews God made like, the Red Sea open—I don't know how exactly—and it came crashing down on the Egyptians.

The band Metallica wrote a song about Passover on their *Ride the Lightning* album. It's pretty cool. It's called "Creeping Death." As you can see, it's on the back of my head.

Misha swivels his frayed cap through 180 degrees to show me his CREEPING DEATH *patch. With the cap still reversed, he suddenly plays a series of portentous, heavy metal riffs. The floor vibrates.*

MISHA: This part I'm not too sure about [*sings*] I AM THE CHOSEN ONE—I really don't know the verses, but the chorus is . . .

Misha sings and plays. Parker sings and plays air drums.

So let it be written! So let it be do-o-one! To kill the firstborn
Pharaoh's son. A creeping death!

MISHA: This part is the part that kinda makes sense. Mostly.

Now let my people go! From the Land of Goshen. I shall be
with thee a bush of fire . . . blood running red and strong down
the Nile.

Come on, Michael! Sing the chorus with us!

The boys sing. I try to lip synch.

So let it be written! So let it be do-o-one! To kill the firstborn
Pharaoh's son. A creeping death!

Good try, Michael. And then there's the guitar solo—which I'll
skip—and then it goes:

Die! Die! Die! Die with me! Killing firstborn men! Die! Die! Die
by my hand!!! Die! Die! Die by my hand!!! Creeping death! Die!
Die!

*Misha blasts off a final riff, ending with a whining slide that starts
my ears buzzing.*

So whaddya think? It's pretty cool. It's pretty heavy too, but it's not
as stupid as some of their older stuff about leather and motor bikes.
It's uh, a pretty famous song with the real diehard Metallica fans.

PARKER: A lot of the music we listen to is really oriented to religion. Lots of the bands sing about Satan. I mean, that's fine, because there are many aspects of Satanism, and some people say it
came first, it was the first religion, and then Christianity was developed, and Satanism was shunned upon, and they decided to take
Satan and blame everything bad on him.

MISHA: Yeah. But I'm not really against Christians for thinkin'
this. I guess it's fine for the Catholics to think it's bad if that's what

they really believe. But y'know, it can be *good*. There are different kinds of Satanism.

PARKER: Right. I think in all religions there is a referral to a Higher Being. I think they all branched off from the same thing, Satanism, Christianity, Judaism. Which came first, chicken or the egg? Same thing. And if there was a way to take everything back to the beginning, that's where you'd find your answers.

Misha repeats the riff from "Creeping Death." The boys launch into the chorus again.

SO LET IT BE WRITTEN, SO LET IT BE DO-O-ONE . . .

What Remains Here?

———— ◊◊ ————

Aaron Lansky is president of the National Yiddish Book Center. A boy-ish-looking forty-three-year-old with an infectious smile, Lansky is en-ergy, enthusiasm, and determination incarnate. He's been collecting Yiddish books since the late seventies, and has so far saved more than a million volumes from destruction. The Center's headquarters—a ram-bling postmodern structure recalling traditional shtetl architecture—are adjacent to Hampshire College in the heart of the Massachusetts coun-tryside. The view from the president's office includes a large open field and a number of old apple trees. In front of the trees, a large Yiddish sign in black Hebrew characters reads: DER SOD. *Underneath, in a smaller sans serif, the English translation:* THE ORCHARD.*

Lansky's telling me about a 1991 trip to distribute Yiddish books to Jew-ish communities in the crumbling Soviet Union.

WE HAD A—LOOKED LIKE A JAPANESE CAMPER VAN, like a Mitsubishi van sort of thing, but with extra-heavy springs and stuff. So it was passable as a kind of touristy vehicle. But it was heavy enough that we could then put books in it and then drive through the Baltics distributing all these books. All this without any visas or anything. It was really a kind of a hairy experience.

Everything worked out along the way. Until we finally got as far as Riga in Latvia. We were in Riga and then we had another twelve hundred books we wanted to bring down to Vilna—Vilnius—in Lithuania. However, the Lithuanians had declared their indepen-

317

dence a little while earlier, and the Soviets had cracked down on them, and there was no gasoline. The roads were closed, but we finally ended up getting a transit visa to White Russia that enabled us to pass through Lithuania. But then we were afraid to go on the roads alone because we knew there had been a tremendous amount of—of hijackings, that kind of thing on the highways.

So we asked our contacts in Vilna to send us some shtarkes, some—some tough guys to travel with us, because we thought it was pretty dangerous. And not speaking Russian, we were particularly vulnerable in all of this. So they sent these two shtarkes, two Jewish guys. Big, tough guys. And they get in the van with us. And then there's this friend of mine who's a reporter, and another very close friend who's a photojournalist, from Houston, Texas, of all places. And they were covering it for an American magazine.

So now we have five of us in this van, and we're driving and driving and driving. We're the only vehicle on the road the whole morning. We must've driven three hundred, four hundred kilometers. Nobody. Nobody on the road. Because there was no fuel. And we were maybe two hours outside of Vilnius. We're just hungry, two in the afternoon. Hungry. We'll have to stop for lunch somewhere. But it's not like here in the States. Here you pull off the road and there's a rest area and you have a restaurant. It doesn't quite work that way there.

So we see a sign for a city called Ukmerge. So we pull off the road, and as we're driving around, it looks like something out of a Roman Vishniac photograph. I mean, it's like The Place That Time Forgot or something. And we see the houses, and we see goats tethered in the yards, and we see women washing clothes down by the river, and guys going on horse-drawn carts through the streets. It was—was almost unimaginable to see this. And we bankrupted— the United States almost bankrupted itself because we were worried about this threat? [laughs]

And so we're driving through it, and I say to our shtarkes, "This

place looks just like a shtetl.* It looks like just out of the books."
He says, "Well, 'cause it *was* a shtetl." I said, "Really? Never heard
of it."

He says, "Before the war this was Vilkomir."

I says, "Vilkomir, I heard of." You know, that's a very famous place.
Lilienthal, I think, had come from there. A number of prominent
scholars had been associated with it. So that was a good size shtetl,
a good size small city. Certainly a place where there must be a lot
of traces of Jewish life. It was a major center—ten thousand Jews
there before the war.

"What remains here?"

He said, "Nothing. Obviously."

So we said, "There has to be a cemetery here. Jews lived here for
years. That at least has to be here." And the shtarkes ask around.
And finally they find somebody who gives 'em directions to where
the Jewish cemetery was.

So we drive to the outskirts of town. It's just a—Just an expanse.
Just a field. It's like this. [*gesturing towards the window*] And kids
playing ball somewhere. And right in the very middle was a little
monument for the Jews. It was in Lithuanian and Yiddish, as I
recall, not in Russian. Which itself is a statement. Lithuanian and
Yiddish, "To the memory of those who—who have died."

And next to it they had this one little matzeiva, this one old, old,
probably early nineteenth-century tombstone, with the Yiddish—
with the Hebrew writing on it. And that's all that remained. Of
course, the Jews were killed by the Nazis, the cemetery was destroyed by the Soviets.

And I have to say that after two trips to the Soviet Union, that was
the only time in all that time that I just broke down crying. It just
got to me, you know. In the sense that here we have our little
Japanese van parked on the street with books in the back of it. And

this other decimation. We saw the way in which a culture had just been—A whole civilization had been uprooted, in the most violent, the most brutal way possible, and how little remained. And here we are, somehow trying to make amends with our little Japanese van and twelve hundred books. *This* is somehow going to make amends? For not one Vilkomir, not two, but hundreds and hundreds and hundreds of shtetlach* exactly like this, of whole towns and whole worlds that were destroyed?

MG: *My great-grandfather came from Vilkomir. I went there in '94.*

[*with surprise*] Oh, that's unbelievable.

MG: *I was actually in that cemetery. I went there with someone I met in Ukmerge. He was an architect working for the town council. He wasn't Jewish, but he'd been appalled by what had happened to the cemetery, and as a kind of personal project he decided to build his own memorial.*

Really . . .

MG: *So what he'd done . . . In one corner of that big field he'd planted a hedge in the form of a Magen David.* *It was a privet hedge. A low hedge, about this high* [hand at knee-height]. *But it just wasn't growing well. It was really sad.*

Like a metaphor yet again, isn't it? Oh that's just awful . . .

MG: *But he'd cared enough to plant it. He'd put it there. I was moved by that.*

You know what I'd say? Accept the metaphor for what it is. It *is* moving, and yet it is . . . somehow . . . somehow it's almost—I mean, it gives me chills a little bit, but it's almost fitting that nothing should grow there anymore. It's over. . . . Too much happened. That is a burdensome history. That's not the memorial.

I think what struck me that day in the cemetery was, whatever continuity there would really be ultimately depended on us, that when all was said and done not only the Jews of Vilkomir but the cemetery itself had been destroyed. Whoever the survivors were [*points to me*] that's you. *You're* the survivor of that town. In the most literal sense. We all in a somewhat more metaphorical sense are the survivors of Jewish life.

And because of that, it bestows upon us, it seems to me, a tremendous sense of responsibility. Because whatever real hemsheich, whatever real continuity there will be is gonna happen here. And the truth is we're very privileged. We have tremendous possibility, tremendous opportunity. We're comfortable, we have financial means, we have freedom, we have access to knowledge, in ways that are almost unprecedented in Jewish history.

And so, for all the devastation in that world, we also kind of stand poised for a possibility of renaissance. Not in the same forms as before—I don't want slavishly to reproduce the past. I'm not the least bit interested in that. What I want to do is to build a future *informed* by the past. And I would say without that there can be no Jewish identity—I think it's almost axiomatic that for Jews—as for all people—but for Jews especially, because we had been landless and powerless for so long that our national identity—our collective identity—has to derive from shared conscience or shared memory.

In other words, if you want to know who you are, you better know where you're coming from. That is a fairly straightforward commonsensical statement. It's not ideology. It's simply seichel.*

Am I Really Jewish?

―――――◁▷―――――

Originally the largest Jewish group in the United States, Sephardis—Jews whose ancestors lived in the Iberian peninsula before the expulsion of 1492—became a minority within a minority following the mass migration of Ashkenazi Jews from central and eastern Europe. For most of the twentieth century, the contemporary American Sephardi experience was either little known or completely ignored by the majority of Jews as well as non-Jews.

Sharon L. is a Sephardi Jew who grew up in a small town in Mississippi during the 1960s. Her grandparents arrived in the United States from the Greek island of Rhodes. They spoke Ladino—Judeo-Spanish. A photograph of a younger Sharon, her parents, and grandparents is lying on the mantelpiece of the family's brand new split-level home on the outskirts of Ann Arbor, Michigan. Sharon, her husband, Simon, and their two young children have only just moved in. Theirs is the only occupied house in this new subdivision—the others are still under construction. Outside the kitchen, a landscaper is laying turf while another unloads a small pile of saplings from the back of a pickup truck.

I ALWAYS IDENTIFIED WITH THE SEPHARDI CULTURE. We lived with my father's mother, and he always spoke Ladino to her. We ate Sephardi food: stuffed grape leaves, feta, olives, yaprakes,* pastillas,* the whole . . .

And it was a very close community. There was a Jewish country club where we lived. They started one because Jews weren't allowed to join the Christian one and then Sephardis weren't allowed to join the Jewish one.

And my father was the first Sephardi to join. I think because he was a doctor they let him join. And then, he somehow wangled himself onto the admissions committee, and made sure other Sephardi Jews got on, and eventually there was no more discrimination. I had many Ashkenazi* friends because we all went to the same schools, but they were . . . one way or another, they were always letting me know I wasn't Jewish.

At Passover we always had rice. Now apparently, they're not allowed to eat rice by certain Pesach* rules. But we did. And they would really give me a hard time on that. And in lots of ways. The service in our synagogue was partially in Hebrew and partially in Ladino. And when my Ashkenazi friends would come, they were very sarcastic about the fact that there wasn't more Hebrew. And when I mentioned this to my father, he said, "Well, these are the same Jews who wouldn't let us into the country club. You can't listen to *them*. They don't have a good spirit."

But I felt confused because they seemed much more religious than we were. My mother was raised Orthodox, but she dropped it—it's sort of a long story about my mother—but my father was more the one who was guiding us growing up and he didn't really believe in God, he believed in Jews, he believed in Sephardi culture. He was president of the synagogue, he took it very seriously and he had no patience for the "I'm a better Jew than you" kind of stuff. He would just think these people were ridiculous.

And at some level it stuck to me, the fact that my friends—my Ashkenazi friends—thought I wasn't as Jewish as them. I felt in some ways, "Am I really Jewish?"

And I still can't answer that question. I don't believe in God. But I love the sound of certain prayers, especially the Kaddish.* I like the prayers over the Chanukah candles. There's something nice about not understanding the language.

I feel very deeply Jewish, I feel very connected if I find someone else is Jewish. I'm always wanting to know people's last names. It was important to my father. I—I should put in . . . [*Her eyes fill with tears.*] that my father died, and that's hard, that's why I feel kind of emotional about this. He was—You can probably figure out most of my feeling, my Jewish feeling comes from him . . . And he was very . . . just a good person, with a great sense of humor, he had a good heart and I think talking about the Kaddish . . . I think . . .

Anyway, he died quite a while ago, four years ago but . . . [*sighs*] It's hard for me to separate what he believed from Jewish belief. I'm very mixed up about these things.

And it was important to my father that I marry someone Jewish—and my husband is not Jewish—but my father really loved my husband, and one time, just before he died—he wasn't sick, we just happened to be together—and I said to him, "I'm really sorry about not marrying someone Jewish, but it just didn't happen. . . . This is who I love."

And he said to me, "Well to me, Simon *is* Jewish." He would do this thing, where if he liked someone, they *were* Jewish. He had very close friends who were not Jewish, but he would bring them over into the camp, into the tribe. I mean, his heart was big enough to do that. On the other hand, it's still like saying, "Non-Jews are not like us, don't feel safe to me." I think that was a weakness of his.

And uh [*pushing a loose lock of hair behind her ear*] I'm trying to be the kind of Jew my father thought a Jew was. Religion meant nothing to him, the people meant a lot to him. And today a lot of my passion about feeling Jewish is sort of, I don't want to let him down. But it's more difficult now that he's dead. Because I can't talk to him about it, and say. . . "My kids aren't going to have a bar mitzvah,* bat mitzvah,* what do you think about it?"

I mean, I *do* have mental conversations, but the problem is he says different things depending on what day I ask him. [*laughs*]

MG: *What does he say?*

Sometimes he'll say, "Oh it's just a pile of bullshit, who cares . . ." Other times, he'll say, "I think they'll be glad that they did . . ." But I much more hear him say the bullshit part. [*laughs*]

Or when I talk about Simon and me arguing about what's a Jew, he would say, "Sharon, you're gonna blow it because of Judaism?" He would think that's crazy.

My husband and I used to argue about what's a Jew all the time. Big, horrible arguments, and some interesting ones too. He very strongly believes that any kind of religion militates against a world where people see each other as whole people. And those arguments have made me more confused than ever about what it is to be Jewish.

I feel that all my life I've been trying to deal with that question. Maybe all Jews do . . . It's hard trying to forge some Jewish identity in my kids, given that I'm mixed up about it. And my husband is adamant: he's willing to go along with this Jewish identity thing— whatever that means—but he resents it too.

The kids know we don't believe in God, but we send them to a Jewish daycare, and when they learn about tzedakah* at school, my husband makes sure they know it's not just Jews who believe in that. And that's a good thing for *me* to learn too. But he thinks they should have a socialist identity. And I tell him, "You're being very Leninist about this, very rigid." Because people need other identities besides their political identities.

He says, "Well, their identity can be they're from Michigan." I think people need more than that. But maybe I'm living in the Old World. I guess that's part of feeling Jewish, feeling the sum of all these inquisitions, the survivor of all these migrations, and killings, and whatever you believe comes from that.

My father would never have a German car, never buy anything that came from Germany. He hated Germans. And it took me a long time to get over that. I'm still not over that. If I meet someone who's German even if they weren't born till after the war—that had nothing to do with what happened, I can't let go. I feel like a bad socialist [*laughs*] and probably a bad Jew. I mean, I have a lot of Jewish friends who don't feel that way, and I feel like they're better people. I tell myself, "You're being ridiculous, Sharon." And then another voice says, "But they're German." It's terrible. It is. But I'm working on it.

The Dead
and the Living

---◆---

She points to the framed picture above the fireplace. It's one of several large wax rubbings that she made of Jewish headstones in Polish cemeteries.

THIS IS THE LION OF JUDAH MOURNING. He's crying at the tree that has been broken. The broken tree is actually a very common image. It probably refers to a passage in Ezekiel about the tree that is cut down in Zion. And considering the post-history of this world, it's a very poignant image.

Whites and blacks abound: black-framed rubbings hanging on white walls, white sofa, white rug, snow—still falling—blankets the street outside. She's wearing black slacks and a bottle-green cashmere sweater. A line of white roots runs the length of the parting in her black hair. Carole P. is a psychoanalyst. She grew up in rural Iowa, the only child of an Italian Catholic father and a Jewish mother. She's forty-six.

Most of my mother's family is now Christianized, and my mother was very anxious to identify herself that way. And when I was a small child, I discovered in our attic a cache of Jewish books. Which were basically taken from me very quickly, and not discussed . . . Or [*laughs*] my mother actually said it was something from my father's family, which is ridiculous in retrospect. But I accepted it, I didn't know.

But my mother's mother gave me a powerful sense of connection with the past, with a sense of spirituality in some way that was unspoken but very strong. So I had a sense of Jewish identity. I remember she played this card game with me called Authors. It had all these images of famous poets and writers, and this was a great, beloved game of mine. And she would tell me how amazingly like Henry Wadsworth Longfellow her own father looked. I found this *fascinating*, to think I had a relative like this.

And later on, I came across Roman Vishniac's photographs of Polish Jews and realized I'd found my grandfather in these bearded folk. And this was a huge thing for me.

And as I grew up, all along I had been reading and learning about it, carrying it along, always under heavy critique, the critique of God, the critique of a patriarchal God, the critique of Zionism, all these things that are influenced by the left and the women's movement.

And yet I had never abandoned it, and years later, when I was working in New York, I found myself drawn to a group of Jewish colleagues, and for the first time I was actually comfortable in relating to them as Jews. They were stunned at the degree of interest and knowledge I had of Judaism, in someone they viewed as very peripheral. These were people who had come through Jewishly-oriented childhoods, and for the first time I found myself being acknowledged and recognized in that world as a Jew. I wasn't the Italian person looking in, I was the Jew who hadn't had very much access.

And this is one of those spooky stories: I was driving through this run-down, working-class white, poor neighborhood, and I saw a wrought-iron gate with the Star of David. And I was just drawn to go inside. And at first I was very disappointed, 'cause it was a very typical, very modern Jewish cemetery with headstones where you have the family name, I would say very much of the Christian sort. But as I drove back, I came to the old section: a lot of vases and urns, trees, the presence of so much Hebrew, the density of the stones, the way the stones have a more anthropomorphic feel to them. And what's so strange is that it felt alive. Alive to me.

It felt like it was a place where the relationships and the lives of these people seemed to be perpetuated in the monuments themselves, even though they'd fallen into disrepair. There was something strangely holding in the way the headstones related to one another; they tended to tilt into one another. Husbands and wives who fought throughout life are now lovingly clinging to one another as the sides of their headstones touch throughout time. Much to their chagrin! [*chuckles*]

And I found some unbelievable comfort there, I was drawn back to this place. And several times, as I would stand and look at these headstones, people would walk by—residents of the area, who mostly walked their dogs. And I realized that for the first time in my life I was being viewed as a Jew— with a degree of suspicion, curiosity, and hostility.

When I entered into that cemetery, it was the only place on earth where I was a Jew, totally a Jew, standing on Jewish ground as a Jew. It was a remarkable experience. And then, the day before I was to leave New York—I was moving back to Chicago to take up a position in one of the hospitals here—I returned to the cemetery.

It was this time of year, a day like this, it was snowing, it was grey, and I stood there *knowing*; it was clear that something had shifted, and with a sense almost of terror and anticipation I knew I was walking out of that cemetery to a different life, to a life as a Jew.

Carole now observes Shabbat, keeps a kosher home, and is an active member of a Progressive congregation. Recently, she has made several

*trips to Poland where she visited Jewish cemeteries in rural Ruthenia.
She intends to return in order to preserve a more systematic video and
photographic record of this fast-disappearing heritage.*

The last time I was in Poland, I persuaded two friends of mine to
go with me to the ohel* of Rabbi Elimelech [*an early Chassidic
master, the subject of a well-known folk song*].

Now I always loved the little song and was intrigued about who
Rabbi Elimelech was. The song is very much about Chassidic
ecstasy: he sings, he dances . . .

Well, I discovered that he was Elimelech of Lezajsk and he was
a well-known follower of the Maggid, one of that first generation of Polish Chassidim, a very powerful guy who taught the
Seer of Lublin. I couldn't believe it, the guy died in the seventeenth century, and there was an ohel, there was some mauso-
leum that was extant. And I got it into my head to go to Lezajsk
because it seemed like it must be a magical place, and my friends
agreed to go.

We went first to Tarnow, where there's a hugely devastated synagogue and very little else that remains. It was difficult to go and
see that. The Jewish monuments are often used as places where
people hang out, drink, walk their dogs, the dogs urinate and defecate on the monuments . . . They don't see many Jews there; it's
off the main Jewish heritage route.

And when they see people who look different, you draw attention.
You see people looking out the windows at you; there's a real
tension. And we all felt very uncomfortable. And to some degree
threatened. Not by a physical threat, but there was something uncomfortable.

And then we drove to Lezajsk, entering into the very heartland of
Polish Chassidism. One sensed it, as we went through the forests.
You could really feel all that wonderful mystical stuff. This was
the world of the Chassidic tales, this was the world of those great

330

Chassidic courts that were in the towns. Bobov, the Bobover Rebbe. Bobov is in this area.

But also . . . there wasn't a Jew left. The Chassids come back now every year, and you can imagine what that must be like for these villagers. They must see them as completely foreign, and undoubtedly sources of curiosity, fear, and contempt. And so as we drove through these villages, picturesque as they may be, it was very sorrowful.

What I have found in the last two years is the return of the Church, is the absolute return of anti-Semitism. I think its embedded in the very fabric of Polish Catholicism. The rhetoric is absolutely the culpability of the Jews in the death of Christ, that the Holocaust was vengeance wreaked upon them. I've seen it myself, whacked by a kid on a bicycle as I was going into a shul. . . .

And then we got to Lezajsk. It's a town that's known for its beers. And that made me nervous anyway. [smiles] I figured there'd be a bunch of Poles drinking a lot of beer, and this is not gonna be good! [laughs]

And there was a sign there, and it gave the sights of the town—including the brewery, of course—but the very last was the Jewish cemetery. I was really amazed. I went into a store and I asked in my fractured Polish for the cemetery, and a taxi driver, who was very helpful, drew a map and showed us how to get there. And we found it!

It was on the outskirts of town surrounded by now quite decrepit houses very much like that Jewish cemetery in New York. And it had a gate, a very high gate. And much to our distress it was locked. But you could look through and see a very modest structure which was, I assumed, the ohel of Rabbi Elimelech.

There was a plaque saying the cemetery had been preserved under the auspices of the Nissenbaum Foundation. This is apparently a very wealthy man, originally from Poland, who I think immigrated to South Africa. But what was so horrendous and so disheartening is that etched onto the plaque was a gallows. And hanging from it was a Star of David. And next to it someone had scrawled in German: JUDEN RAUS! JEWS OUT.

And it was like . . . there was not a Jew living within fifty miles! And I think we all just imploded. It was so disheartening, to think that even when there is no Jewish presence, there's still somehow a need to kill in the place of the dead, rekilling the dead, over and over again.

The fact that Rabbi Elimelech's ohel had survived at all was incredible. But looking at that plaque, thinking about the neglect, the resurgence of anti-Semitism, the vandalism, the desecration, just the passage of time, we all said, "This will not survive."

It had a very profound impact on me to try to do something at least to preserve the visual images. Unlike the wooden synagogues, which were burned down, the headstones were tough enough to survive but I don't think they're tough enough to survive much longer. The great cemeteries in Cracow and Warsaw will survive; they're tourist attractions. The Poles aren't stupid, they want to make money. They'll preserve the monuments and make allowances for people like the Nissenbaum Foundation. I can see that. But in the remote rural areas, as the stones are slowly toppled over, defaced or just worn away by time in these small towns in Ruthenia, no one notices or cares.

MG: *You have a very passionate response to these cemeteries and to the defense of this lost world. I wonder what kind of emotional meanings they have for you.*

Is it the child without a family wanting to keep alive the memory of a vanished world? Certainly. I can't underestimate the role of Roman Vishniac's photographs on me when I was child. I took them out of the library over and over and over again.

And I think I've probably always had a fascination with the dead, and the world of the dead, perhaps in part because I had little family and experienced a lot of deaths at an early age. But ultimately, there is no one else to preserve these stones, because the generations after them died. These are people for whom there is no one, and for me it's an affirmation that the dead and the living can coexist. It's a kind of affirming place.

I think I do see myself in this odd space between the two worlds and I can inhabit it. And on Shabbat, when I light the candles in this room [*indicating the rubbings*], I feel this brings them in, in a way.

Running on a Beach

Linda Hirsch is a photojournalist and a member of the social action group Artists for Survival. She began taking photographs in high school.

THE VERY FIRST PICTURE I TOOK that I really liked was of a young girl running on a beach, with a spray of sun just coming through the clouds onto her like a spotlight.

A young girl features in another of Linda's photographs.

In the early eighties, when I traveled to the Netherlands, I went to Amsterdam. And I should preface this by saying, when I travel, I am not the kind of Jewish person that goes looking for temples, Jewish cemeteries et cetera et cetera which is what many of my friends do. I don't do that. I just sort of find what I find.

Well, I will confess that in Amsterdam I did go to the Anne Frank house, 'cause I was curious. That's something I would not have avoided. But I found myself very sort of [*pausing to consider the right phrase*] unaffected? by the experience.

I watched other people going through it—going through the house. And I saw them really reacting. I don't know if they were Jewish or non-Jewish, no idea. But I felt flat. Strangely flat. And when I left the house, and was walking around the city, I was puzzled. I found myself thinking, "Why am I so disappointed by this experience?" I thought I'd be upset or moved or . . . something. And it troubled me.

The very next day I went to Utrecht. Totally different city within the Netherlands. [*on a heavy outbreath*] And I was just walking down the street, I forget what I was looking for, I was just wandering, gathering an impression. And I came across—from a distance I saw a statue.

As I got closer I saw it was the statue of a young girl. And sort of all at once—within two milliseconds—I realized it must be Anne Frank. And when I walked around the back, I saw a swastika painted on the back of the statue. On the base of the statue. Graffiti.

And all the feelings that I hadn't had—and I still get very emotional about this because it was a very powerful feeling because it came so by surprise—that all the feelings that I had not felt the day before I felt immediately. Like anger. Because it was such a deep offense. It was a cowardly act. I mean, it was cowardly anyway, but this was like shooting someone in the back.

And I photographed it. Without any thought as to how I was framing the image—I had to document this. I just did Boom! From the back, not the front.

And I knew the rest of that whole day and that whole trip that I had to do something about this. It just wiggled around in my brain. "Oh, this is upsetting, and I'm going to do something about it." It rankled.

And there was one other image that I took on that trip, that was also graffiti that had to do with racism, just a very graphic scrawl: "Racism takes human lives." That's how it translated from the Dutch. And it was on a post office wall in front of which were these heavy chain links. It was just a great image. It just talked to me about slavery basically.

So I came home with these two images, printed them, and then I thought, "OK, now I'm in the States, what do I do with this stuff?" And I found that the Anne Frank Foundation is based in New York, so I sent the images with a letter. They forwarded the information about the pictures to the Anne Frank Foundation in Amsterdam, full circle! Whereupon the graffiti was removed. And also the statue was physically removed and placed in a more secure setting. Well, what was deemed more secure, with its back closer to a building. It was harder to get behind it. And if anyone did deface it, it would be that much more visible.

And the pictures were put into a permanent collection. And then they toured; there was an exhibit that traveled around the world. My two little pictures . . . It was like, "Wow!" And those were some of the most important pictures I will ever have taken, all because I acted on my conscience.

I went back to the Netherlands several years later. And my children were with me. And I took a picture of them standing next to the statue. It was like, "Ha!" I felt so wonderful. It's like when you see these movies about the future, and people time-traveling. I felt like, "Yeah, I changed something here. And you know what? I changed myself." And . . . ah . . . Ah! It was wonderful.

Prescription for Life

She describes her look as stylish but not too corporate: black pumps, black stockings, black skirt and jacket, and a velvet choker. Also black. Other stylish items include the swivel chair, an L-shaped desk, and a large private office on the corner of Sixth Avenue and Forty-second Street in New York City. On the wall in front of her there is a large map of the world of a decidedly more corporate character. As Vice President of European Programming Operations in the International Department of cable company HBO, Pam Spector is responsible for new business development and strategic planning and operations of HBO businesses around the world. In work-related travel she has seen firsthand the social and economic conditions of Jews in post-communist Eastern Europe. Pam explains to me how she became involved in an aid project for Eastern Europeans. She's thirty-seven years old.

MY SISTER IS PART OF THE YOUNG leadership program of the UJA,* and last February she told me about something called the Washington Conference, which is something that happens every year. And it's a four-day conference in Washington, D.C. I'd never been to anything like it, and the UJA here in New York tends to have a bit of a stereotype, UJA is always asking for money, and there's a certain, I guess, kind of person socially who goes to these Jewish parties and things, and I *never* associated myself with them.

MG: *What kind of person are you thinking of?*

Oh God! [*laughs nervously*] uh . . . Let's see if I can come up with

some tactful word for this . . . The people that go to these functions I either would find sort of . . . I'm tryin' to keep this . . . 'cause
I don't mind if you put my name in, but if you do, we need to find
a way to . . . Let's say, they're a little more . . . awkward . . .

MG: *Awkward?*

Well, between you and I, dweeby, nerdy, whatever, OK? Not the kind
of people I'm used to spending time with either at work or friends.
And this is the general feeling of a *lot* of people in New York. But I
decided to go to it, because it sounded very, very different than anything I had gone to, and the appeal was that it was going to be a
national conference, and there'd be people from all over the U.S.

And it was amazing! There were three thousand people there, mostly
Americans and some Israelis. I met Jewish people from all over,
from Omaha, Nebraska, and different places where I honestly—It's
not that I didn't think Jews existed there, but you just don't meet
Jewish people from Omaha, Nebraska, all the time. And in some
ways they're different, and in some ways they have that core, that
connection, that certain understanding, a certain level of knowing.

So getting back to the conference, this conference was *incredibly*
inspirational, and I learned a lot. They discussed political issues,
having to do with Judaism and Israel, and pluralism, and cultural
issues—like why there are more Jewish singles in the United States
than anywhere else in the entire world. And religious issues–It
was a *wonderful* conference.

And there were all these different panels, and different breakout
groups—five or six a day—and then at night everyone would get
together, we had a teleconference with Netanyahu, and Al Gore
came to speak, and they had some Jewish comedians come down,
and they had some Israeli singers . . . it was just unbelievable. And
it was *very* social, and just a lot of fun. It was just a real eye-opener.

And there was a project, and it was called Prescription for Life.
This guy from Florida came up with the idea that everyone at-

tending the conference, which was more or less three thousand people, to ask them to put together a bag—He sent out the bags, a plastic bag to everyone, it said Prescription for Life on it. And he came up with a list of about six items, basic items, that were needed, desperately needed in the former Soviet Union: like aspirin, bandaids, eardrops, and I can't remember the others right now, and he wanted—The former Soviet Union is in bad shape to begin with, but the Jewish people there, because, communism and World War II, they sort of got the double hit, so he asked people to bring these small incidental items.

And I saw tables and tables, *rooms* filled with these bags, and this sight was just unbelievable to me. It had such an effect on me, this wasn't writing a check, this was—Because you knew that if you brought a bottle of aspirin, you knew that you were helping a person in the FSU.

And my region, I work with eastern Europe, I have a kinship with them even on a professional level, and my family roots are there . . . And being at a point in time in my life where I really felt that I wanted to start giving back—I'm not married, at the moment—and when I saw all the things that people were doing, it struck me that, "OK, I'm not religious. But I feel Jewish, what have I done to give back?"

And when I saw these bags, I said, "I would like to join this project." But I found out that it was only a project for that drive, so what I decided to do was take the idea, capitalize on it, and make it an ongoing project, try to target a different audience and then try to make it a national project, to target corporations, to ask for goods in kind that meet the needs of the JDC [*Joint Distribution Committee, a rescue and relief organization under the umbrella of UJA*]. And so I started attending the meetings of the Young Leadership.

But here in New York so many thousands of people are volunteering, it's broken up into professions, and I joined the entertainment division, and one of the organizers said that *they* were a team without a project, and I was a project without a team, so I became a member of the steering committee. And together with the co-chair, we targeted twenty-five companies, wrote letters asking for everything from sunscreen, adult diapers, clothing, all these different things—and this is all only two months ago—and as of last week we received the first goods in kind, from a corporate donor here in New York. Which is pretty amazing in such a short period.

But the project started getting too big to follow up on all the wild ideas we had for growing it. So the UJA Young Leadership decided to give us a staff person to suppport this project. And so now we're planning to do a walkathon here in New York . . .

And I've subsequently touched base with the guy who initiated this conference, and asked him if he'd like to join forces and make it a national project, get the name Prescription for Life trademarked, so that only people affiliated with us can use it. And people are getting involved in every way: we've got someone designing a web site, someone working on a logo, someone's writing copy for publications . . . the lawyers are working on the trademark, we're hoping to do some spots . . . and who knows, maybe get someone like Noah Wiley from *ER*, y'know, related to prescriptions, and maybe get it on the air at HBO—this *is* the entertainment division!

The list goes on and on . . . we're designing brochures for it, we had someone show up two nights—a guy who works at Pfizer—so he is trying to get either X amount of prescription drugs or a twenty-thousand-dollar grant from them.

And we cater to Jews and non-Jews. It's not just for Jews, and in addition, if there's a disaster somewhere, like Nicaragua or somewhere, I wouldn't for one second hesitate to say, "You know what? We've got some clothing, let's send it to them there also. Once you start helping people, you realize that there are a lot of people out there who need to be helped. The motto is "To save a person is to save a world," and I feel lucky that I can finally do something concrete.

340

What's Not to Like About That?

Sam L. and Sophie K. are ceramicists who create teapots, mugs, and vases, as well as milchik* and fleishik* crockery holders, chanukiyot,* mezuzot,* and Hebrew (SHALOM!) fridge magnets. Fugitives from New York City, the couple have lived in Oregon for fifteen years. Their split-level home, studio, kiln block, and showrooms overlook the ocean. We're in a large light-filled living room. Thirty yards beyond the French doors, the surf, spangled with late afternoon light, breaks on a pine-fringed beach. Unfortunately, my view of this idyllic scene is obscured by a pair of long hairy ears.

SOPHIE: Harold! Off! [*scoldingly*] No no, no! [*to me*] He's really being obnoxious. And you have our permission to push him away. *HAROLD! GET OFF OF MICHAEL NOW!*

Harold the cocker spaniel stops licking my face. Starts chewing my hand instead.

SOPHIE: Harold, if you don't calm down, I'm takin' ya out!

MG: *I'm sure he'll settle—*

Fifty pounds of frenzied affability leaps onto my chest.

Shortly afterwards, Harold is seen romping on the beach. Sam and Sophie, both a little breathless, are back on their sofa. I'm a little breathless, too.

341

SOPHIE: Oh, I must tell you this. We were in shul* last night and the regular rabbi had to go to a bar mitzvah* in Houston or somewhere.

SAM: Dallas, I think.

SOPHIE: Wherever, and the, the woman who was filling in happens to be a mohel.*

SAM: Shouldn't that be mohelette?

MG: [*laughing*] *I didn't realize there were women in the business these days.*

SOPHIE: Oh, yeah, she was saying there's about a hundred of 'em now. Anyway, she's very nice, and just before she started, one of the congregants there, he said, "I wonder what's it gonna be like having a mohel leading the service." So I jumped in without thinking, and I said, "Oh, she'll cut it short!" And the whole congregation cracked up. [*laughter*] It was hysterical! Did I turn red!

But seriously, to answer your question, What does it mean to be Jewish . . . The reason I went to shul last night, was because it was my mother's Yahrzeit*—she passed away two years ago—and for the last week, I knew I was going to go to the synagogue, and thoughts of her came welling back up . . . And for me, being Jewish is knowing the community supports me when I stand up and say Kaddish.* And I was very moved . . . It was very healing. I felt held by the congregation, and that's important, especially when you've had a major loss.

And for *years* I wasn't affiliated with any Jewish organization. I never felt right going to my family's synagogue.

SAM: Well, *they* never felt right there either.

SOPHIE: Yeah. Well, my mom didn't believe in God, because God wasn't there for her and her family during the Holocaust. She lost almost everyone. Same with my dad. I mean, they gave my brother and me a Jewish education, but I didn't feel God was present in our lives, and I didn't set foot in a synagogue for like, fifteen years, until I met Sam and we went together.

SAM: Yeah, it was right after the congregation formed, and they'd just received this Torah scroll from Poland that'd somehow survived the War, and been repaired. And we unrolled the whole scroll that evening, and held it. It was like it was being reborn into the community. It was quite an emotional experience.

SOPHIE: Yeah ... And I was coming from a world where a woman would *never* touch the Torah. It was taboo. It would invalidate the scroll. And here I was holding it in my hands. And I felt very included for the first time. So it's a great shul. It's quite a drive to get there, but we go. We teach Sunday school there too. It's really important for us to be involved. I mean, we're also involved here in the town. I'm a member of our local business association, we're both active in our craft guild ...

SAM: It's very important for us to be involved in our communities.

SOPHIE: Plus we're both also very involved with our families. I'll tell you about the wedding—Well, we went to Poland with my uncle last year, to see where he and my mother had grown up. And that was just an incredible trip ... And when we got back— Well, we always try to make it to family simchas* if we can, and my cousin was getting married in New York. It was like the poshest New York restaurant. You know The Four Seasons? Very, *very* sophisticated, upscale, really fancy-shmancy! And there we are—

Well, you have to know that Sam likes to shop, and I *don't*. And so she shops for me, but she just kind of doubles up on everything, and so we have two identical winter coats, identical sneakers, identical everything. We're kind of like Siamese twins, it's hard to miss us! We're two of a kind: members of the short Jewish lesbian potters with glasses club!

SAM: Yeah, and we'd heard about how fancy this party was going to be, and I was concerned about not looking like country bumpkins. At the same time, not wanting to spend too much on outfits that we'd probably only wear once. So I went shopping in Portland, and saw this black velvet pants suit.

SOPHIE: And what does she say? "Gimme two of those!" [*laughter*] And there we were at like, the poshest restaurant in New York, sitting next to each other, both dressed in black velvet pants suits and frilly white blouses. And we looked *great*! Absolutely identical clothes.

SAM: Similar

SOPHIE: They were *identical*!

SAM: One of the blouses was altered.

SOPHIE: Almost identical. It was *hysterical*. And my cousin—Well, he's in a position where he's probably got everything he wants already, so it wasn't like we needed to buy him something on the bridal registry. And so what we gave him was a very nice framed calligraphic reproduction of the translation of this marriage certificate we found when we went to Poland, which basically said when his great-great-great—

SAM: great—probably—

SOPHIE: great-grandfather got married, and it had his signature on it—in Yiddish—and *his* parents' names! Back in the seventeenth century or whatever.

SAM: It was a marriage certificate, not the ketuba,* the legal certificate.

SOPHIE: And that was especially important to me, because being born in America—I was the first person in my family born here—my brother was born in a DP camp in Germany—and I really never felt I had much family. I really felt I was severed from my past. So having that certificate, it was a nice piece to put—[*smiling with relief*] Yeah, so . . . whenever someone passed away in my family, the sense of loss was doubled, because it was the loss of continuity as well. The family was shrinking. But now, my sister's had a child, my younger brother's just had a third child . . .

SAM: My sister's just adopted a little girl from China . . . and uh . . . [*glancing at Sophie inquiringly*]

SOPHIE: [*nodding*] Are we gonna tell 'im now? OK. We weren't sure if we were going to say this, but you're so sweet, you're not going to make us look bad, right? . . . *We're* also adopting a little girl from China.

I mean, the two of us live and work together, we're together twenty-four hours a day, been together thirteen years now, and we've *always* been happy just being . . . well, just *being*. But it was at Purim last year, like, we made two hundred hamantashen* and sent 'em out all over, and we had a party, and . . . and we're here in the kitchen, and we both said, "We shouldn't be doing this by *ourselves*." We should be doing this with a little kid. We need to share this. A holiday's kind of empty without a child to share it with.

SAM: We'd already thought about it for a long time: How can we take a Chinese child, bring her to this snow-white fishing town, and raise her here as a Jew with lesbian mothers? That stopped us for years.

SOPHIE: Yeah, we would've adopted years and years ago. Then a friend at shul said, "You're thinking about it the wrong way. You're thinking, 'Poor kid . . .' But look at it another way instead, 'This kid's gonna grow up in a very loving family, and is gonna be very strong, very empowered, very capable. Just imagine what *access* she will have. She's gonna make a difference in the world.'"

SAM: And in fact there are now several adopted Asian children in our synagogue, so our daughter will not be the only Asian there, which will be very nice for her. And as I said, my sister and brother-in-law in Seattle have adopted a Chinese baby. And I think that was the clincher. Our daughter would have a relative that looked like her.

SOPHIE: First cousin!

SAM: Right. And we thought that between the shul and the family she'd have some anchors in the sea of differences.

SOPHIE: And of course, she'll have not one, but *two* Jewish mothers! [*laughs, then becoming serious*] We're actually going to call her after my dad's mom, who was killed in the Holocaust. For some reason nobody ever named a child after her. My brother's oldest kids are named after Mom's parents, and the new baby has Mom's name, but nobody took my *dad's* mother's name. It's like she completely disappeared. So we're going to call our child Lily. It's a nice name, huh?

SAM: We'll have a conversion and naming ceremony. And we have a mikvah* here.

MG: [*surprised*] *Really?*

SAM: Mikvah, meaning a running body of water.

MG: [*puzzled*] . . . *The Pacific Ocean?*

SAM: Right. So if it's warm enough, we'll convene the rabbis here. We're basically ready, just waiting for that phone call. We've done all the workshops, we've got the house child-proofed, and we're expecting to go to China sometime over the summer. Lily's probably born already. . . . So now we're getting things ready, clothes and stuff, but also . . . like for my niece's birthday, we bought her this mezuzah* that was made out of mahjong tiles, and I want to get one for our daughter too. A mezuzah with Chinese characters!

SOPHIE: [*reaching behind the sofa*] And we already have a Jewish teddy bear! Note the Magen David* on the yarmulke.* [*handing it to me*] It's still a little damp, Harold tried to eat it before.

MG: *Looks like you're all set.*

SOPHIE: I think so. I really think it'll be a good place for a child to grow up. We hope . . .

I mean, we're very, very fortunate. It was obvious to me right from the start that Sam and me were meant to be together—we meshed right from the start. And now we have this beautiful home, and we do work that we love.

It really makes me believe in God, that certain things reveal themselves, and it's up to us to act on them. Like the idea we had to leave New York and come here . . . And other people come here now, buy our pots; and they're taking home a piece of us, and their memories of being here. You make a good product, you're proud of it, and people are happy with it, and it gives 'em pleasure. What's not to like about that?

Outside, on the beach, Harold barks affably at a terrified cormorant.

I mean, the world can only get better, if we keep *making* it better! I mean, I *do* worry about our daughter. Being discriminated against is *not* fun. As we all know. But it really does make you stronger. Just look at us Jews! It's the twenty-first century, and we're still around, after thousands of years, still goin' strong as ever. I figure Hitler will just be rolling over in his grave—He tried to get rid of us, he failed, and now Jews are poppin' up everywhere! We're even recruitin' new ones . . . In China!

Glossary

The terms below may have more than one meaning. They are defined here to help the reader understand their usage in the context of the interviews.

Adon Olam—"Lord of the Universe," a prayer popularly used as the concluding hymn at synagogue services

aggadot—legends

aliyah—immigrating to Israel; often, "making *aliyah*." Also, a Torah honor.

Ashkenazi—Jews of eastern European origin

avoida—Ashkenazi/Yiddish pronunciation of the Hebrew *avoda*, meaning "duty, service"

Avraham, Yitzchak, and Yaakov—Abraham, Isaac, and Jacob, patriarchs of the Jewish people

Aza—Gaza

bar mitzvah (masculine), *bat mitzvah* (feminine)—a child who has reached the age of religious maturity; also, the ceremony marking the rite of passage

Baruch Atah Adonai Eloheinu—"Blessed art Thou, O Lord our God," the opening words of most Hebrew blessings

Baruch, baruch Atah—"Blessed, blessed are You"

Baruch haShem—"Praise the Lord"

Ben-Tzion—Son of Zion

Beth Din—religious court

bimah—podium or raised platform from which synagogue services are conducted *bris, brit* — circumcision ceremony

brocha — blessing

Chabad — the Lubavitcher Chassidic Movement

chagim — Jewish holidays

chai — Hebrew word meaning "life," consisting of the letters *chet* and *yud*, which are often fashioned into a charm and worn as an amulet or as a symbol of personal identification with Judaism

chalav Yisrael — milk handled only by a Jew

chanukiya (plural, *chanukiyot*) — nine-branched candelabrum used to celebrate the holiday of Chanukah

chavruta — studying in pairs

cherem — excommunication

chuppah — marriage canopy

daven, davening — pray, praying

Dvar Torah — commentary on the Torah reading

dvekus — attachment, devotion

Eretz Yisrael — the Land of Israel

Falashas — Ethiopian Jews

feribel — umbrage

fleishik — made of or associated with meat or meat products

frum — pious

Gemara — commentary on the Mishna. *see* Talmud

gesundter heit — in good health

get — Jewish divorce document

goy (plural, *goyim*) — non-Jew (usually derogatory)

goyishe — non-Jewish

haftarah — reading from the Prophets

halacha — Jewish law

halachic, halachically — in accordance with Jewish law

hamantashen — traditional triangle-shaped pastries for the holiday of Purim

HaShomer HaTzair — "The Young Guard," a Socialist Zionist youth movement

Haskalah — the Enlightenment, an eighteenth-century movement that sought to introduce general culture to Jews *hatafat dam*—drawing of a droplet of blood symbolic of the act of circumcision

havdalah—ceremony concluding the Sabbath and ushering in the new week

hechsher—written certification that a product is kosher

heimishe—warm and inviting, homelike, friendly

Kaddish—the mourner's prayer

kapos—Jewish prisoners in a concentration camp who were appointed by Nazis to oversee their fellow inmates

kashrus, kashrut—kosher dietary laws

kavanah—spiritual concentration

ketuba—Jewish marriage contract

Kiddush—prayer over wine sanctifying the Sabbath; also, the name of the collation that sometimes follows synagogue services

kipa—skullcap

kipas—anglicized form of *kipot*; plural of *kipa*

kishkes—guts

kneidlach—matza balls, dumplings made from matza meal

Knesset—Israeli parliament

Kohen—Priest; individual descended from the Priestly class

Kol Nidre—the name of the Yom Kippur eve service; also, the prayer with which the service begins

Kotel—Western Wall

Kristallnacht—literally, "Night of Broken Glass," November 9, 1938; also, the commemoration of that infamous day when Nazis burned synagogues, destroyed Jewish property, and attacked Jews throughout Germany

l'shana haba'a b'Yerushalayim—"next year in Jerusalem," a refrain recited at the conclusion of the Passover seder

landsman—fellow countryman

laying tefilin—putting on phylacteries. *see* tefilin

Levi—Levite; individual descended from the Levites, chosen to assist the Priests in the Temple

Litvish—Lithuanian

loshen horeh—"evil tongue," malicious gossip

Lubavitch—Chassidic sect of Ukrainian origin

Maccabee war—second-century B.C.E. conflict between the Syrian-Greeks and the Jews

macher—big shot, person of influence

Magen David—Star of David

mashgiach (plural, *mashgichim*)—supervisor of kosher dietary laws

mazel tov—"good luck," congratulations

mechitzah—barrier separating men from women in Orthodox synagogues

menorah—candelabrum

mensch—decent person

meshuga—crazy

mezuzah (plural, *mezuzot*)—small case housing a parchment containing a selection from the Bible, affixed to the doorpost of a Jewish home

Midrash—rabbinic commentary on the Bible

Mi Kamocha—phrase used in Jewish liturgy, meaning "Who is like unto Thee?"

mikvah—ritual bath

milchik—made of or associated with milk or dairy products

milchiks and fleishiks—dairy foods and meat products, which Jewish dietary laws prohibit from being mixed

minyan—religious quorum, composed of ten congregants; quorum of ten Jews required for public worship; sometimes used to mean religious service

mishpocha—family

Mitzra'im—Egypt

mitzvah—commandment, good deed

Modeh Ani—first prayer of the day, which begins with these words, meaning "I give thanks"

Mogen David—see Magen David

mohel—ritual circumcisor

Moshe—Moses

Moshiach—Messiah

neshuma — soul
ohel — tomb
Oneg Shabbat — Sabbath social gathering
oy gevalt! — oh, woe is me!
parsha — Torah portion
pastillas — chicken pies, a Sephardic specialty
Pesach — Passover
platzing — bursting with emotion
rebbe (plural, *rebbei'im*) — teacher, rabbi; also, the leader of a
    Chassidic sect
Rebbe, the — the Lubavitcher Rebbe
Rochl — Yiddish form of Rachel
Rosh haShanah — Jewish New Year
seder — the traditional Passover meal; also, the name of the
    festive Tu B'Shvat meal; also, any festive meal
Sefer Torah — Torah scroll
seichel — "brains," common sense
Sha'ar Zahav — Golden Gate
Shabbat — Sabbath
Shabbat shalom — "[have] a peaceful Sabbath," a greeting
Shabbat Shira — "Sabbath of Song," the Sabbath on which the
    Torah portion containing the Song of Moses is read
Shabbos — Sabbath
Shavuot — Pentecost
Shechinah — Divine Presence
sheitl (plural, *sheitls, sheitlach*) — wig worn by some Orthodox
    Jewish women to cover their natural hair for purposes of
    modesty
Sheva Brachot — seven wedding blessings
shiksa, shiksas — non-Jewish women (derogatory)
shiur (plural, *shiurim*) — Talmud classes
Shiva — the traditional seven-day mourning period
shlof — nap
Sh'ma — central testament of Judaism, which begins with the
    words "Hear, O Israel"

Sh'ma al haMitah — the *Sh'ma* prayer recited at bedtime

shochet — kosher slaughterer

shtetl (plural, *shtetlach*) — small eastern European Jewish town or village

shtum — quiet

shul — synagogue

siddur — prayer book

simchas — celebrations

Slichot — penitential prayers

smicha — ordination

Sukkot — Festival of Booths

talit — prayer shawl

Talmud — commentary on the Bible consisting of the Mishna and Gemara

Tanach — the Bible, consisting of the Torah, Prophets, and Holy Writings

Tanya — teachings of the first Lubavitcher Rebbe

tefilin — phylacteries; two black leather boxes to which straps are attached and which contain parchments with texts from Scripture

tircha — trouble

trop — Torah cantillation marks

Tu B'Shvat — the fifteenth of the Hebrew month Shvat, the New Year for Trees

tzedakah — charity

tzitzis, tzitzit — fringed ceremonial garment

UJA — United Jewish Appeal

Westerbork — transit camp for Dutch Jews en route to concentration camps

Yad VaShem — Holocaust museum, archive, and memorial in Jerusalem

Yahrzeit — anniversary of a death

Yahrzeit candle — memorial candle

yaprakes — stuffed chard leaves, a Sephardic specialty

yarmulke (plural, *yarmulkes*) — skullcap

Yerushalayim—Jerusalem
yevarechecha—first word of the Priestly benediction pronounced
   at synagogue services
yichus—pedigree
Yid—Jew
Yom HaShoah—Holocaust Memorial Day
Yom Kippur—Day of Atonement
yom tov—holiday
Zlochover niggun—Chassidic melody from the Ukraine
zman—time

Index

About the Author

⌣

MICHAEL JAFFE GARBUTT grew up in Manchester, England, and was educated at the Durham University, where he was president of the Jewish Society. He holds a Ph.D. in applied linguistics from Macquarie University, Sydney, Australia, and has worked extensively in the analysis of patient narratives in psychotherapy. Currently a resident of Sydney, Dr. Garbutt has also lived in Israel, Italy, Indonesia, and the United States.

Dr. Garbutt's interest in narrative studies also extends to the visual arts and architecture. He is the co-director and presenter of the popular Australian ABC-TV series *Garbutt's Way*, which explores the quality of the built and natural environment, and director of Tunguska Events, a multimedia design studio based in Sydney. The author of several English language textbooks, he is currently working on a book about sacred spaces in architecture and a feature film about Jewish life in the Diaspora.